IMAGES
of America

African Americans of San Francisco

I0807686

ON THE COVER: In the photograph are the members of Third Baptist Church of San Francisco, which was under the leadership of the Reverend J.A Dennis. According to church records, Dennis served as pastor of Third Baptist Church from 1917 to 1924. He is credited for paying off the mortgage on this church at Hyde and Clay Streets and giving the church stability. Under his leadership, the usher board and a morning choir were organized. This building was constructed within two years after the first church was spared by the 1906 earthquake but destroyed in a fire. Pastor Dennis and his wife, Mildred, are seated in the first two seats of the first row. (Courtesy of Third Baptist Church of San Francisco Inc.)

IMAGES
of America

AFRICAN AMERICANS OF SAN FRANCISCO

Jan Batiste Adkins

ARCADIA
PUBLISHING

ISBN 978-0-7385-7619-0

Published by Arcadia Publishing
Charleston, South Carolina

Printed in the United States of America

Library of Congress Control Number: 2011931766

For all general information, please contact Arcadia Publishing:
Telephone 843-853-2070
Fax 843-853-0044
E-mail sales@arcadiapublishing.com
For customer service and orders:
Toll-Free 1-888-313-2665

Visit us on the Internet at www.arcadiapublishing.com

I dedicate this book to the many African American pioneers who struggled to establish a viable community in San Francisco that survives today. Also, I dedicate it to the families and community organizations of San Francisco who have preserved the history, photographs, and stories of the city's African American residents. I hope this book provides San Francisco's youth and community members with a much-anticipated overview of the history of its African American community.

Contents

ACKNOWLEDGMENTS

Many individual have supported my efforts at researching the history of San Francisco's African American community. I express my sincere thanks and gratitude to the many librarians and archivists who served as invaluable resources for this project: Robin Walker, librarian and archivist at the International Longshore and Warehouse Union; Alison Moore and other reference staff at the California Historical Society; the reference staff of the Oakland African American Museum and Library; Jeff Thomas and Christina Moretta, photo curators at the San Francisco Public Library; Gina Bradi of the San Francisco Maritime National Historical Park; Marie Browning and Gaynell Armstrong, staff at the San Francisco Redevelopment Agency; Kelly-Ann Turkington, archivist of the Royal BC Museum; Dr. Jeffrey M. Burns, archivist for the Catholic Archdiocese of San Francisco; Bryan Caston of the African American Historical Society of San Francisco; and Peter Fitzsimmons, historian and curator of San Francisco's Jazz and Heritage Center.

I also want to thank the many friends whom I met along this journey: Ellen Carr and Ethel Pitts-Walker, historians of Third Baptist Church; Jerry Sumner; mother Rose Westbrook; LaZelle Westbrook; and others who have shared their families stories and photographs.

I would also like to thank researchers Christina Boykin and Karis Ingram for their assistance in the layout of the book. Gathering and sorting the images were very time-consuming, and I express a special thanks to Chris Boykin and Jittaun Jones for continual support and assistance. I could not have completed this project without my researcher, Jittaun Jones, who provided her invaluable historical insight and dedication to details.

I want to express a special thanks to Susan Shillinglaw of San Jose State University for her overall wisdom and insight that guided me throughout the project.

Most importantly, I want to express a special thanks to my family and my husband, Walter Adkins, for the endless encouragement and inspiration expressed every day throughout the project.

And finally, thanks to my acquisitions editors, John Poultney and Tiffany Frary, for their wisdom and continued support for this book.

Introduction

African Americans of San Francisco documents the city's history for a century and a half, focusing on groups and individuals who contributed to an evolving, energetic community. It is an overview of black pioneers of the 19th century. Some had overcome slavery, and many had to face the great odds of racial discrimination and economic setbacks to develop communities in San Francisco. It also documents the work of 20th-century leaders who protected the rights of San Francisco's black residents. This book examines life and conditions for black residents and also chronicles the social, political, and cultural contributions of the city's African American communities.

The theme of traveling to the continent's end in search of new opportunities is prevalent throughout San Francisco's history. In the 19th century, many slaves came to the city with their owners and then sought and found freedom in the free state of California. Many free men and women came in search of gold and opportunities for business and land for the family home. These early African American settlers developed churches, businesses, schools, newspapers, and social and cultural organizations that continue to serve as foundations for viable, ever-changing communities that exist in the city today. Throughout the history of African Americans in San Francisco, some black residents have left San Francisco in search of better opportunities in cities of the Pacific Northwest, Canada, and in southern and eastern regions of California. Some black migrants became disillusioned and left San Francisco to go back home. But while many moved on to other places, many more African Americans continued to migrate to San Francisco from as far away as Barbados, all in search of new opportunities in the city on the bay. The early black pioneers faced discriminatory laws prohibiting blacks from testifying against white citizens of San Francisco. Many faced employment biases that limited work options. Black children could not attend school with white children, forcing the black community to develop schools known as "colored schools." Many church members who were black could not worship in the same seating areas as whites in churches and therefore built their own churches. Even though segregation took root in San Francisco and continued into the 20th century, many African Americans continued the westward movement to California in search of a better life. With this steady growth, San Francisco's black population grew from 425 in 1850 to 1,654 by the late 19th century, and neighborhoods and businesses were established. For African Americans, San Francisco was a place of hope.

In the early 20th century, African Americans continued traveling to San Francisco from the South in search of jobs and new opportunities. The black population grew to 4,846 by 1940. African Americans came to San Francisco in the early wave of a great American migration. According to Isabel Wilkerson in *The Warmth of Other Suns: The Epic Story of America's Great Migration*, "Over time, this mass relocation would come to dwarf the California Gold Rush of the 1850s with its 100,000 people from Oklahoma and Arkansas to California in the 1930s." By the end of World War II, the African American population exploded to over 43,430. Many came to San Francisco to work in the shipyards and in other wartime industries. This influx expanded the African American community into new neighborhoods of San Francisco. In many cases, it resulted in newly established black businesses that served the needs of residents of black neighborhoods. After the war, African Americans confronted racism and segregation in labor, education, housing, and economic opportunities.

By 1970, the number of African Americans in San Francisco reached a high of 96,000, which was 13.4 percent of the total population. But since then, the number of black residents has steadily decreased, in large part because of the expensive housing market. In spite of the challenges of rapid population growth, people from all over the world continue to travel to San Francisco seeking new beginnings, fortunes, and a chance to realize dreams.

Documenting the narrative of African Americans of San Francisco required oral interviews of many existing leaders and community residents. All of the photographs were acquired from local residents, museums, libraries, government agencies, churches, universities, and social organizations. Reviewing historical records and documents was necessary for understanding the evolution of the black communities of San Francisco, and the references listed in the bibliography were essential for examining and understanding the early history of San Francisco's African American community.

Over the last 165 years since the first early black settlers, African Americans in San Francisco have confronted and overcome tremendous obstacles in order to establish communities where black residents could live in safety and raise families. The aim of this book is to inspire conversation about the efforts of the early pioneers and 20th-century leaders who envisioned new lives in the West. Hopefully, this book will inspire new ideas within black communities of the city to continue focusing on economic, social, and cultural contributions to the overall history, cohesion, and livability of San Francisco. This is only a start. *African Americans of San Francisco* is a survey that does not attempt to include all contributions and leaders, but it will hopefully stimulate future researchers to continue documenting the local history of African Americans in the San Francisco area.

One

1840–1900

San Francisco's Early Black Pioneers

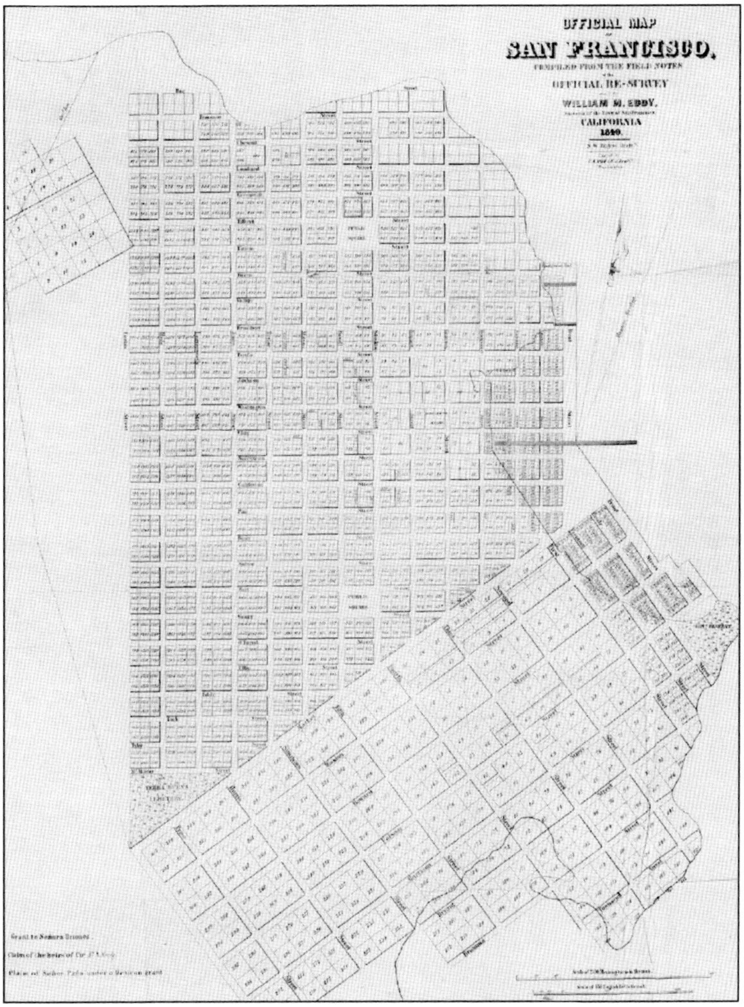

San Francisco offered opportunities for African Americans. Many came, from every state and the West Indies, traveling to San Francisco to establish businesses, get a job, seek gold, obtain land, find freedom, or to start a new life in the California free territory. Both slaves and freemen worked in the goldfields, while others worked as domestics. By 1860, the black population in San Francisco reached 1,176, and it grew to 1,654 by 1900. (Courtesy of Ramsey Maps.)

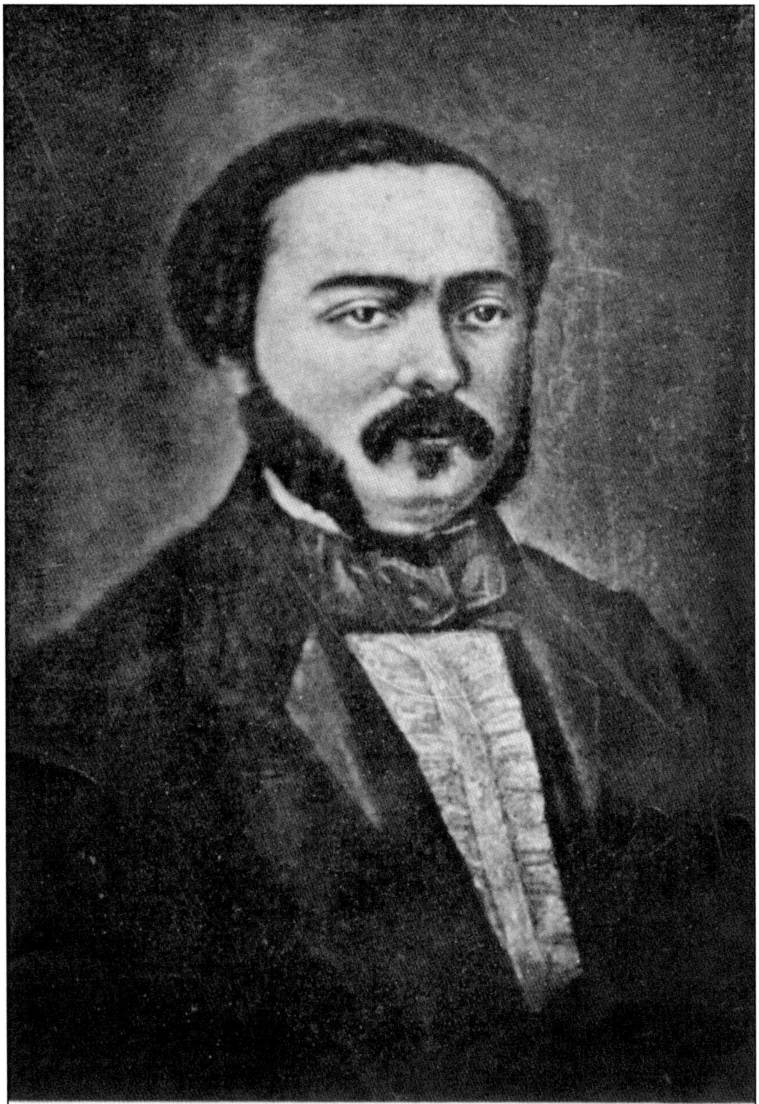

WILLIAM ALEXANDER LEIDESDORFF

According to *Blacks in Gold Rush California*, in 1841, merchant captain William Alexander Leidesdorff settled in San Francisco—the Mexican territory of Yerba Buena. Born in 1810 in St. Croix, Danish West Indies, he was of African and Danish heritage. Before settling in San Francisco, he lived in New Orleans and worked in the shipping business. Many in San Francisco, as well as in New Orleans, considered Leidesdorff white. In 1845, President Polk appointed Leidesdorff as an American vice consul because of his pro-American sentiments. Elected to San Francisco's town council in 1847, Leidesdorff, with others, started the public school system. He established several businesses and built the City Hotel. He was the first to bring his steam vessel, the *Sitka*, into the waters of San Francisco Bay. Leidesdorff was a wealthy businessman by the time of his death in 1848. He was buried at Mission Dolores in an elaborate ceremony "befitting his prominence and social virtues," writes Delilah Beasley. After his death, his mother in St. Croix was contacted, and the truth of his heritage became known to many. (Courtesy of San Francisco History Center, San Francisco Public Library.)

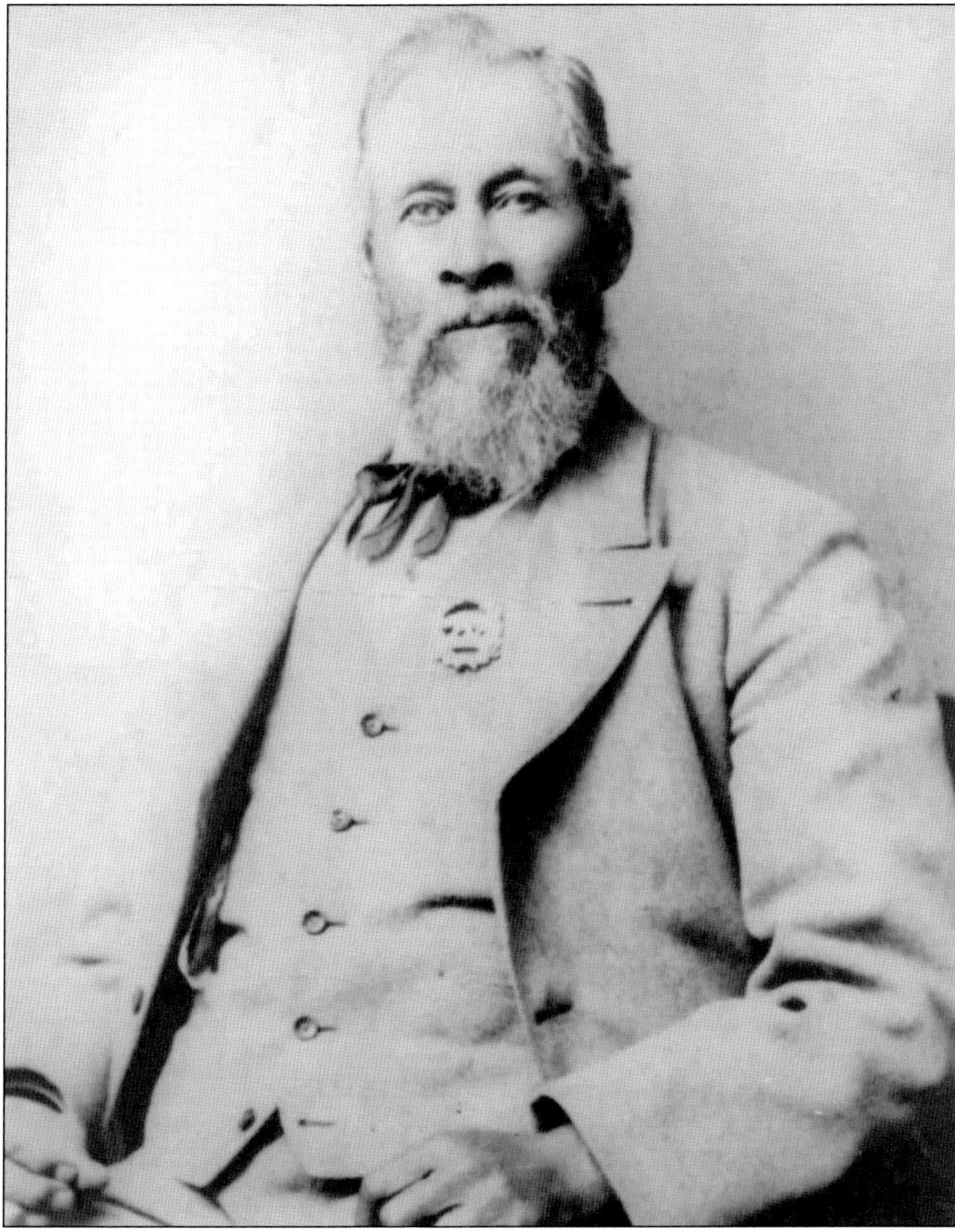

Many slaves were brought to California from slave states to work in the gold mines during the Gold Rush. Often, slaves were able to buy their freedom with money earned doing odd jobs in their spare time for their owners or other white miners. Alvin Coffey, born in 1822 as a slave, was first brought to California in 1849 by Doctor Bennett of Missouri and worked for a short time in the gold mines. In 1854, Coffey returned to California with another owner and bought freedom for himself and his family by working in the gold mines of Placer. Sue Bailey Thurman notes that after Coffey's death in 1902, several members of his family—including his granddaughter Ora Williams James, San Francisco's first black nursery school teacher—settled in San Francisco and worked to improve education and civil rights for African Americans during the early 1900s. (Courtesy of the African American Museum and Library at Oakland.)

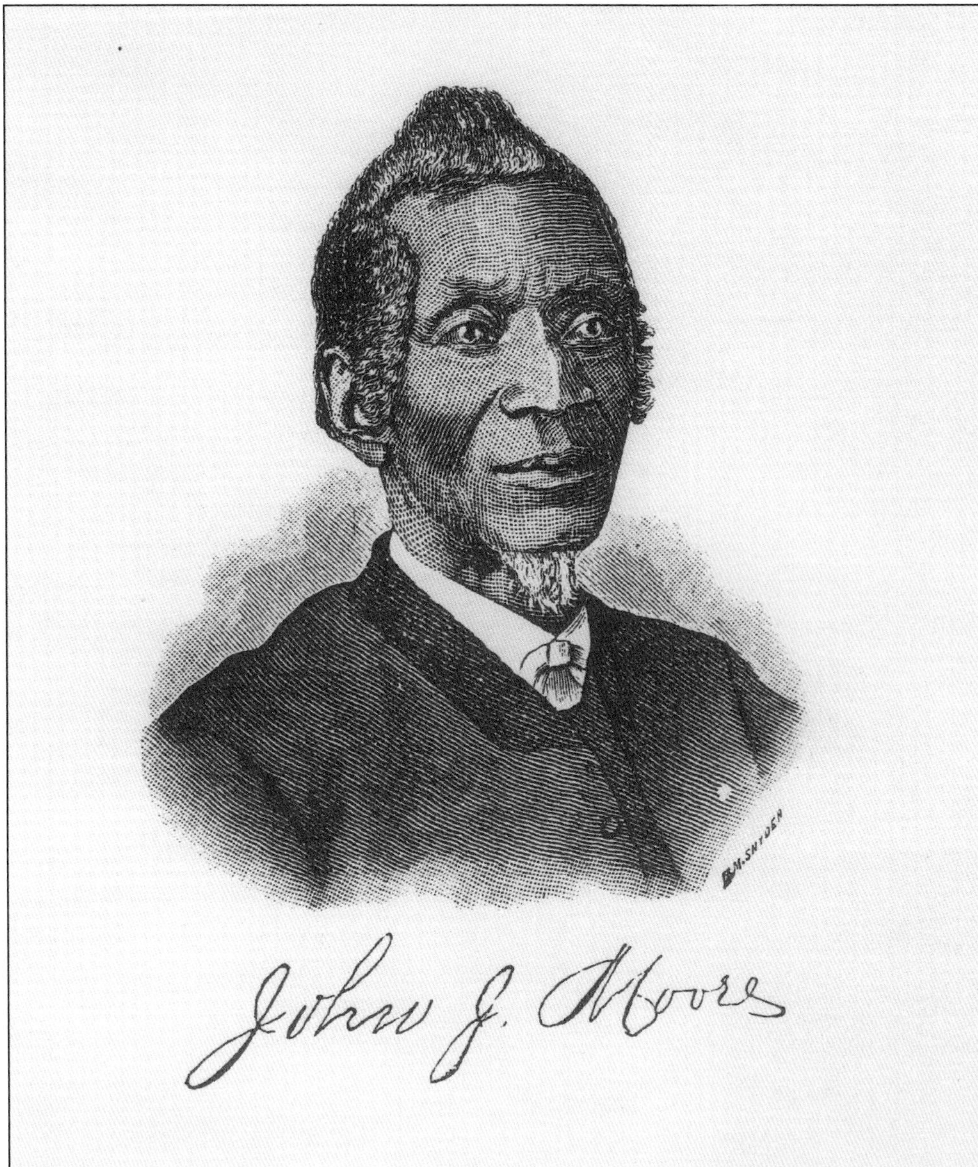

Church records state that John Jamison Moore, a slave, was born in 1818 in what is now West Virginia. Once freed from slavery and before slaves were emancipated, Moore joined the African Methodist Episcopal Zion Church as a young man and began traveling by day and preaching at night. In August 1852, Moore established the First Africa Methodist Episcopal Zion Church, located on Stockton Street between Broadway and Vallejo Streets in San Francisco. Moore was a prominent citizen of San Francisco. In 1855, he organized San Francisco's colored school, located in the basement of St. Cyprian's Church on Jackson and Virginia Streets. He was its first principal and teacher. In 1862, Moore published the first black, short-lived periodical, the *Lunar Visitor*. He also traveled throughout the Bay Area cities of Napa, San Jose, and Watsonville, ministering to African Americans. In 1855, Moore was the chaplain at the first Colored Convention of California. In the spring of 1868, Moore left San Francisco for Washington, DC, and accepted an appointment as bishop. (Courtesy of First AME Zion Church.)

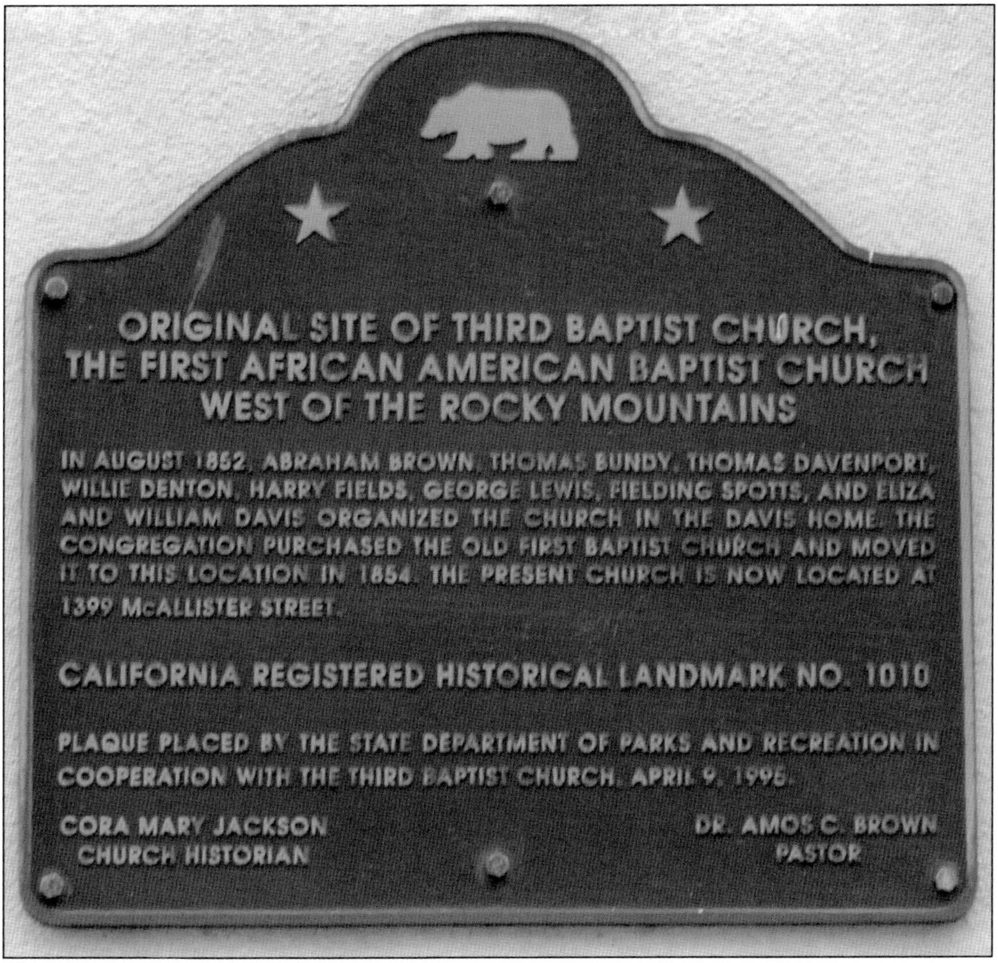

In 1852, Eliza and William Davis established their home as a meeting place for a group of nine black parishioners who decided to no longer worship in the segregated section of the First Baptist Church of San Francisco. According to church records, the First Colored Baptist Church of San Francisco, established in August 1852, was the first African American Baptist Church in the West. For five years, white ministers from the First and Second Baptist Churches of San Francisco provided communion services to church members until the first pastor, Rev. Charles Satchell of Cincinnati, was called in 1857. In 1854, the group bought the old First Baptist Church on Dupont Street. In 1855, the First Colored Church became the Third Baptist Church; however, its legal name was not changed until 1908. (Courtesy of Third Baptist Church.)

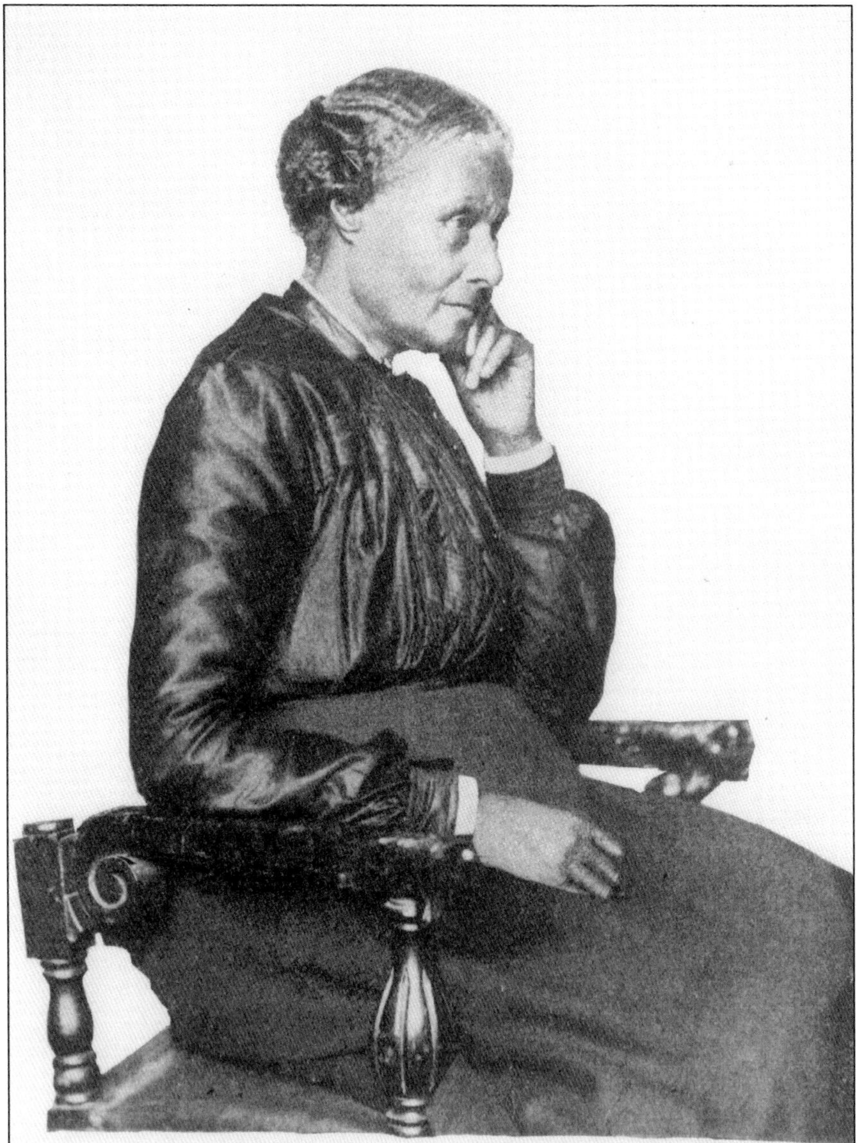

MARY ELLEN ("MAMMY") PLEASANT AT 87 YEARS OF AGE
The first and only photograph taken since she was 13 years old

In April 1852, Mary Ellen Pleasant, born a slave between 1814 and 1817 in either Virginia or Georgia, moved to San Francisco from Virginia. Delilah Beasley writes that after being freed when young, Pleasant was sent to Massachusetts for an education. During the 1840s, Pleasant and her husband helped many slaves escape to freedom through the Underground Railroad. With her husband's money after his death, it is believed Pleasant helped finance the John Brown raids. In San Francisco, she was a successful businesswoman, civil rights activist, and philanthropist. She started the first boardinghouse and provided housing for homeless girls and women. Pleasant, worth at least $30,000 in real estate in 1870, died penniless in 1904. In 1975, the city placed a memorial plaque and six eucalyptus trees at Octavia and Bush Streets as a tribute Pleasant's legacy. (Courtesy the California Historical Society, FN-22860/CHS2011.512.tif.)

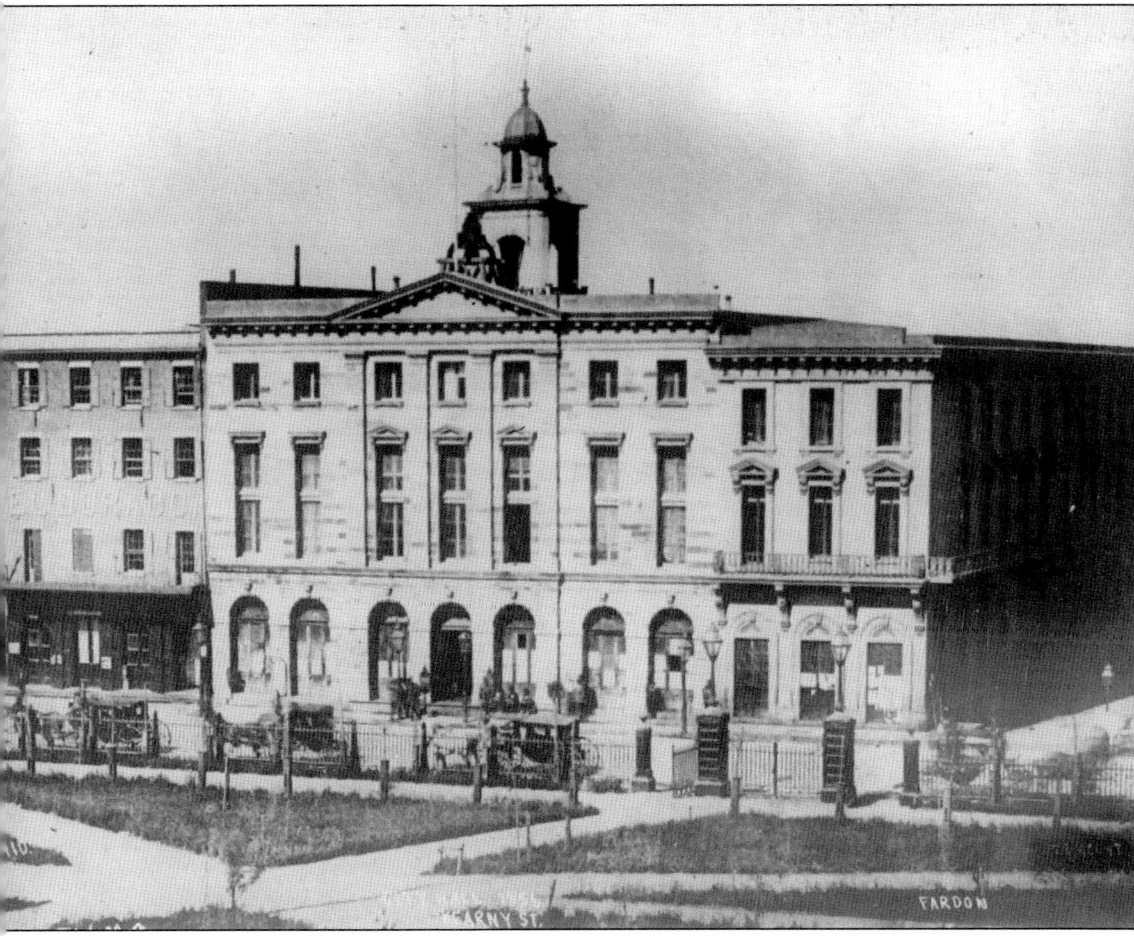

According to *Blacks in Gold Rush California*, in 1858, the Kearney Street Hall of Justice was home to Archy Lee, a fugitive slave, until he became a free man. At 18 years old, Lee was brought to California in 1857 by Mississippian Charles Stovall and worked in the gold mines. When Stovall decided to send Lee back, Lee resisted and hid in the black-owned Hackett Hotel. When found, Lee was tried under the California fugitive slave law, won his case, and was declared a free man. But a state supreme court justice reversed the decision under a fugitive slave law. When Stovall moved Lee to San Francisco to board a vessel traveling to Mississippi, black leaders George W. Dennis, Mifflin Gibbs, and Peter Lester hired a team of white lawyers to appeal Lee's case. Lee won his case, but a US marshal rearrested him in the courtroom under the national Fugitive Slave Act of 1850. Soon, riots broke out in front of the courthouse on Kearney Street, and Lee's case was retried. After winning his case, Lee joined San Francisco's black families who resettled in Victoria, British Columbia. (Courtesy the California Historical Society, FN-29364/CHS2011.576.tif.)

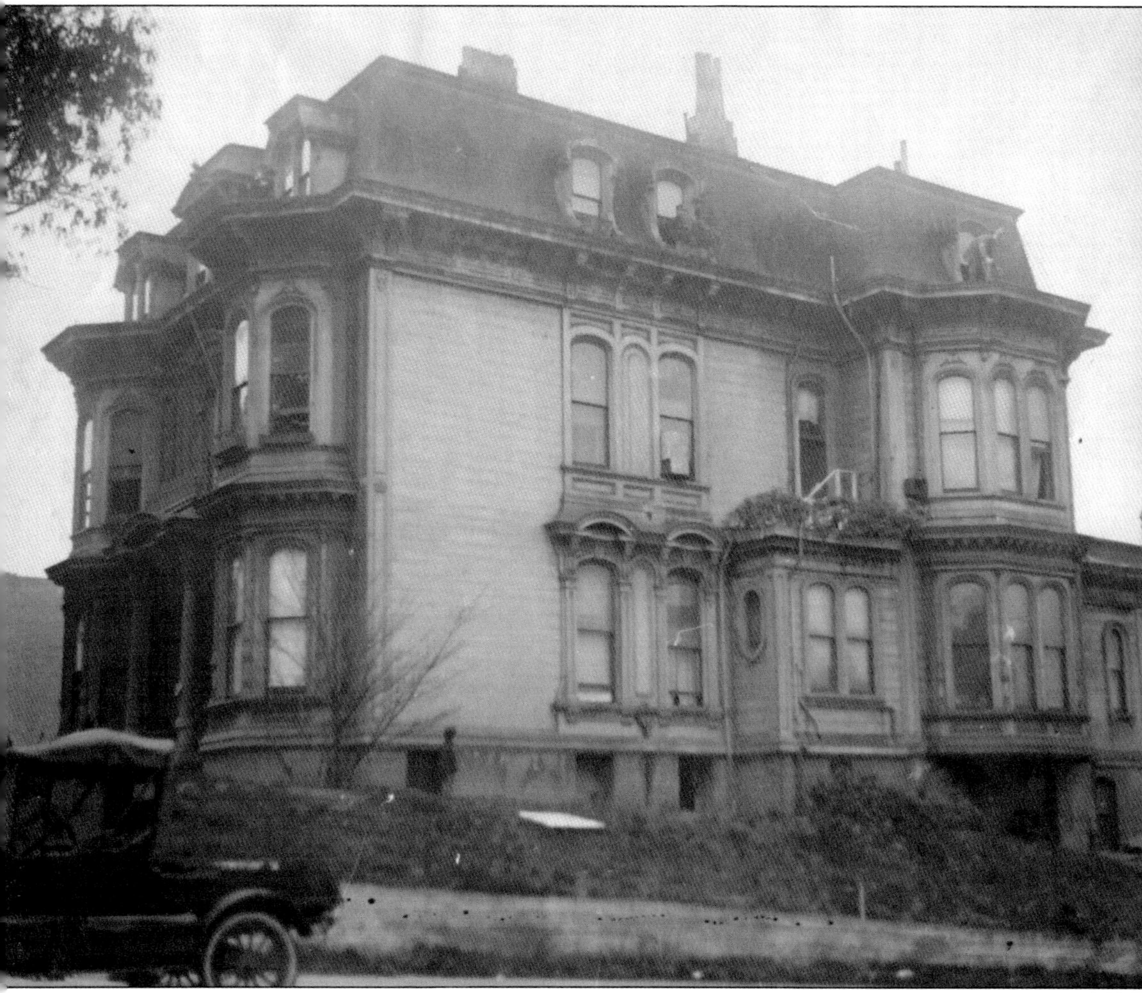

This is the Thomas Bell house on Octavia Street, where Mary Pleasant lived between 1860 and 1870 as a housekeeper to Bell and his wife. Prior to living with the Bell family, Pleasant was considered by some one of San Francisco's most notorious madams. In addition, she continued to provide financial support to both individuals and organizations for specific community needs. She is known today as the "Mother of Civil Rights" for her efforts to secure the rights of San Francisco's black citizens to enjoy equal access to the pubic railroad-transportation system. After Charlotte Brown won her case against the Omnibus Rail Company, Pleasant sued the rail company in 1868 on behalf of black citizens and won. This case protected the rights of African Americans to ride the public rail system. It is believed that on April 14, 1858, Pleasant provided housing for Archy Lee when he was declared a free man. According to historians, Pleasant provided funds to help in Lee's defense. (Courtesy of San Francisco History Center, San Francisco Public Library.)

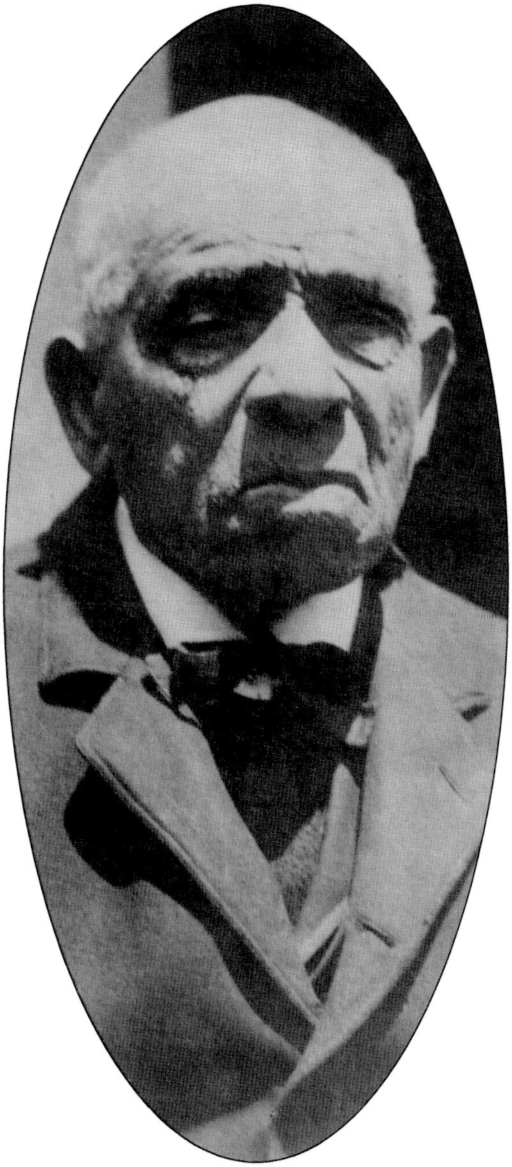

According to researcher Randolph Lapp, George W. Dennis came to California in 1849 as a slave to his white father's company of gamblers who desired to profit from gold miners. After three months, Dennis, who had a mind for business, was able to buy his freedom from his father with the money he had earned as a porter at the El Dorado Hotel located at Washington and Kearney Streets. Dennis saved his earnings, and along with his winnings from the gambling table, he bought his freedom for $1,000 and started a business. Dennis later owned several properties in San Francisco as well as the largest horse livery business in the city. In 1858, he helped finance the Archie Lee defense team. In 1855, Dennis married Margaret Brown, the sister of Charlotte Brown, and raised 11 children, who eventually raised their own children in San Francisco. Members of the Dennis family members were outstanding leaders in San Francisco. The Dennis children became teachers, lawyers, and businessmen/women in the city. A desire to succeed in business and to achieve in leadership lasted through many generations of the Dennis family. (Courtesy of the California Historical Society, de Young Collection, FN-19961/CHA20111.513.tif.)

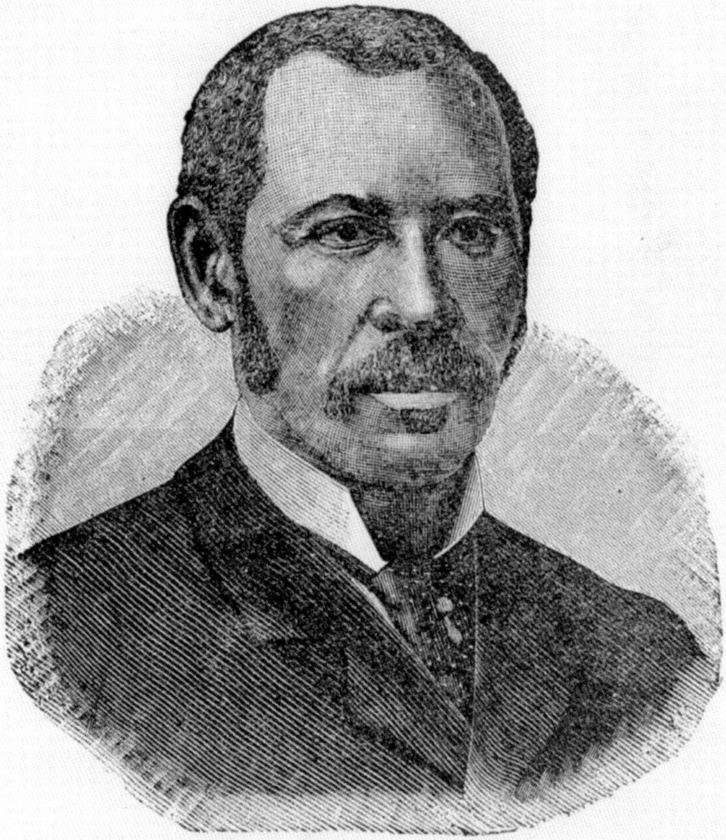

HON. MIFFLIN W. GIBBS.

Rudolph Lapp writes that Mufflin Wistar Gibbs, born in Philadelphia on April 12, 1823, worked with Frederick Douglass as an abolitionist lecturer throughout the Northeast and Midwest. In 1849, Gibbs came to San Francisco and worked as bootblack (a person who shines shoes). In the 1850s, Gibbs started a clothing business in San Francisco with Peter Lester, a fellow Philadelphian. In 1855, Gibbs was cofounder of San Francisco's first black newspaper, the *Mirror of the Times*, which lasted from 1855 to 1857. The *Mirror of the Times* led to two successful newspapers that followed five years later and lasted through the end of the century. In 1858, Gibbs left San Francisco because of the growing racial prejudice towards African Americans. He led the migration of 200 other black families from San Francisco to Victoria, British Columbia. In Victoria, Gibbs became a very successful and wealthy coal shipper. Later, he returned to the United States and lived in Little Rock, Arkansas, where he became a judge and, later, US consul to Madagascar. He retired in Little Rock and lived there until July 11, 1915. (Courtesy of the California Historical Society, FN-10675/CHS2011.516.tif.)

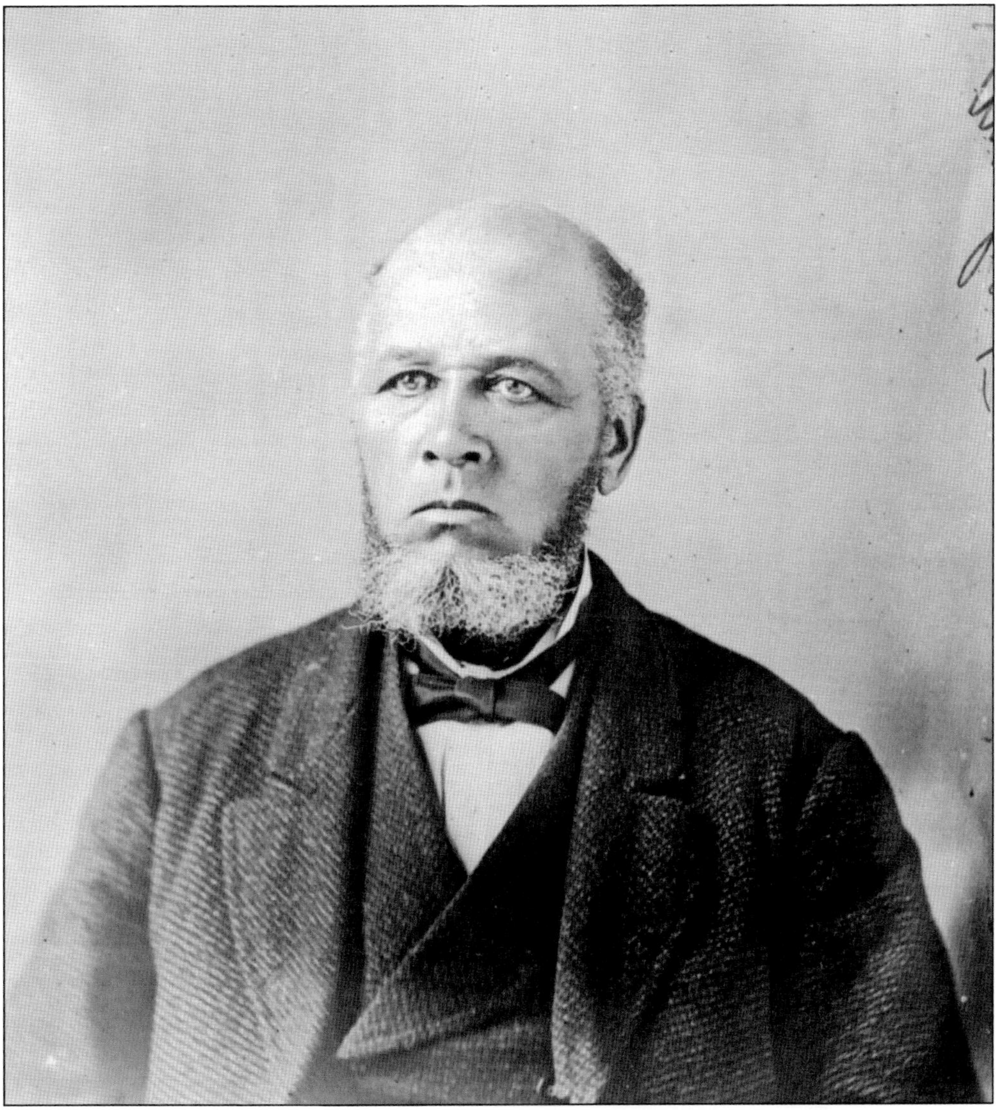

Peter Lester, a bootblack and boot maker, moved to San Francisco from Philadelphia in 1850 with his wife and five children. Opposed to slavery in the free state of California, Lester made his home a safe place for slaves to learn about their rights and to sing antislavery songs. In 1851, Lester and Mifflin Gibbs established a shoe store named Emporium for Fine Boots and Shoes, imported from Philadelphia, London, and Paris. This business was successful, and Lester and Gibbs became very wealthy. Despite this success, Lester despised the way blacks were treated in California. Once, two white men assaulted Lester in his store with a cane and stole a pair of shoes. Lester could not press charges against the men because the courts did not allow blacks to testify against whites. Given this event and a new measure by the California legislature to ban further black immigration to California, Lester and his family participated in a mass exodus of African Americans from San Francisco to Victoria, British Columbia, Canada, where he lived until his death after 1891. (Courtesy of Royal BC Museum, BC Archives, image A-01626.)

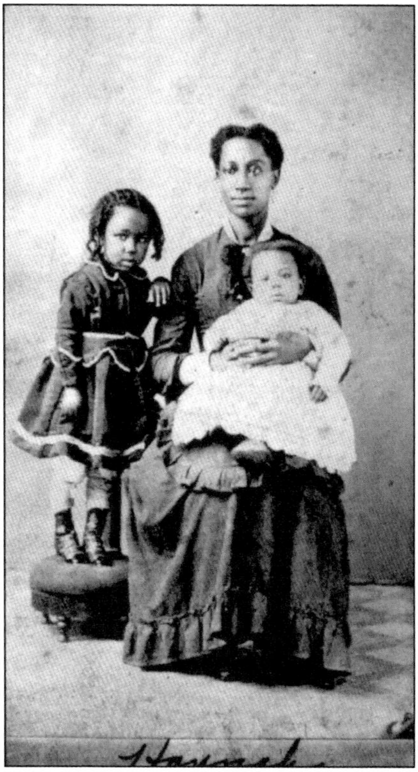

According to information in the Salt Spring Island Archives, Hannah Estes and two of her children, pictured at left, departed California in the 1850s with other African Americans and settled in Victoria, British Columbia. Like Peter Lester, some were fed up with the lack of progress toward equality in San Francisco and left in a mass exit to Canada. Some 200 families emigrated from San Francisco. Many of these pioneers settled in Salt Spring Island and purchased land, built homes, and established a small community of farmers and fishermen. During the 19th century, schools were established, and black teachers from America traveled to the island to provide instruction to black children. The photograph below shows an unidentified family that also settled in Salt Spring Island during the 19th century. Today, there is a community of descendants from the original black families—some from San Francisco—who still live on the island. (Both, courtesy of Salt Spring Island Archives.)

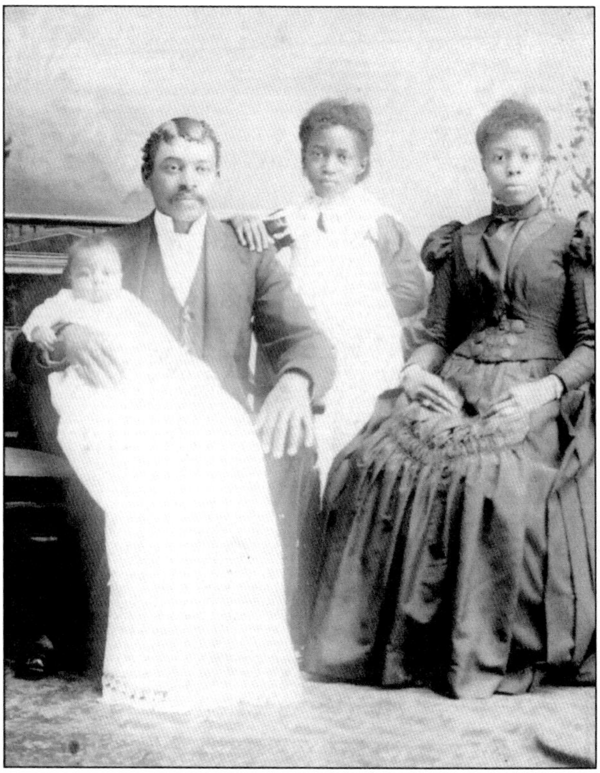

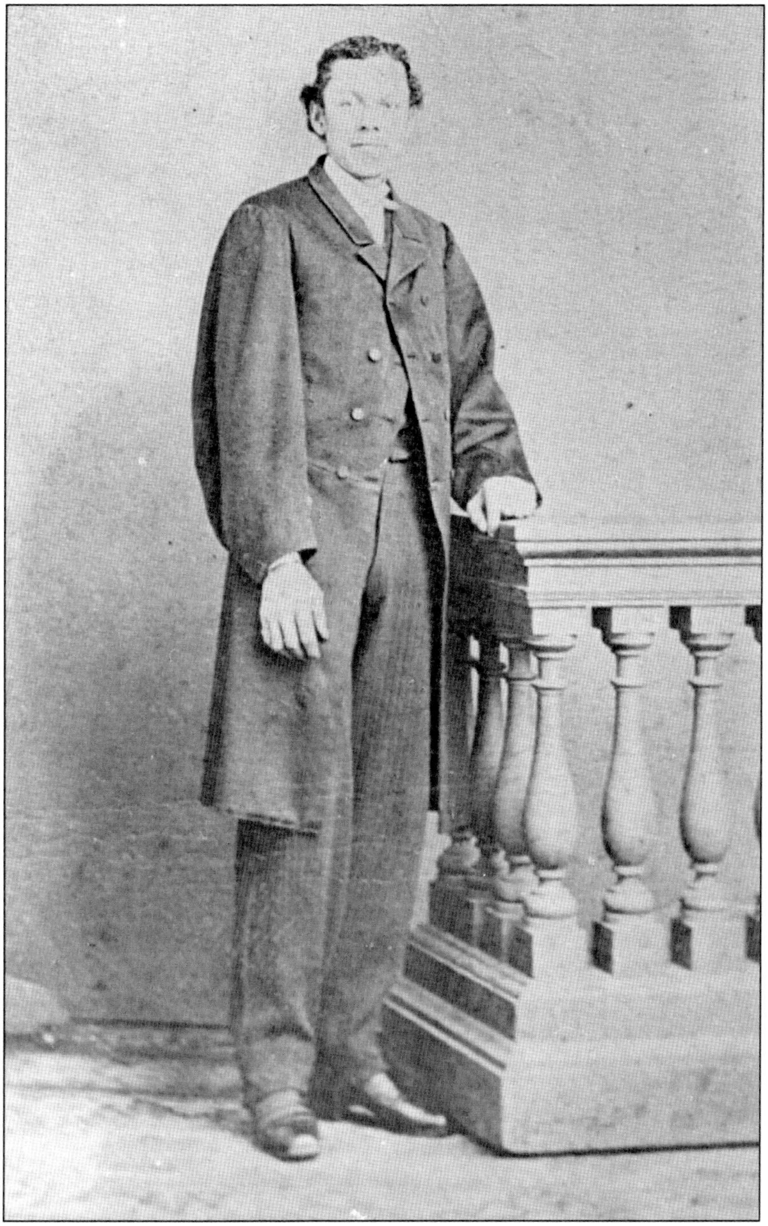

In 1821, Jeremiah Burke Sanderson was born in New Bedford, Massachusetts, and became a prominent black leader in Massachusetts and an associate of Frederick Douglass in New York. He immigrated to California in 1854. In 1855, Sanderson, an antislavery activist and speaker, opened the first meeting of the convention of Colored Citizens of California at the AME church in Sacramento. In 1857, Sanderson served as a preacher at Little Pilgrim Church, located on Scott Street. In 1859, he was a teacher and then eventually principal of a segregated black school in San Francisco. This school was located in the basement of St. Cyprian's Church. After eight years as school principal of the "colored school," Sanderson left San Francisco, moved to Stockton, and established another school for black students, where he taught from 1868 to 1875. (Courtesy of the African American Museum Library at Oakland.)

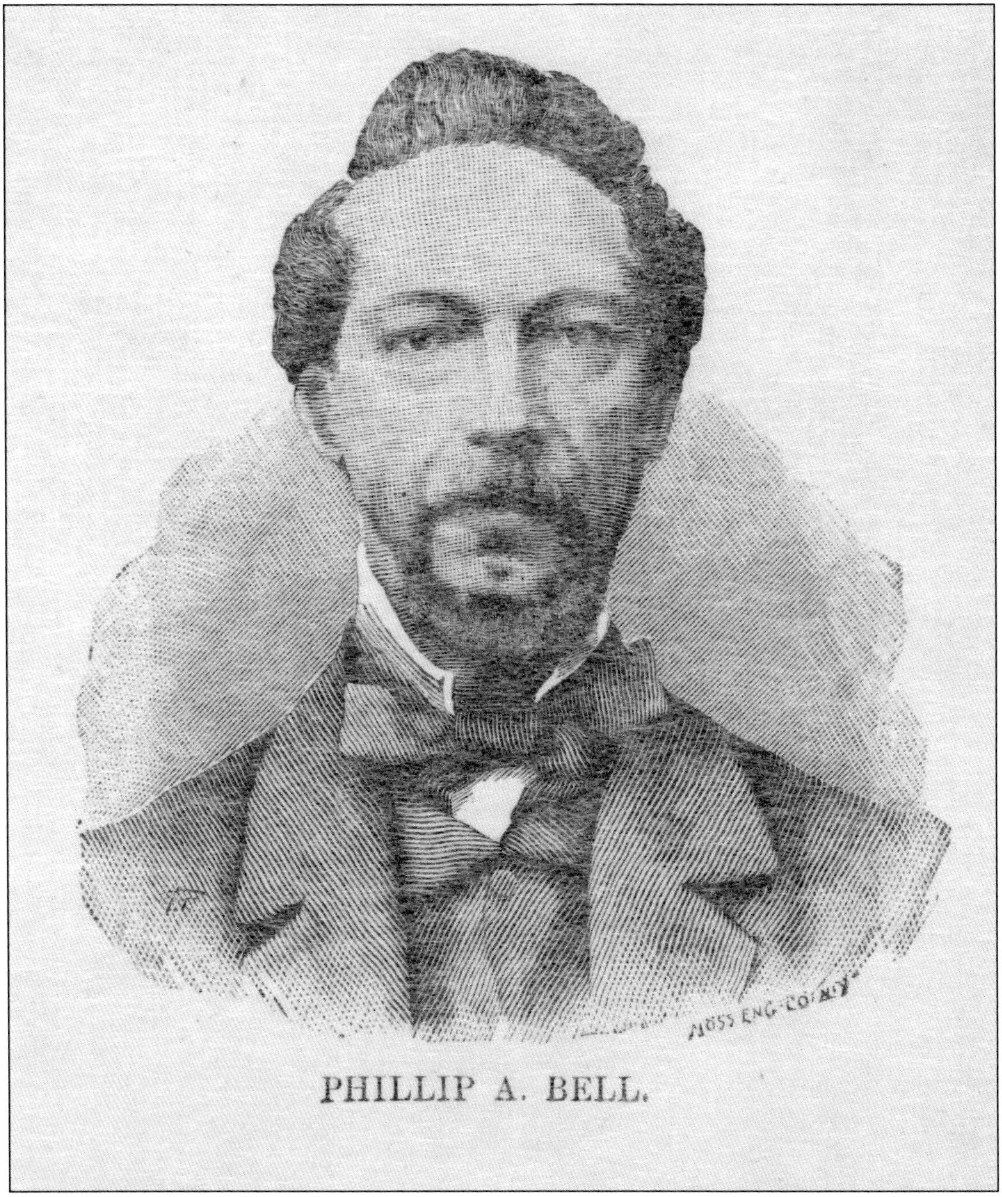

Phillip A. Bell served as coeditor of San Francisco's second black newspaper, the *Pacific Appeal*, from 1862 to 1864 and as editor of the *Elevator* from 1864 to 1879. Bell was born in 1808 in New York City. Before relocating to San Francisco, he worked in New York for William Lloyd Garrison and Frederick Douglass in abolitionist politics. In 1860, he moved to San Francisco and reported on Bay Area community events and black political and economic opportunities on the West Coast. Because of political differences and issues about the direction of the *Pacific Appeal* newspaper, Bell discontinued as coeditor and started the *Elevator* newspaper in 1864. Bell's *Elevator* became the longest-running black newspaper during the 1800s. Bell used the newspaper to promote local events, civil rights for black citizens, and education for black children. Bell died in San Francisco in 1879. (Courtesy of Manuscripts, Archives and Rare Books Division, Schomburg Center for Research in Black Culture, the New York Public Library, Astor, Lenox, and Tilden Foundations.)

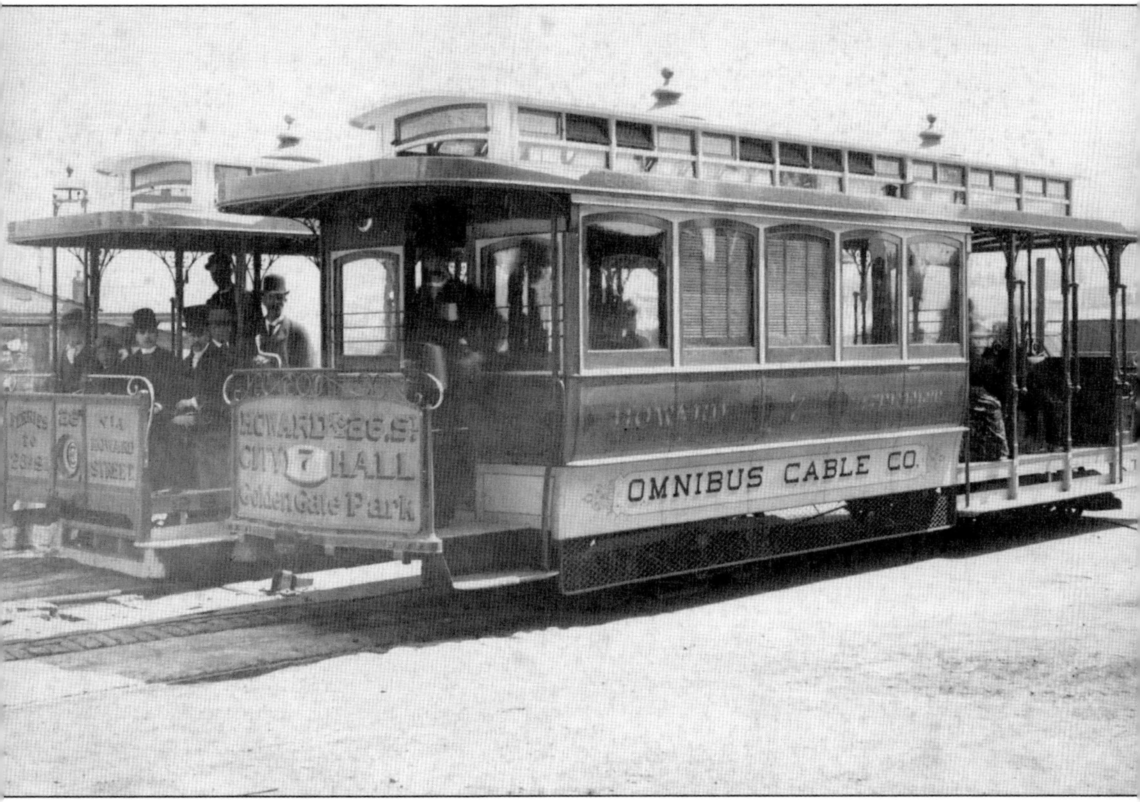

In April 1863, Charlotte L. Brown, a black citizen from San Francisco, rode an Omnibus cable car and was told by the driver that she must give her seat to a white woman who could not find a place to sit. As stated in court transcripts, Brown sued the Omnibus Cable Co. and was awarded $500 because she had been allowed to ride the bus in the past. However, her award only applied to her case and did not prohibit Omnibus from preventing other African Americans from riding the bus. Because of the Brown v. the Omnibus Cable Co. case, Mary Pleasant in 1866 successfully sued the railroad in Pleasant v. North Beach and Mission Railway, which disallowed segregation of the city's public conveyances. (Courtesy of the California Historical Society, de Young Collection, FN-23845/CHS2011.511.tif.)

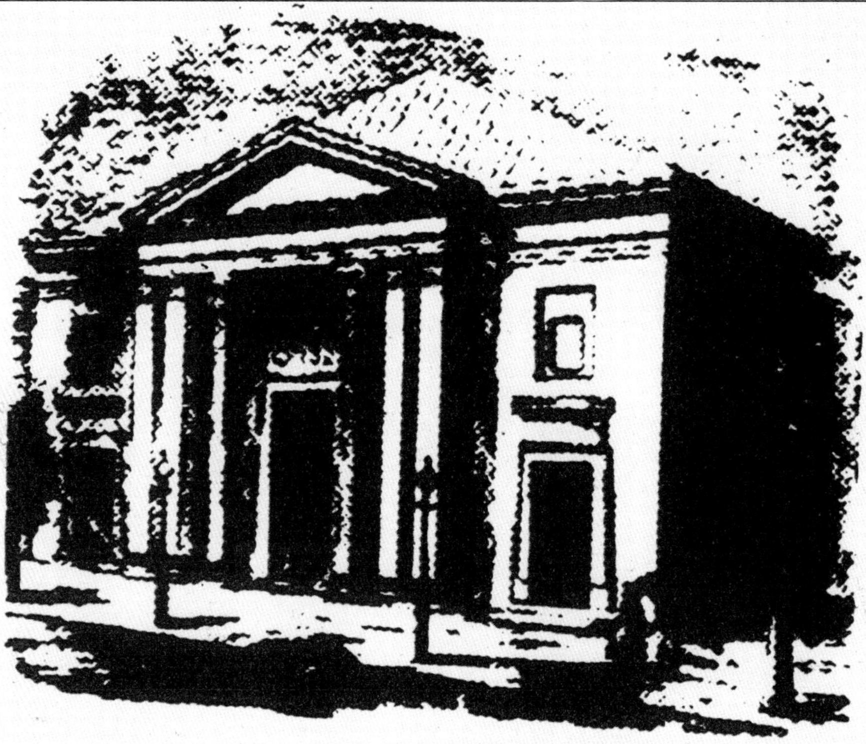

FIRST A.M.E. ZION CHURCH
(Organized 1852)

First Church Home Pictured Here
Stockton Street
(between Broadway and Pacific)

In 1864, the congregation of the First AME Zion Church purchased its first building on Stockton and Pacific Streets from the First Unitarian Church, which was pastored by a white minister, Rev. Thomas Starr King. From 1864 to 1906, the congregation met in this church building. From 1852 to 1855, before purchasing this building, the congregation had met in a makeshift, primitive structure. Then, the congregation moved to a church on Stockton Street between Broadway and Vallejo Streets and became known as the Stockton Street AME Zion Church. From 1855 to 1864, this congregation called themselves the Starr King Methodist Church, out of reverence to Reverend King, who wanted to see this congregation thrive. In 1870, the congregation became officially known as the First African Methodist Episcopal Zion Church. They continued to focus on educational, cultural, social, and political activities as well as spiritual sustenance. The First AME Zion Church stayed in this building until 1906, when it was destroyed in the fire that immediately followed the earthquake of 1906. (Courtesy of First AME Zion Church.)

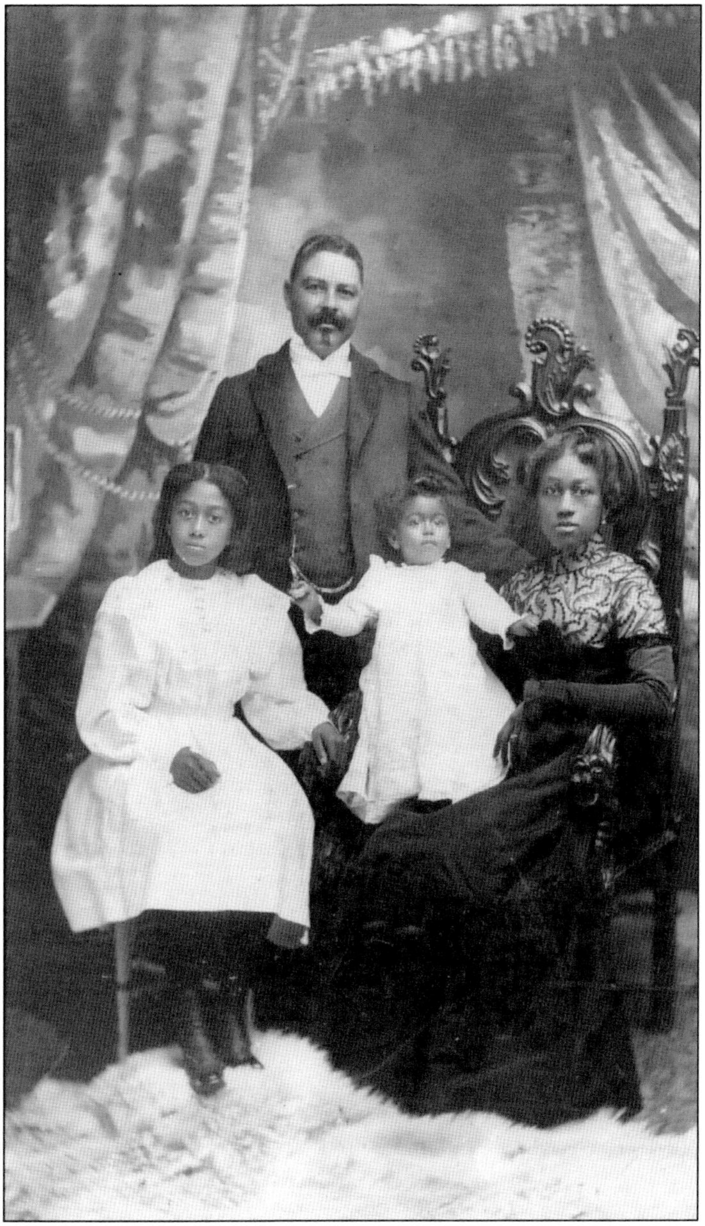

Capt. William Shorey and his wife, Julia, were prominent citizens of San Francisco. Shorey was born in 1859 in Barbados. He learned navigation while serving as a crewmember of a British vessel in 1875. In 1878, Shorey came to San Francisco on the whaler *Emma F. Herriman*. After 10 years at sea, Shorey became the only black captain on the West Coast. Historian E. Berkeley Tompkins notes that as a whaling captain and entrepreneur, Shorey was nicknamed "Black Ahab" by his crewmen. Black men often found work on whalers and grain vessels. In 1887, Shorey married Julia Ann Shelton, the daughter of a prominent San Francisco black family. While in the city, he commanded whaling vessels and other cargo ships based in San Francisco. In this 1910 photograph, he is pictured with wife, Julia, and daughters Zenobia (left) and Victoria. Shorey died in Oakland in 1919. (Courtesy of the California Historical Society, FN-13157/CHS2011.518.tif.)

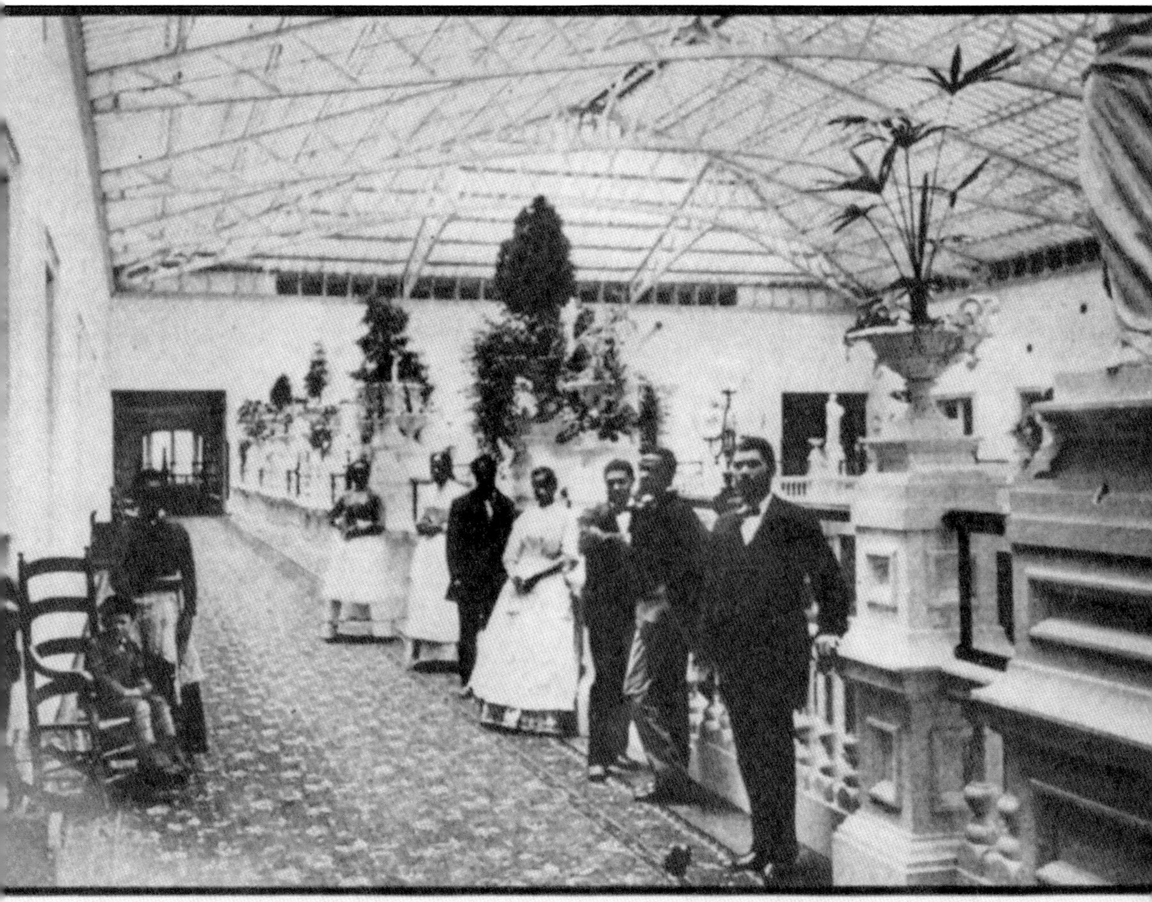

Negro Chambermaids and Porters on the Upper Balcony of the Grand Court

Black chambermaids and porters are seen in 1878 on the upper balcony of the Grand Court in the Palace Hotel of San Francisco. "Negroes' tradition of excellent service accounted for the presence of nearly 200 black employees at San Francisco's famous Palace Hotel from 1875 to 1889," says Douglas Henry Daniels. Many African Americans worked as butlers, domestic workers in homes of wealthy white citizens, barbers, seamstresses, janitors, and other jobs. Black citizens of San Francisco had their own social clubs, owned businesses, and invested in stocks and savings at local banks. (Courtesy of the California Historical Society, CHS2011.514.tif.)

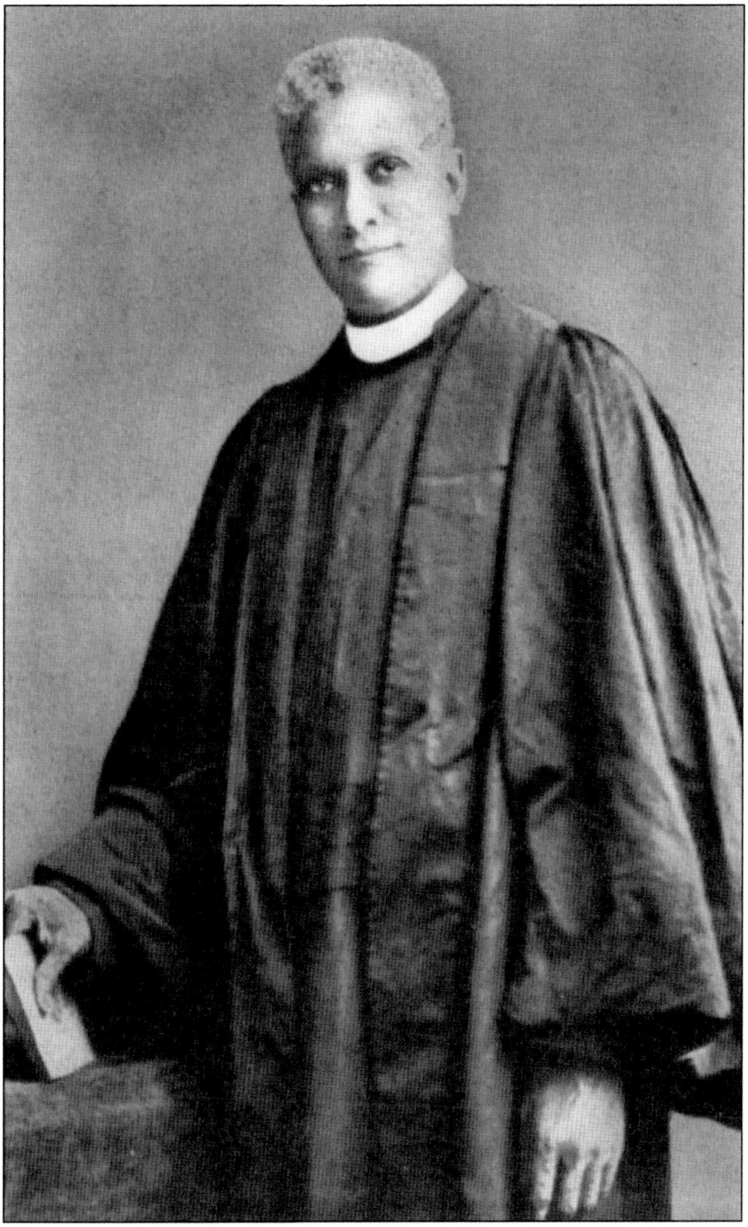

According to church records, Rev. Alexander Walters, a civil rights leader, was born a slave in 1856 in Bardstown, Kentucky. He served as pastor of San Francisco's First AME Zion from 1883 to 1888. The church building was located at Stockton and Pacific Streets. In 1888, Walters left San Francisco to return to the Mother Zion Church in New York. He was appointed bishop and reassigned to another conference. In 1900, he became a member of the Niagara Movement and met on the Canadian side of Niagara Falls with W.E.B. Du Bois and others to address issues of discrimination, lynching, and other violations against African Americans. In 1889, he represented Zion Church in London at the World's Sunday School Convention. Walters was considered one of the most influential black clergymen at the time. He was one of the original founders of the NAACP in 1909 and its president in 1911. In 1917, he died of natural causes. (Courtesy of First AME Zion Church.)

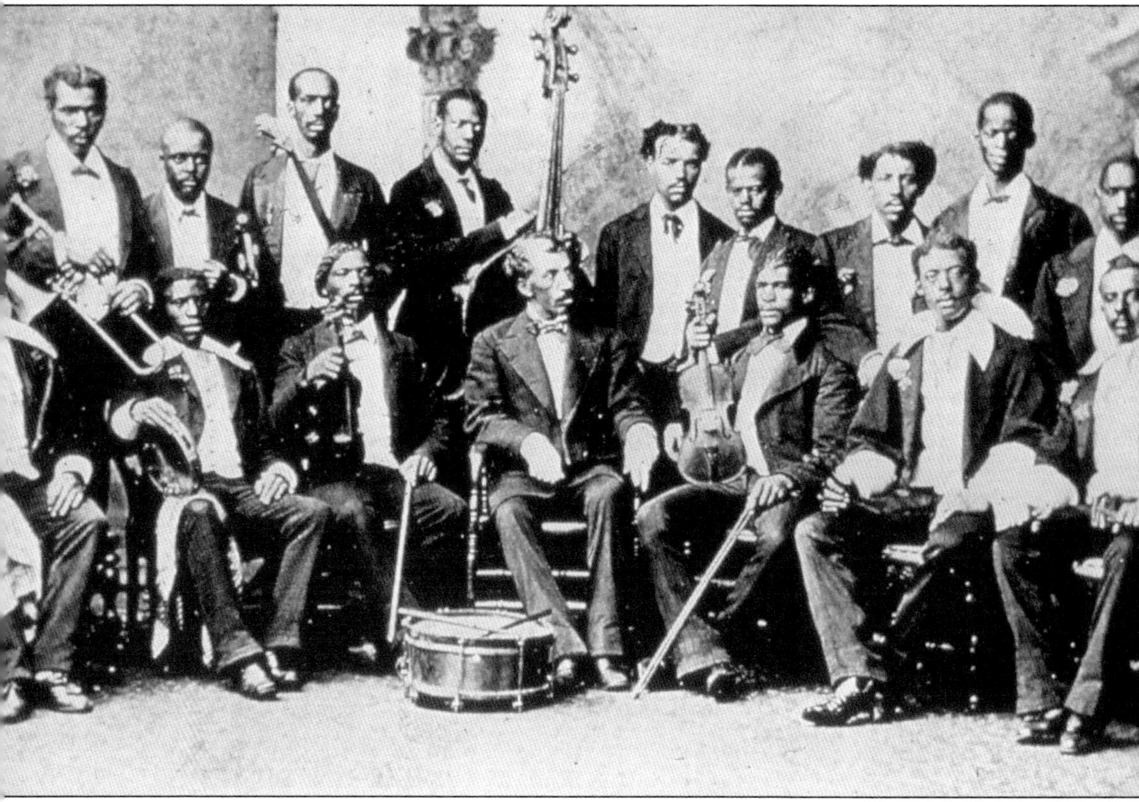

According to researcher Patty Yancey, minstrel shows began performing in California during the Gold Rush days and continued to the turn of the century. Originally, whites performed in minstrel shows; however, after the Civil War, African Americans began performing to both black and white audiences. (Courtesy of the Museum of Performance and Design.)

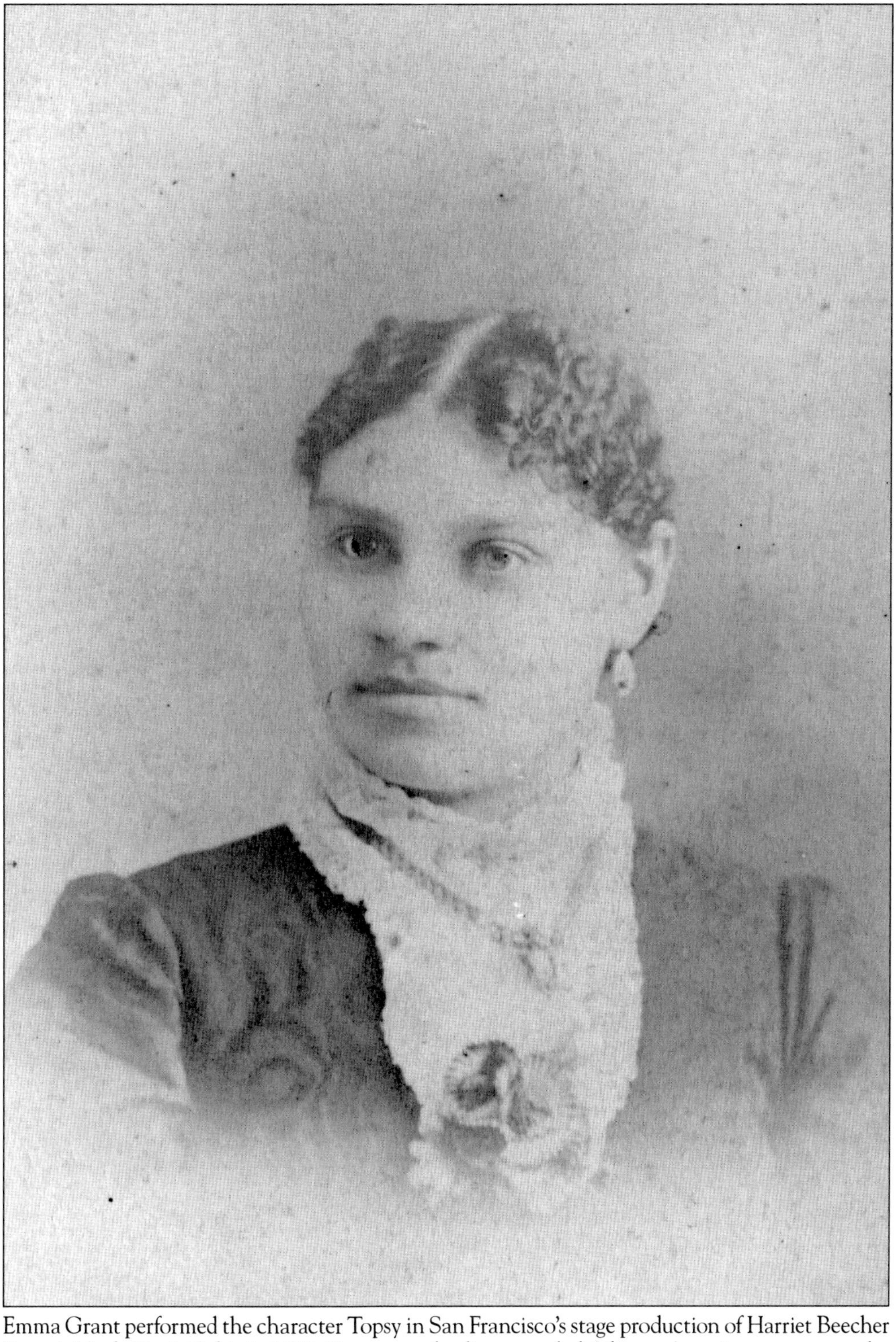

Emma Grant performed the character Topsy in San Francisco's stage production of Harriet Beecher Stowe's *Uncle Tom's Cabin* in 1876. Grant was the first recorded African American actress on the American stage. (Courtesy of the Museum of Performance and Design.)

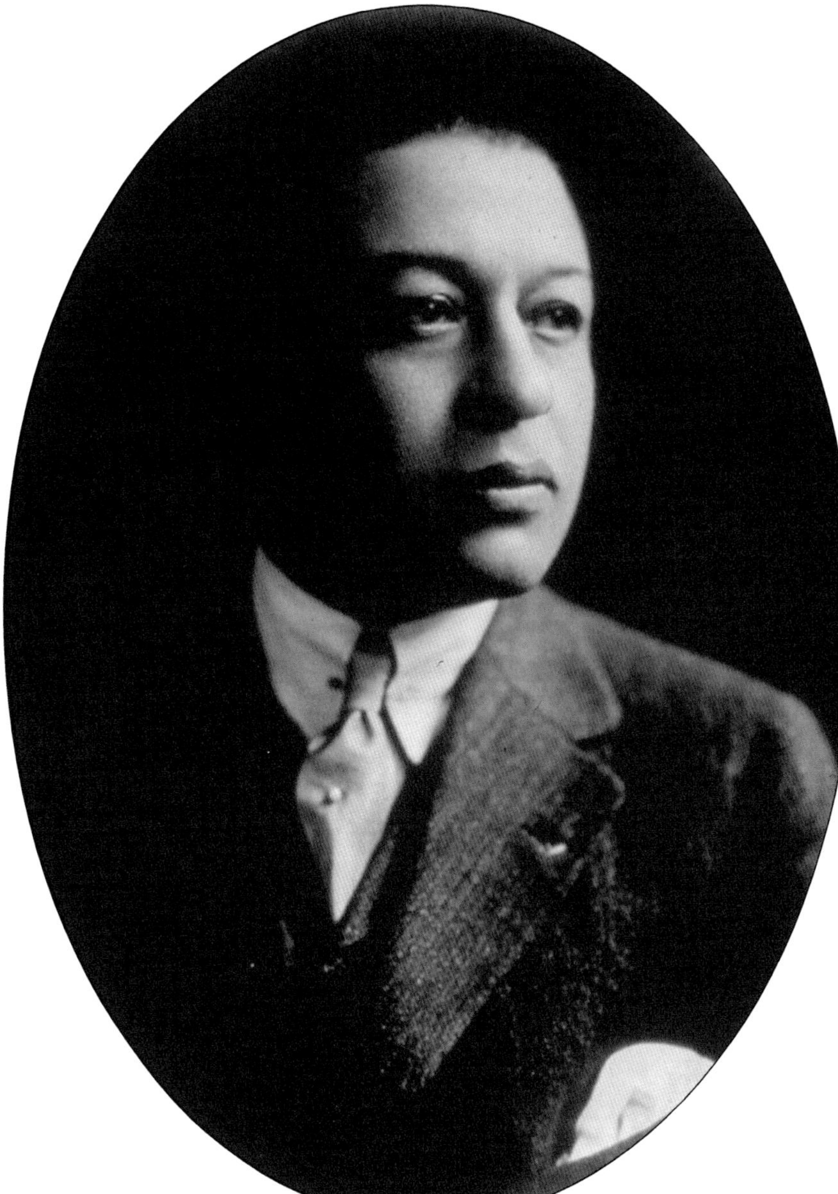

Egbert "Bert" Austin Williams is considered one of the greatest vaudeville performers in US history. He was an actor, mime, singer, dancer, and songwriter. Bert was born in the West Indies in 1874 and relocated with his family in 1885 to Riverside, California. Bert wanted to attend Stanford University in the field of engineering. However, he did not have the money to pay for studies. To make extra money, Bert and his friend traveled to small towns performing as clowns who sang and danced. Through this experience, Bert gained a desire for entertaining. He started performing in San Francisco's Barbary Coast saloons. In 1893, Bert joined the minstrel shows touring cities of Northern California. From 1910 to 1919, he performed with the Ziegfeld Follies and traveled around the country. He was the only black performer and gained recognition for his many talents. In 1922, Bert caught pneumonia while performing on Broadway and died. (Courtesy of the Museum of Performance and Design.)

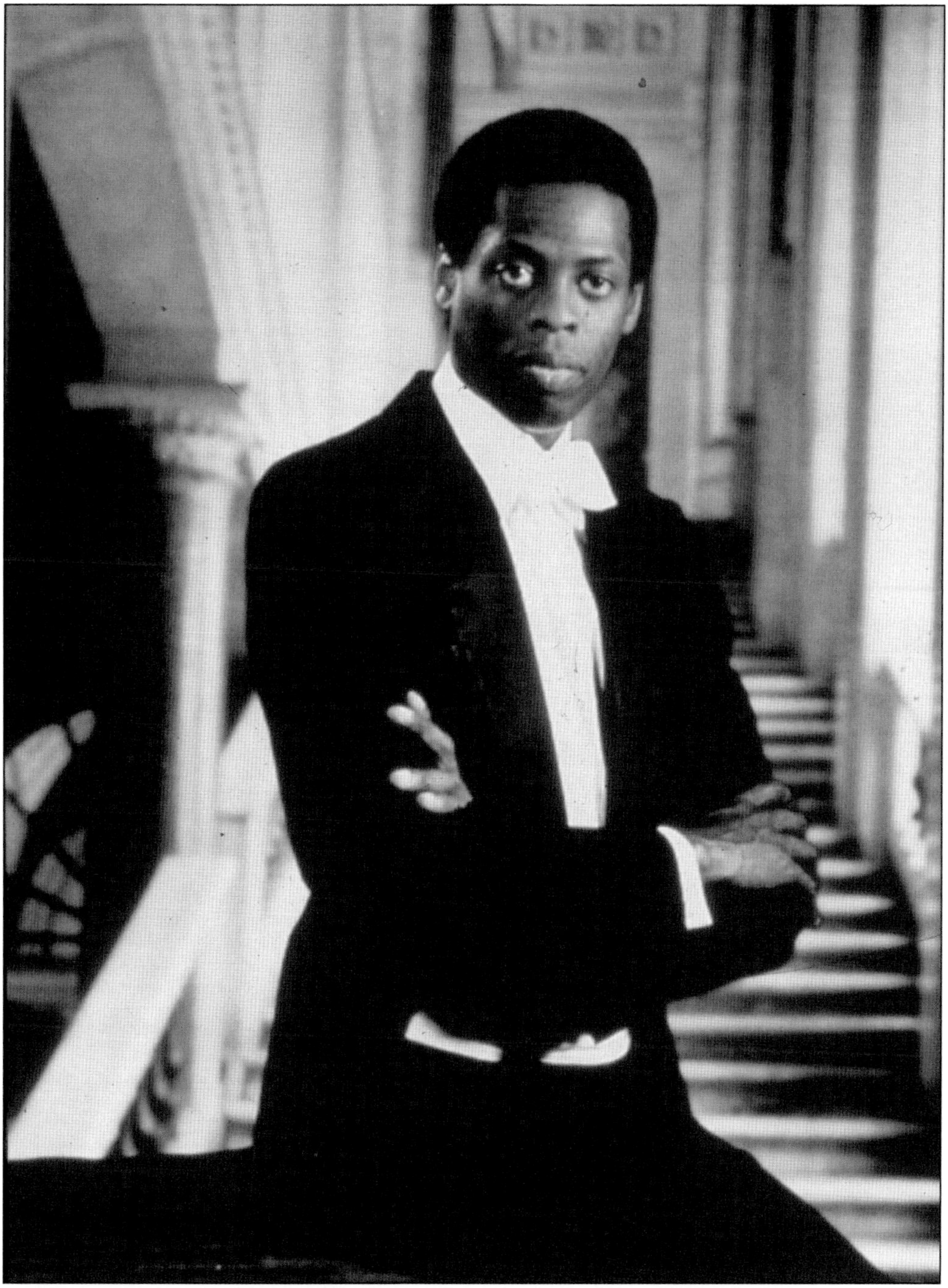

George Walker performed with Bert Williams for 15 years before Walker retired in 1908 due to illness. After their Broadway appearance, they created pioneering vaudeville shows that toured the United States and Europe. Many of their musicals appeared on Broadway. (Courtesy of the Museum of Performance and Design.)

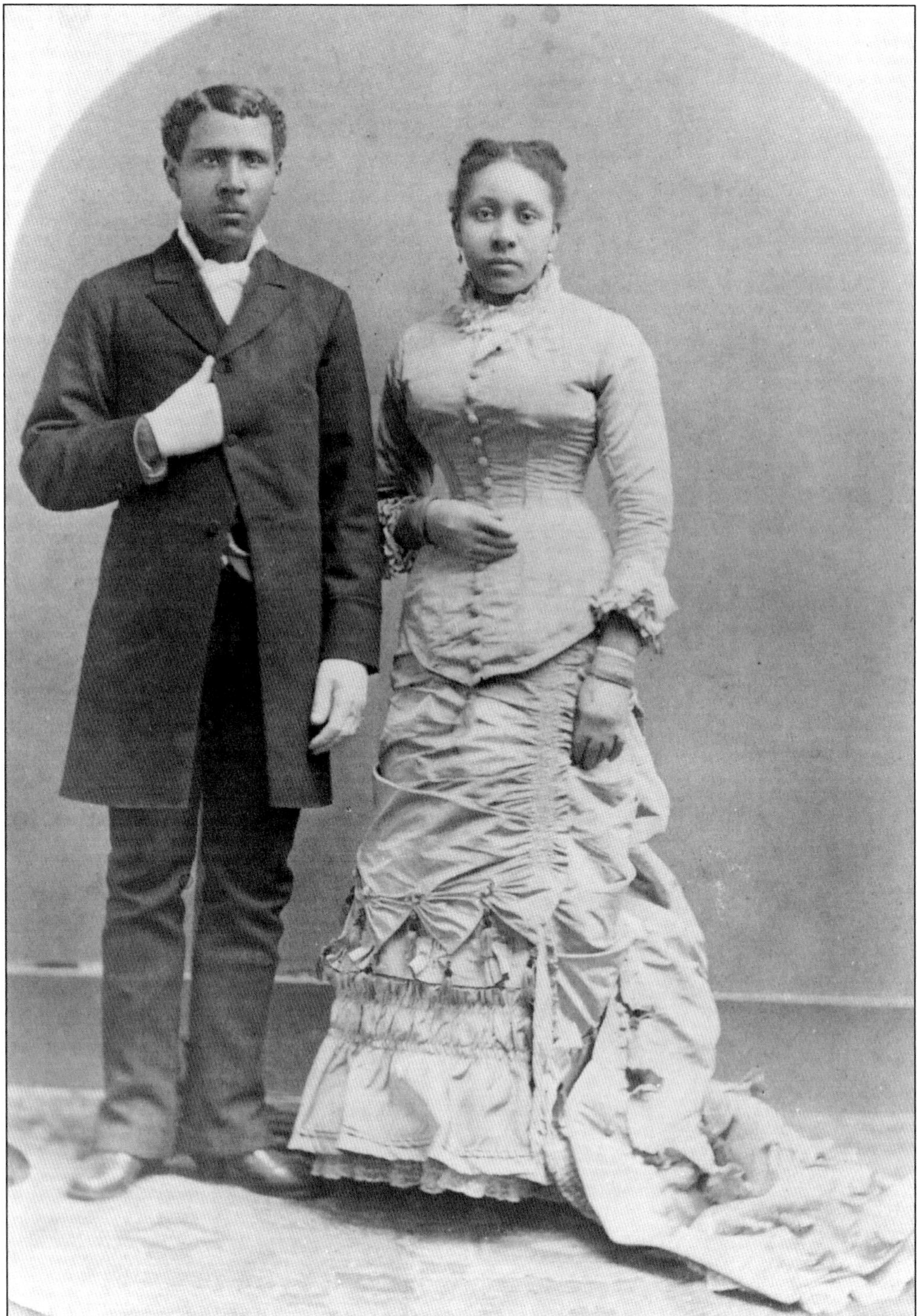

San Francisco residents Richmond and Lilla Bozier were married on June 25, 1880. They celebrated their 50th wedding anniversary on June 25, 1930. (Courtesy of the California Historical Society, FN-12800/CHS2011.515.tif.)

Two

1900–1950

War, Migration, Employment Opportunities, and San Francisco's Emerging Black Community

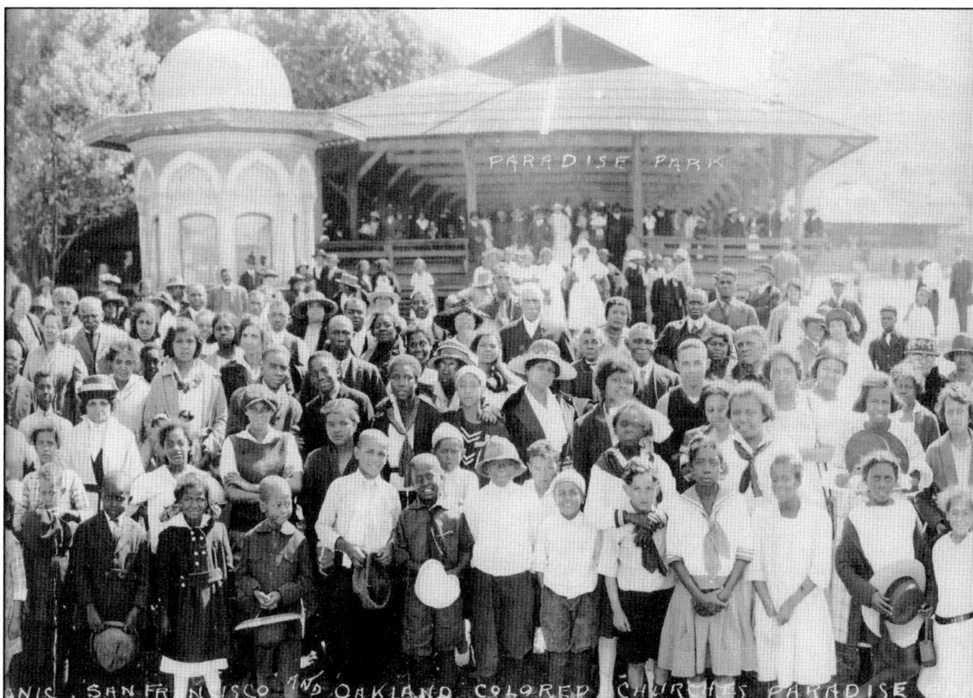

Between 1900 and 1950, the migration of African Americans to San Francisco increased drastically as employment opportunities in the war industries expanded. The African American population grew from 1,654 in 1900 to 4,846 in 1940 and to 43,460 by 1950. Here, African American churchgoers from San Francisco and Oakland attend a church picnic at Paradise Park on July 14, 1914. (Courtesy of Third Baptist Church of San Francisco Inc.)

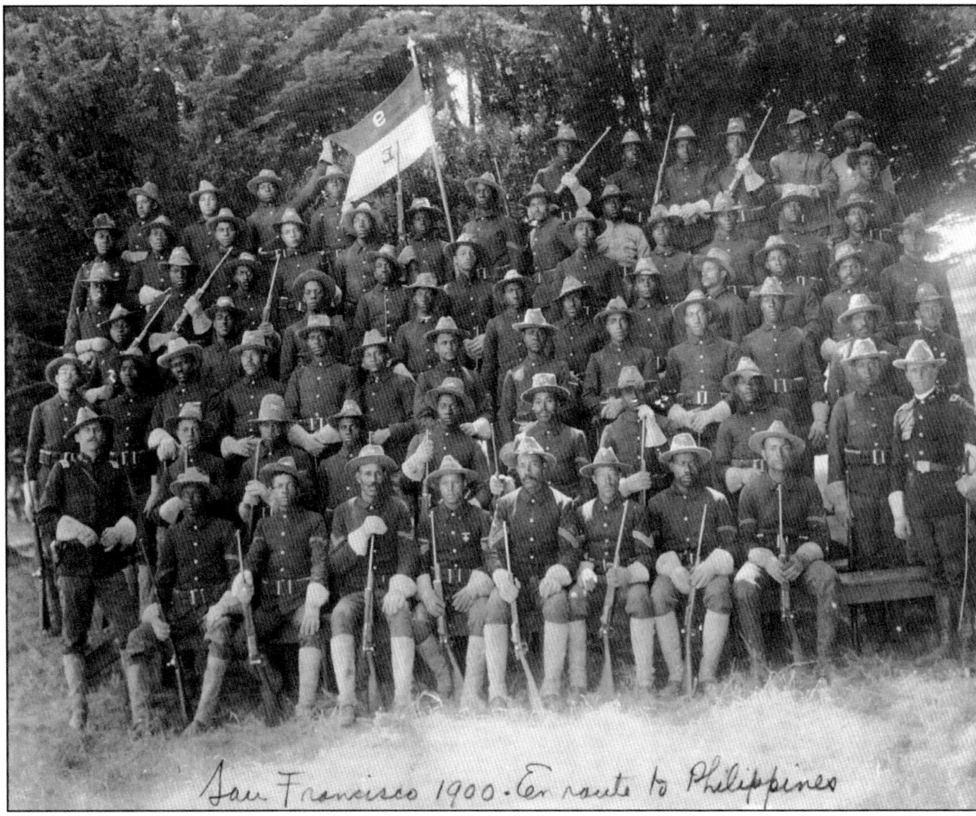

African Americans have defended America since the Revolutionary War. Since the Civil War, black soldiers were known as buffalo soldiers and served in segregated military units. San Francisco has been a major military installation since the 19th century, and often the buffalo soldiers were stationed at the Presidio in San Francisco until they were reassigned to new fronts. African American units were posted on regular garrison duty at the post. Members of the 9th Cavalry were stationed at the Presidio in 1900 prior to their shipping out to the Philippines. In the photograph below, these segregated barracks were assigned to black soldiers of the cavalry and infantry at the Presidio. Today, the National Park Service has preserved the barracks used by the buffalo soldiers. (Above, courtesy of US Army Military History Institute; below, courtesy of Golden Gate National Recreation Area Archives and Research Center.)

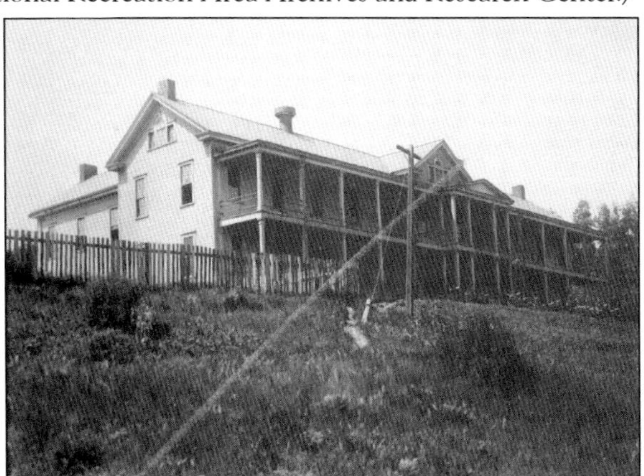

Regiments of the buffalo soldiers were stationed at the Presidio of San Francisco. In 1894, African American soldiers served in the 10th Cavalry Color Guard. In the photograph below, soldiers from the 9th Cavalry stationed at the Presidio serve as the escort of honor for Pres. Theodore Roosevelt during his 1903 visit to San Francisco. This was the first time African American troops were given this esteemed role. (Both, courtesy of Golden Gate National Recreation Area Archives and Research Center.)

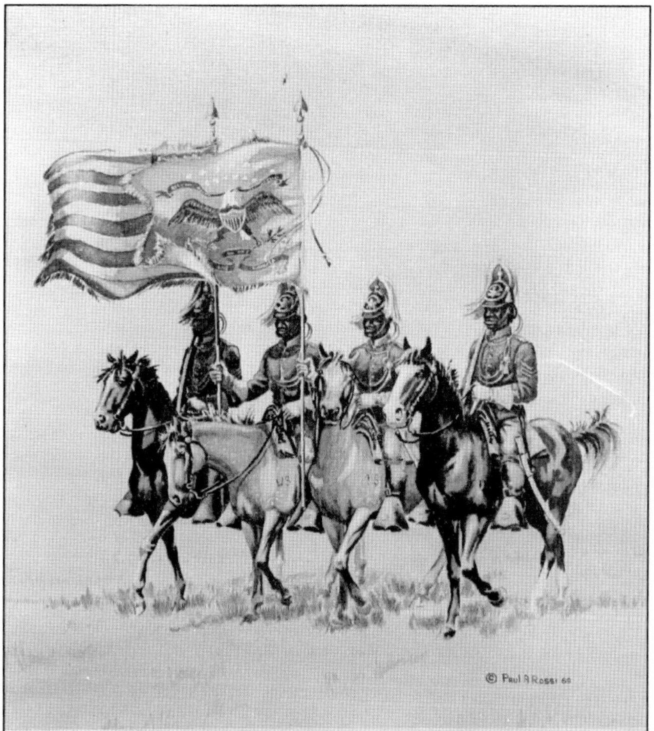

10th Cavalry Color Guard, Full Dress Uniform, 1890

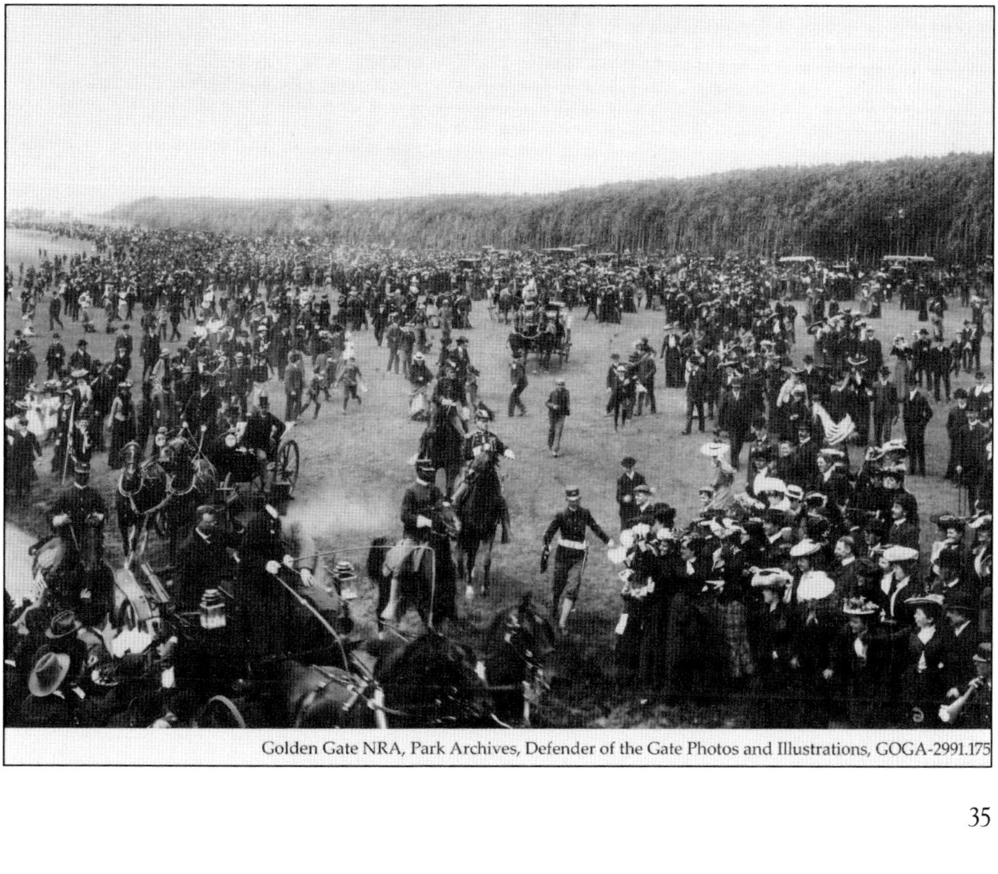

Golden Gate NRA, Park Archives, Defender of the Gate Photos and Illustrations, GOGA-2991.175

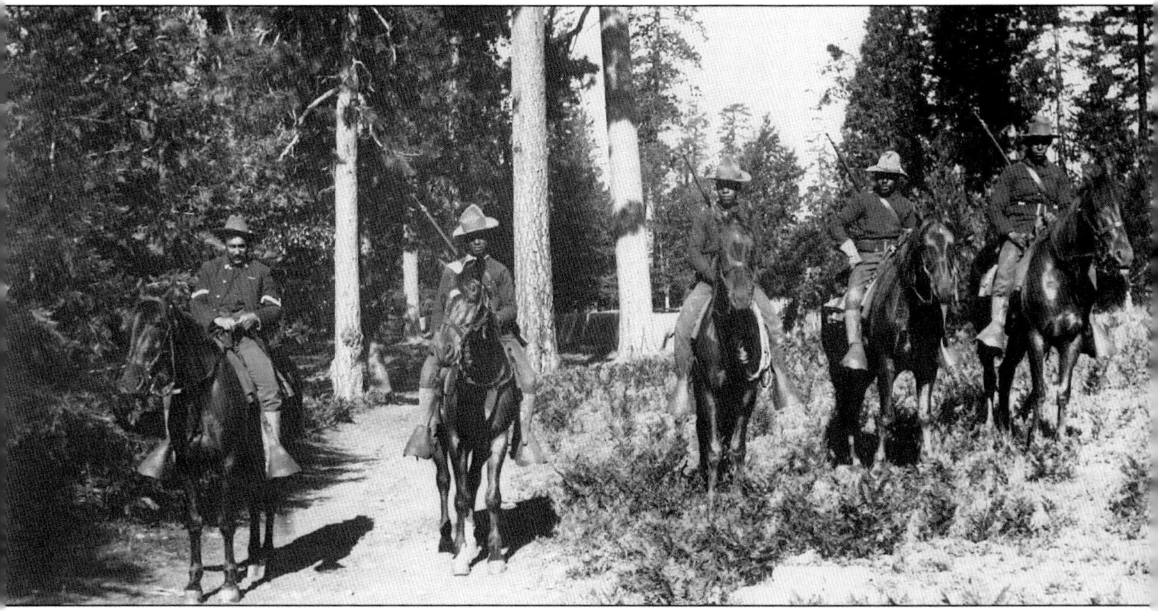

According to the National Park Service, companies from all four African American regiments reported to the Presidio in San Francisco in 1899. Since the Civil War, many African American men had served with pride in segregated units. Some black soldiers went to war, and some in California served as forest rangers in national parks. Here, members of the 24th Infantry patrol Yosemite National Park. In 1899, these were the first black units to guard the park. In May 1903, Charles Young, the third African American to graduate from West Point, led 9th Cavalry troops from the Presidio to Yosemite, Sequoia, and Kings Canyon National Parks. (Courtesy of Yosemite National Park Library.)

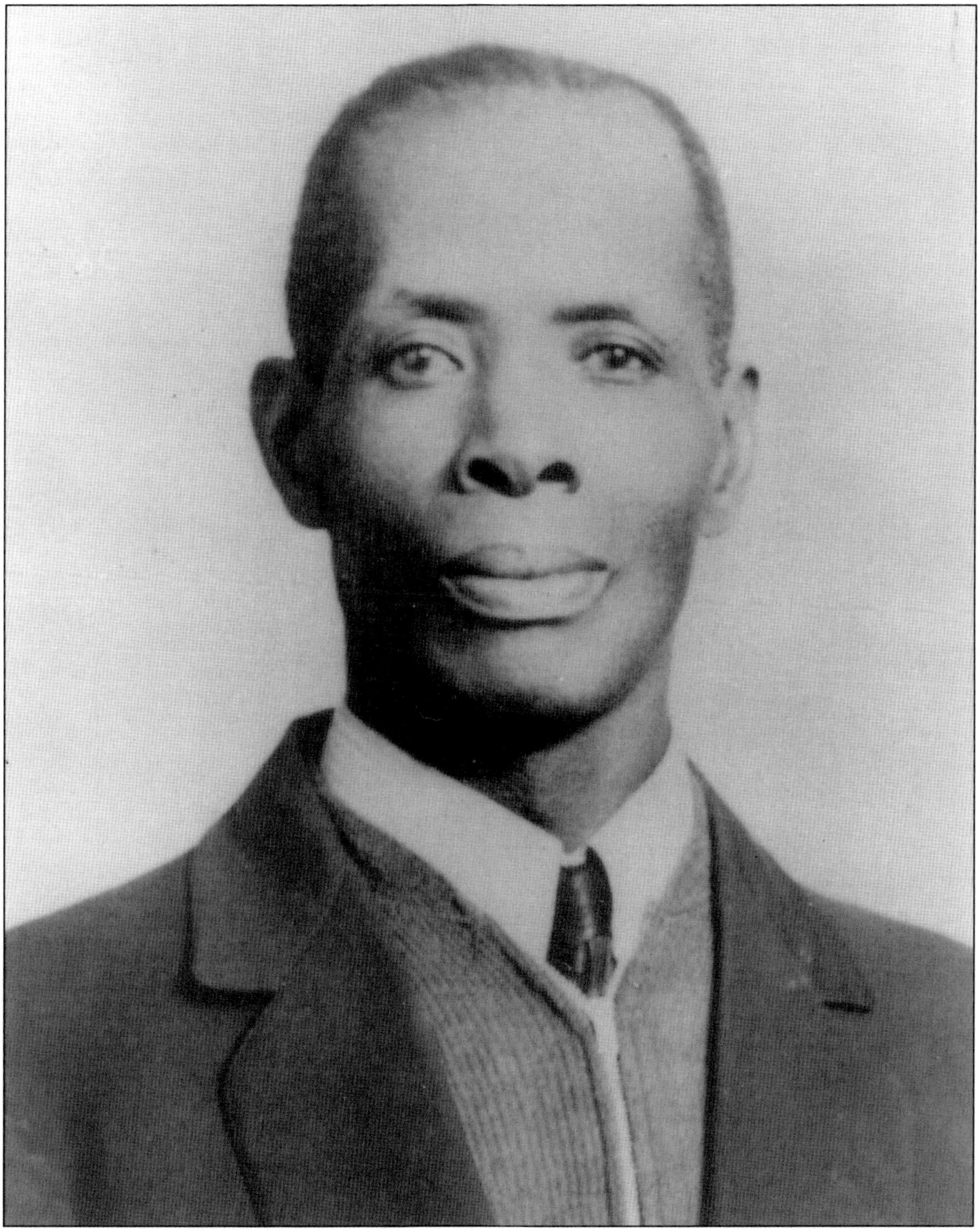

On August 16, 1907, James Henry Thomas arrived in San Francisco from Barbados. Thomas was born in Barbados in 1884. According to immigration papers, Thomas was a crewmember on the vessel SS *Peru* and traveled from Panama City, Panama, to San Francisco. As with others who migrated from islands in the West Indies during the 19th century, Thomas desired to find work in the maritime industries in San Francisco. According to family members, Thomas left San Francisco in 1910, traveled north as a crewman on another vessel, and settled in Portland, Oregon. There, he married, bought a house, and established a family whose descendants still reside in Portland. As immigrants from the West Indies increased, social groups and churches were developed for the West Indian community in San Francisco during the early years of the 20th century. (Courtesy of the Thomas family.)

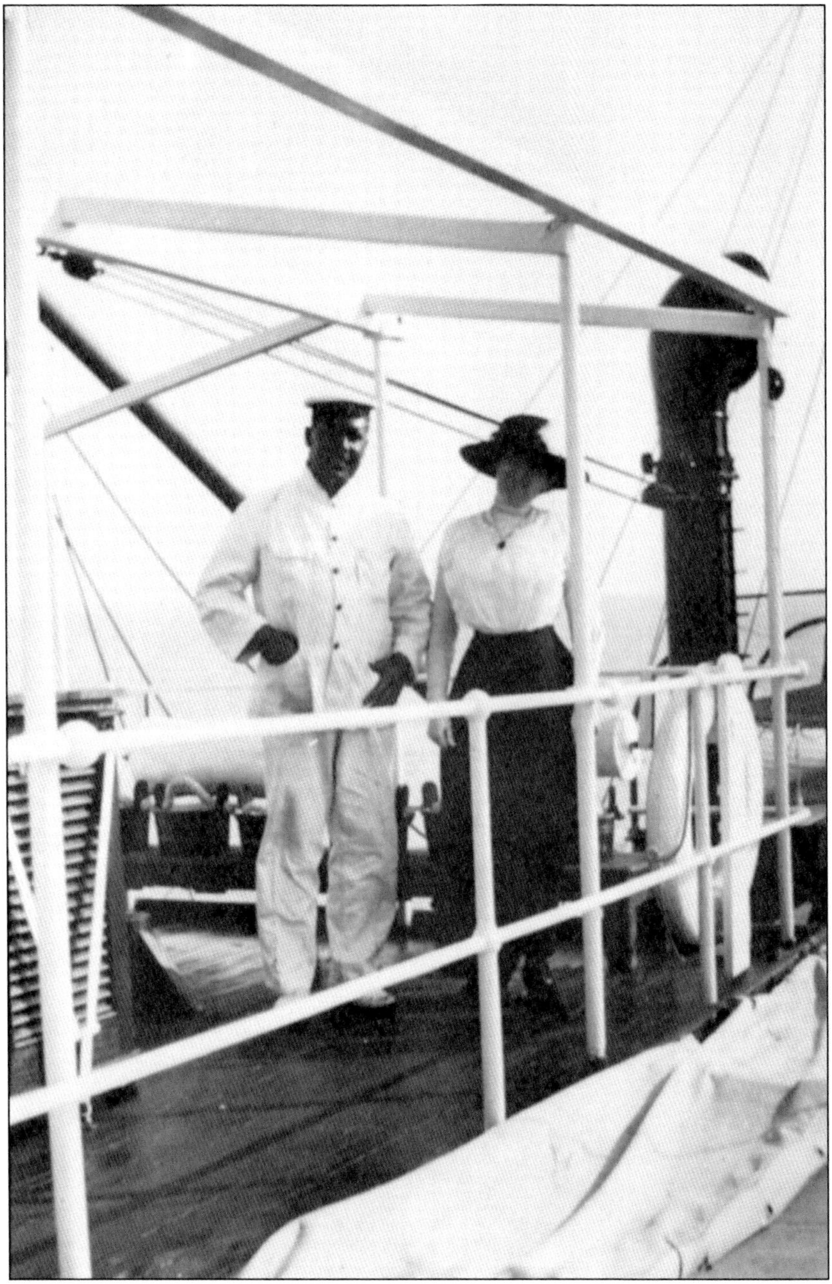

In this photograph, a steamship steward enjoys the company of a passenger. Many ship laborers and steamship stewards were of West Indian heritage, and had at one time worked on the Panama Canal and migrated to San Francisco after the completion of the canal in 1913. Many sought work on vessels in the Bay Area docks and ports. Most were raised in the Church of England, and many black Americans who were affiliated with the Episcopal faith and migrated to San Francisco from other states joined forces with the West Indian immigrants to build their own Episcopal church. These immigrants established St. Cyprian's Church. The name was chosen in 1923, and St. Cyprian's Episcopal Church at Sutter and Lyon Streets was constructed in the 1930s. (Courtesy of the California Historical Society, CHS2011.510.tif.)

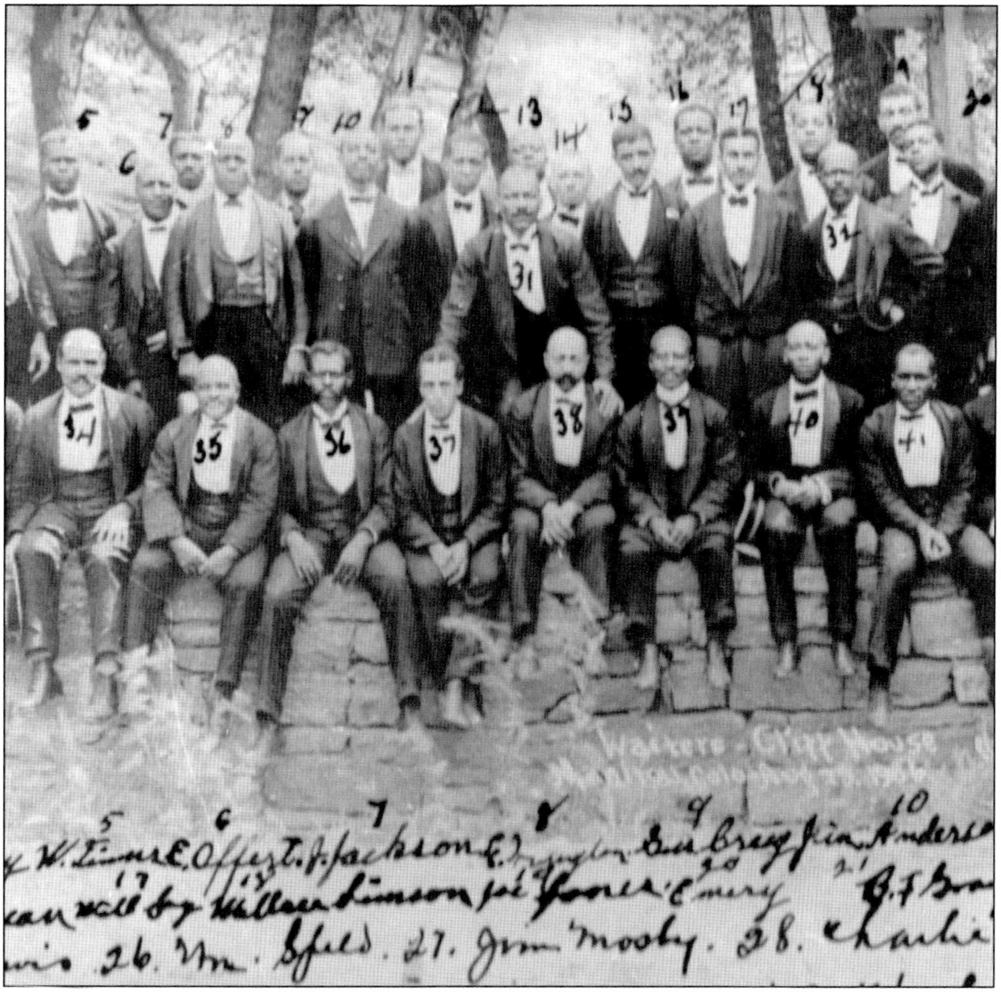

Many African American men living in San Francisco found employment in San Francisco's hotels and restaurants. In the photograph above, these men from Third Baptist Church worked at the Cliff House in 1906 as waiters. In the photograph below, members of Third Baptist Church pose for a photograph in front of the Hyde Street church in the 1920s. Both young and old men pose in an outgoing manner. This may indicate a sense of hope for a better life in San Francisco. (Both, courtesy of Third Baptist Church of San Francisco Inc.)

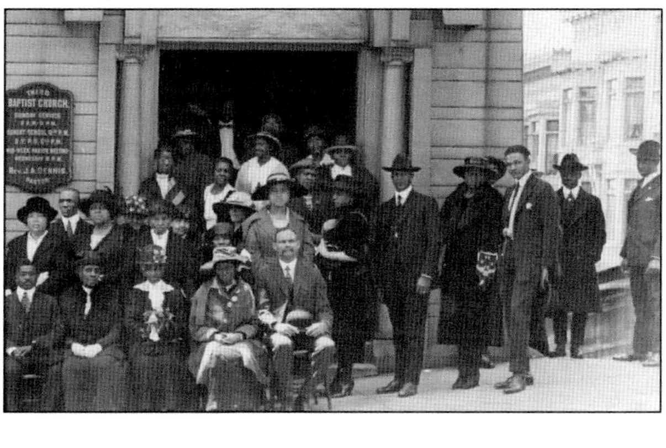

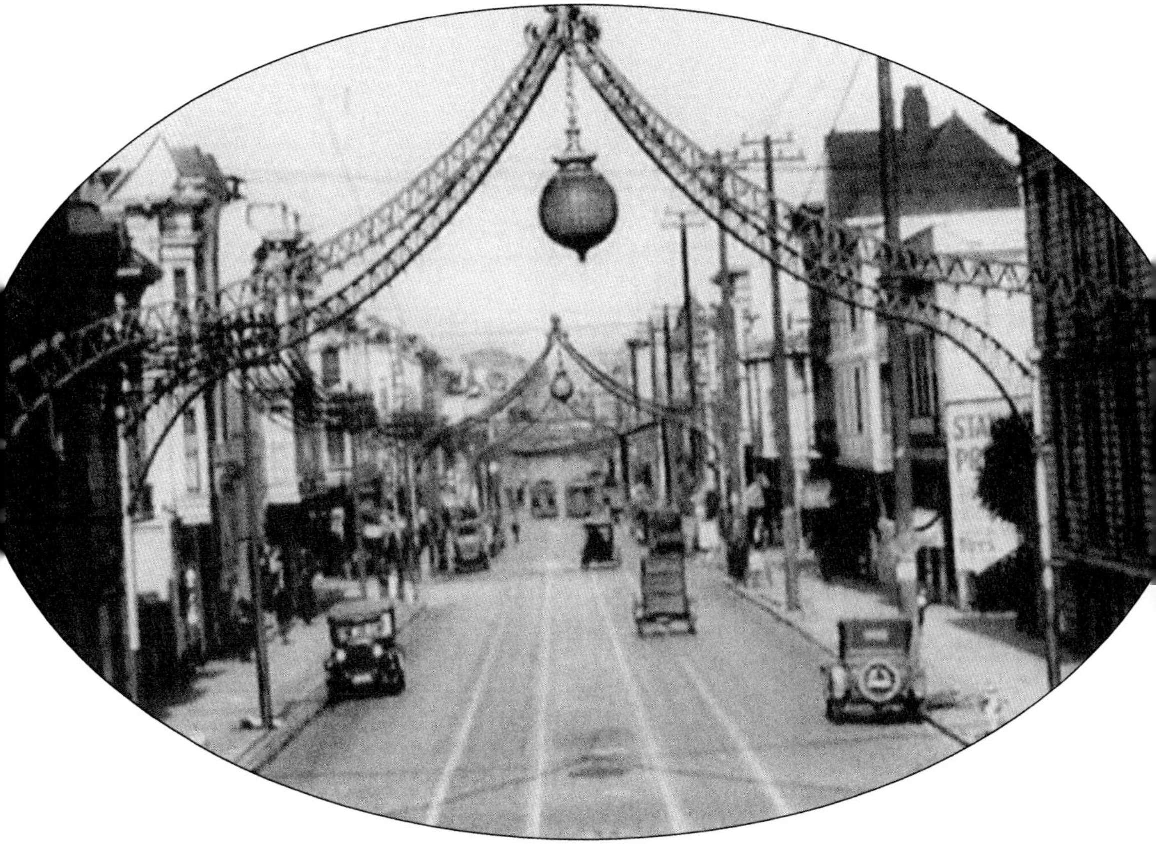

After the earthquake and fire of 1906, many of the businesses previously located on Market Street moved to Fillmore Street so that the Market Street area could be rebuilt. Fillmore Street became the new financial district and downtown for San Francisco. Arches were built on every corner to attract people to the Fillmore District. According to Lewis Watts and Elizabeth Pepin, Fillmore Street became the center of the jazz world for black musicians in the 1930s. In the 1940s and 1950s, Fillmore Street was the center of the black community both economically and socially. During World War II, the arches on Fillmore Avenue were removed and used in war industries. (Courtesy of the Jazz Heritage Center of San Francisco.)

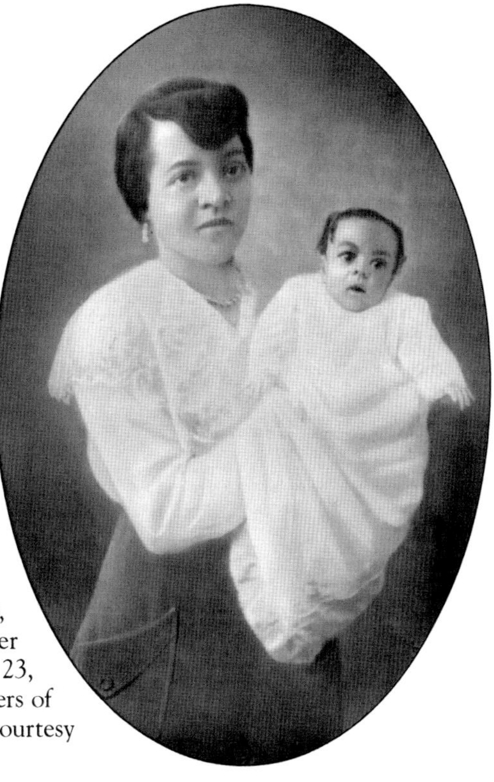

Pictured below, Julian Clarence Hicks was born in 1880 in San Francisco and died on March 21, 1947. He is holding his daughter Marguerite Betty Schumpert. In the image at right, Bertha Marie Hicks, who lived from December 8, 1889, to February 18, 1965, is holding daughter Marguerite Betty Schumpert, born on March 23, 1918. Members of the Hicks family were members of Bethel AME Church in San Francisco. (Both, courtesy of Bethel AME Church.)

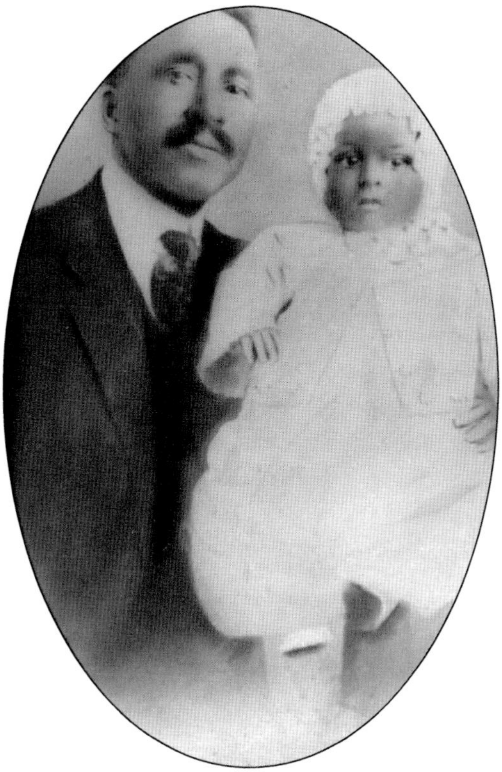

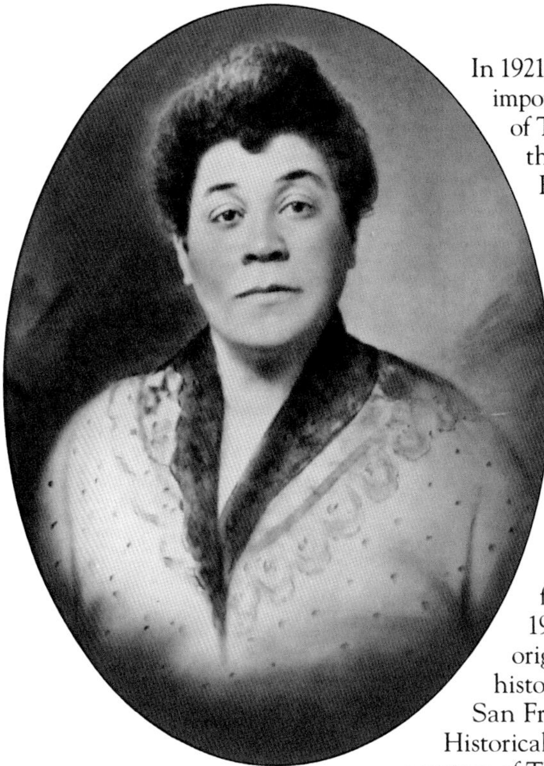

In 1921, providing housing for women and girls was important to Irene Bell Ruggles, an active member of Third Baptist Church. Church records state that Ruggles was cofounder of the C.J. Walker Home for Girls, located at 2066 Pine Street. She also served as the first president of the home. The C.J. Walker home provided single African American women and girls housing and employment counseling. It also became a community resource for social gatherings. Local residents could reserve the home's kitchen and social hall for gatherings. Ruggles, a leader in the black community of San Francisco, served as president of the California State Federation of Colored Women's Clubs. The home was named after Madam C.J. Walker, a cosmetics entrepreneur who became the first African American female millionaire. In 1972, the home moved to Hayes Street. The original location on Pine Street has been given historic preservation designation by the City of San Francisco. (Left, courtesy of the California Historical Society, FN-12889/CHS2011.517.tif; below, courtesy of Third Baptist Church of San Francisco Inc.)

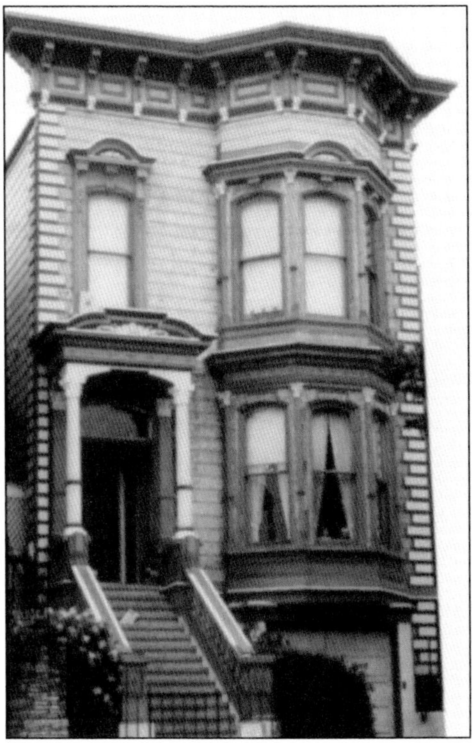

Garland Anderson was born in 1886 and went on to work in a San Francisco hotel as a bellhop. In his spare time, he wrote plays. In 1924, Anderson wrote *Appearance*, a play that was performed on Broadway in 1925. With the help of Pres. Calvin Coolidge, Anderson was the first African American to have a full-length drama produced on Broadway. Anderson died in 1939. (Courtesy of San Francisco History Center, San Francisco Public Library.)

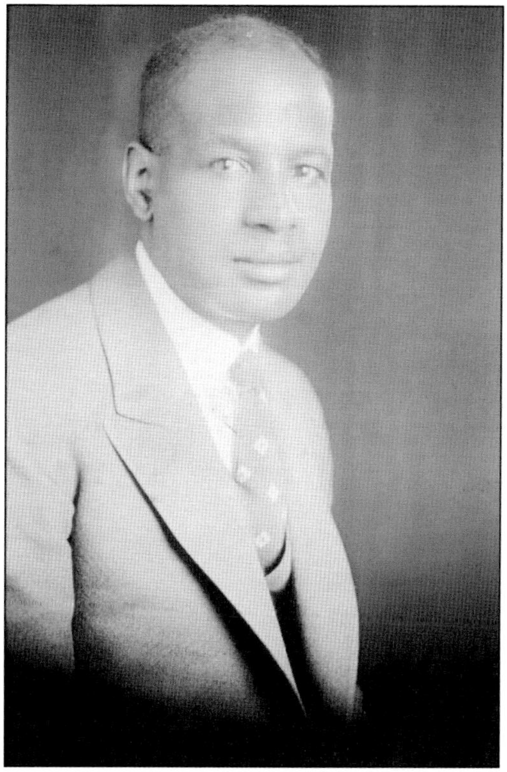

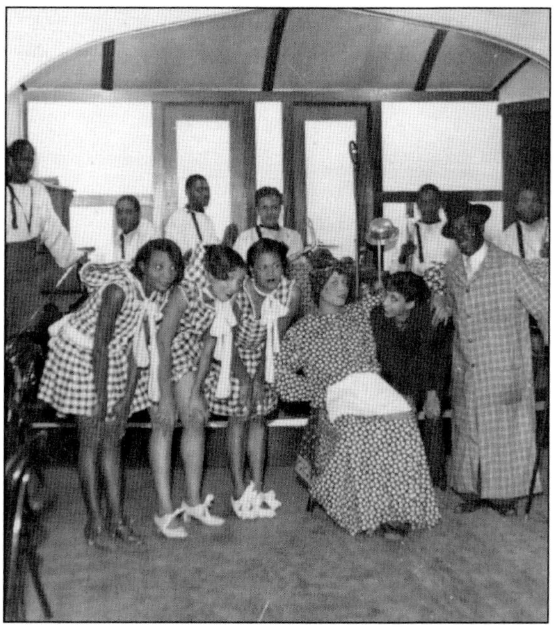

Dance halls in the Barbary Coast attracted enormous crowds. Purcell's, the Dew Drop Inn, the Squeeze Inn, and the So Different were termed as "Negro" establishments that employed black women but catered to white men and white slummers. According to information in the San Francisco Public Library's photographic archives, "Purcell's, located on Pacific Street between Montgomery and Kearney, had a bar, a few rough tables and chairs, and many wooden benches that faced a splinter dance-floor." The turkey trot, the bunny hug, the chicken Glide, and other dances that swept America were first performed in clubs of the Barbary Coast. The dance halls were some of the largest on the Pacific Coast. (Courtesy of San Francisco History Center, San Francisco Public Library.)

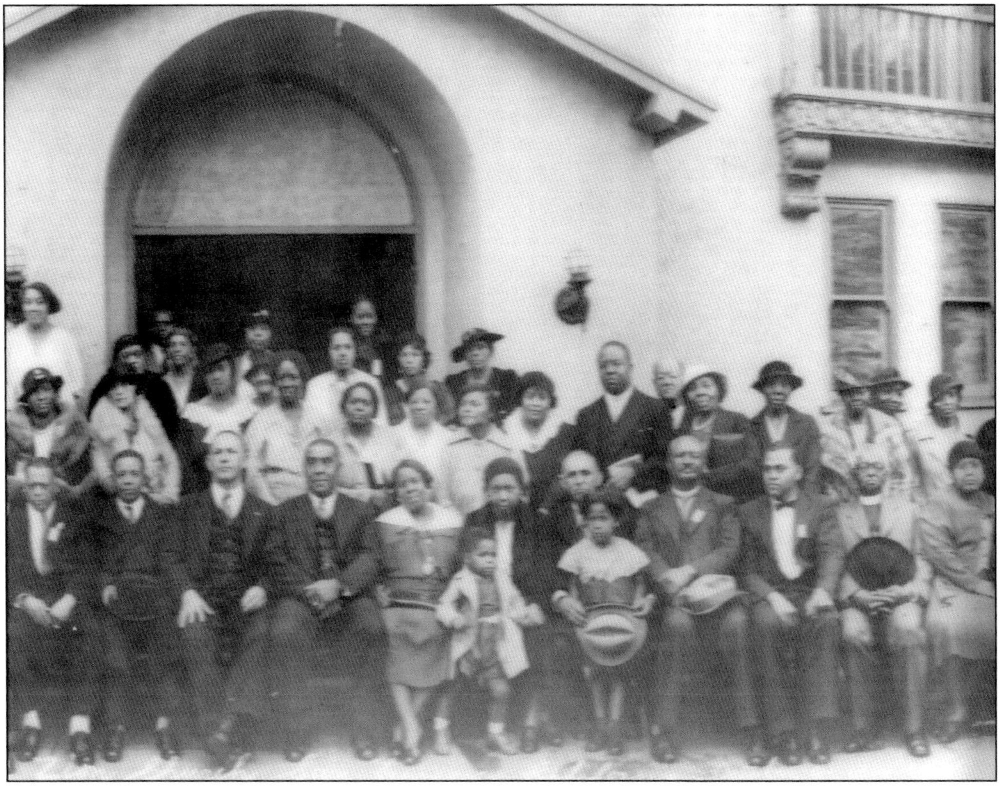

After the devastating earthquake and fire of 1906, First AME Zion moved to a new site at 1669 Geary Street between Webster Street and Buckingham Way in 1914. In the photograph above, taken in 1935 and in front of the Geary Street church building, church members and attendees of the First AME Zion California Conference of AME Zion Churches surround Rev. E.J. Magruder and Bishop J.W. Martin, who was from the Los Angeles Conference. Standing in the rear is John W.E. Ekleberger, secretary of Christian education for the AME Zion Church denomination. The building pictured below is a church-owned apartment house, which also housed the pastor and his family. Rev. E.J. Magruder served as pastor from 1926 to 1941. (Both, courtesy of First AME Zion Church.)

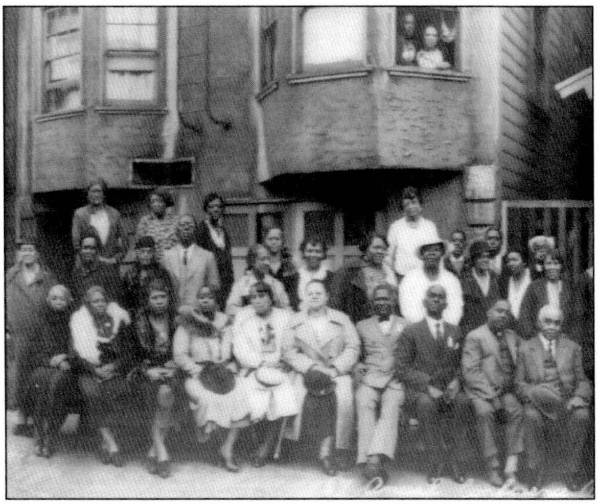

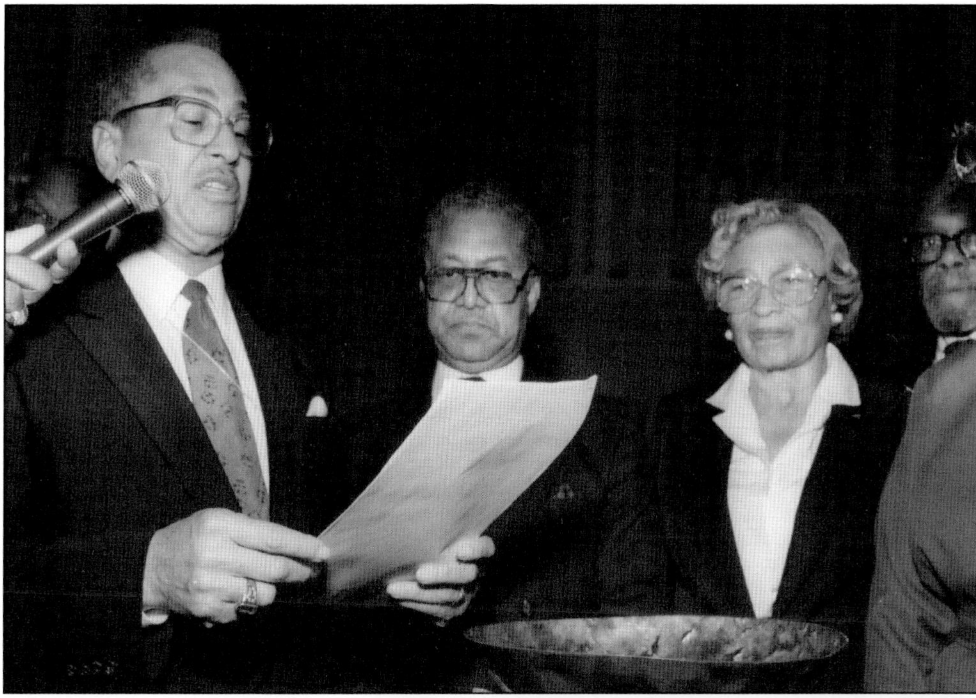

In 1932, Rev. Fredrick Douglass Haynes Sr., a local civil rights activist, led the Third Baptist congregation of 150 members at the church on Hyde and Clay Streets. According to church records, "He found the members of the church scattered and discouraged, and he began to rebuild the church—reorganizing the internal functioning, developing a sound financial program to make it a spiritual lighthouse in the community." Rev. Haynes was not only a church leader but was also highly respected throughout San Francisco's black communities. He participated in the Black Ministerial Alliance, which advocated equality in employment, housing, and public accommodations for blacks. He also pushed for the election of an African American to the board of supervisors. (Both, courtesy Third Baptist Church of San Francisco Inc.)

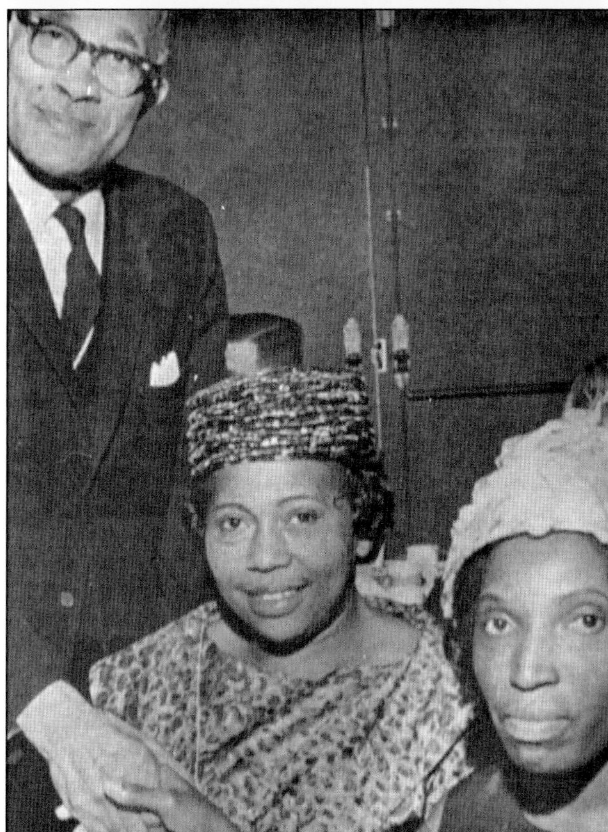

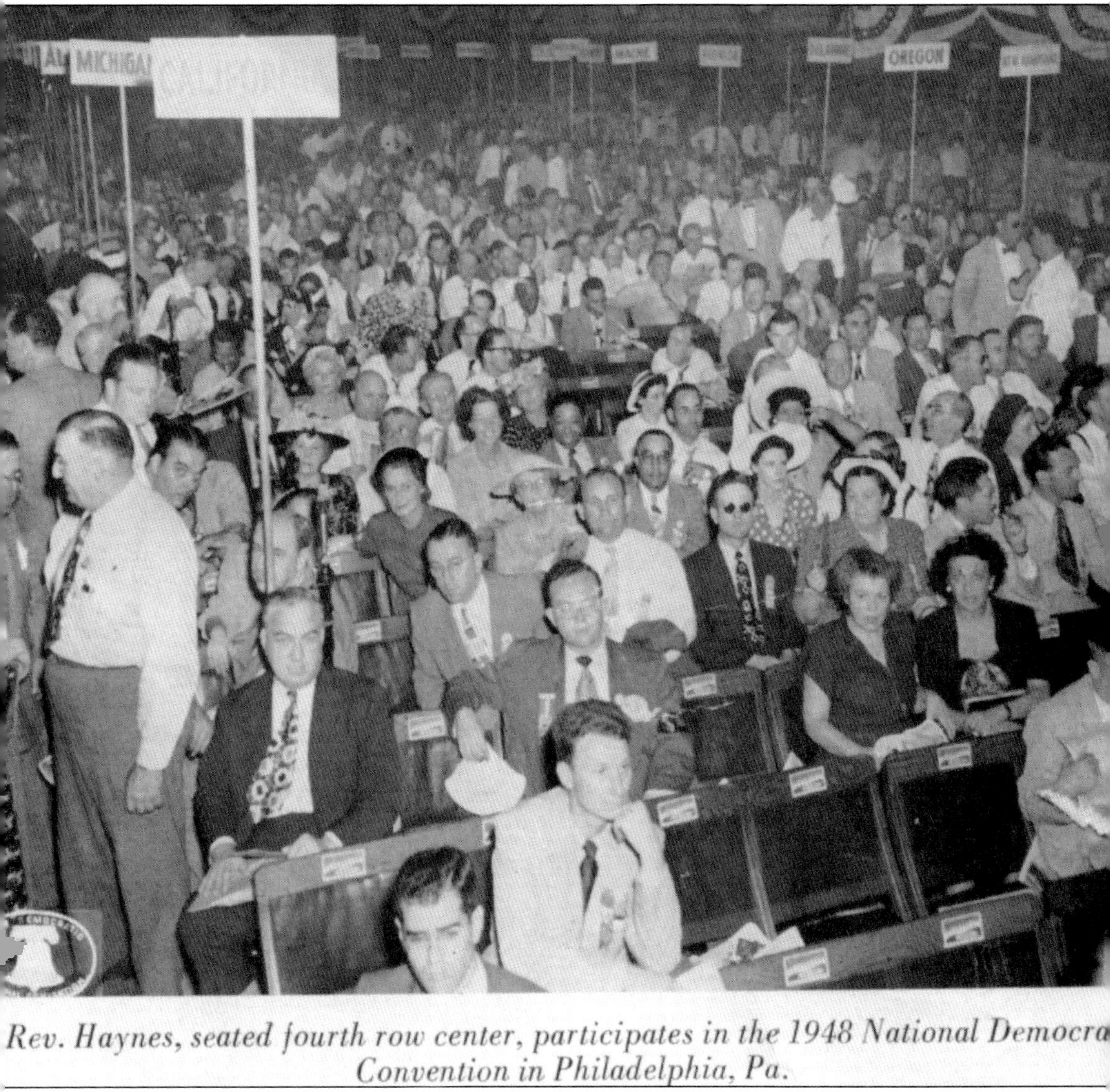

As a community activist, Rev. Haynes attended the Democratic National Convention in 1948. (Courtesy Third Baptist Church of San Francisco Inc.)

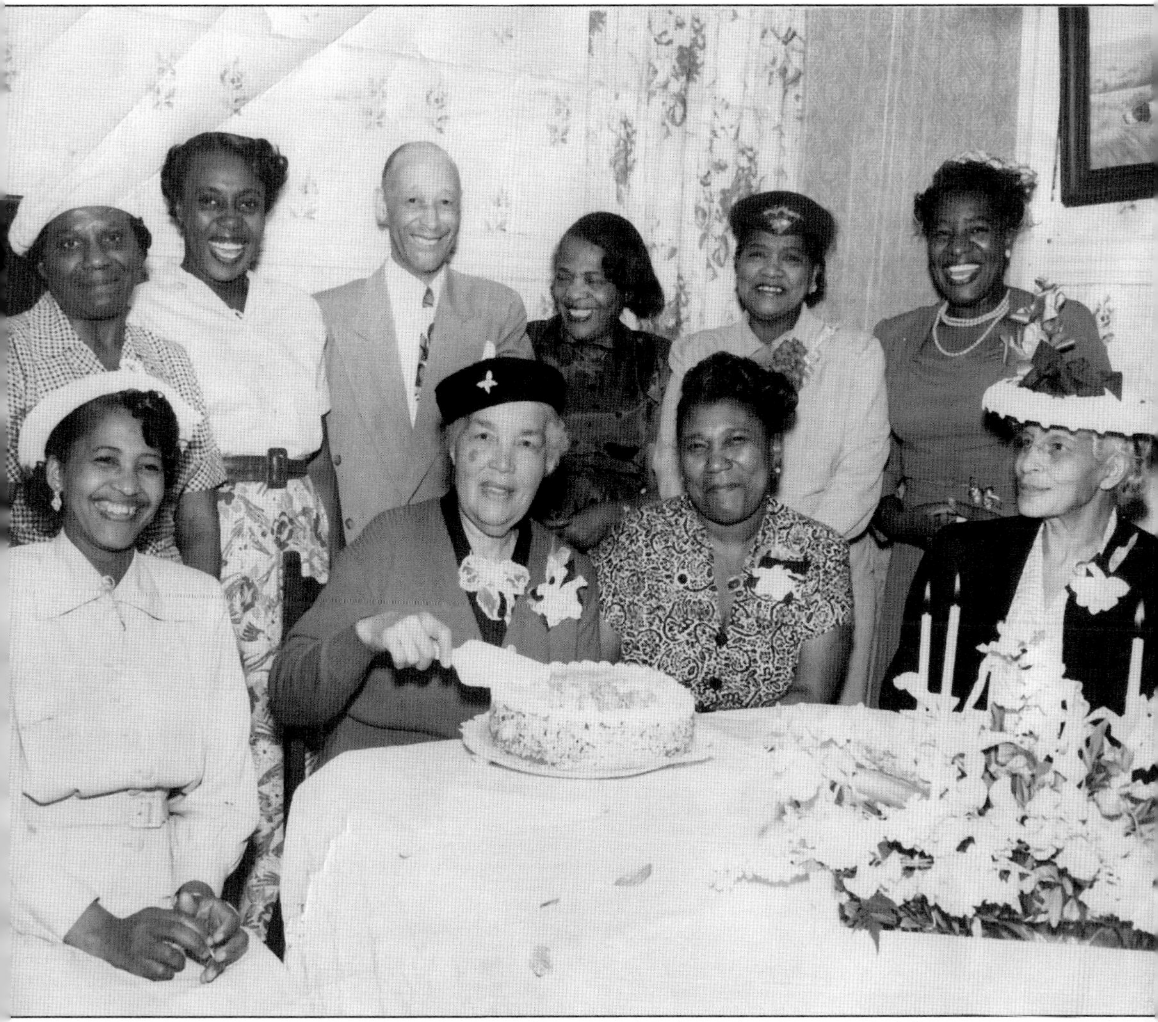

Mother Anderson, sitting in the center, is celebrating her birthday party with fellow women's ministry members. She was a church leader and was highly respected by the church community. She was the oldest member of the church in 1952. (Courtesy of Third Baptiste Church of San Francisco Inc.)

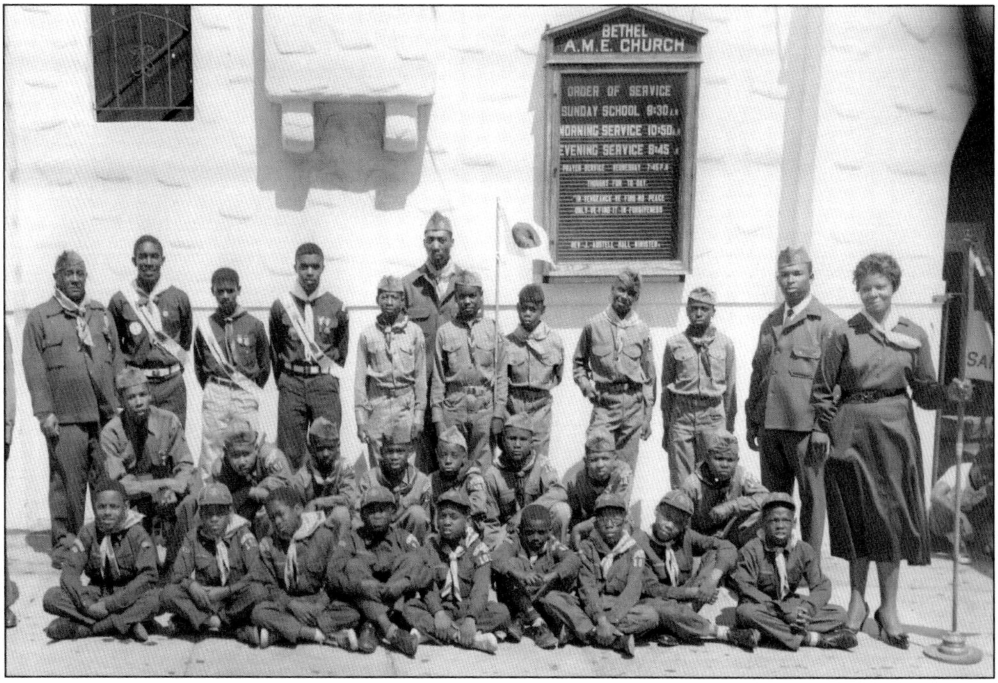

Boy Scouts played an integral role in the development of black male youths through the black church during the early 1900s. In San Francisco, Bethel AME and Third Baptist Church were among the many black churches to introduce young men to Scouting. The Boy Scouts helped uplift the youth by instilling leadership, fostering civic engagement, and helping boys become strong men. Through their efforts, many Scouts received religious emblems of recognition for their contributions and impacts on the church community. Since the 1940s, church leaders of several African American churches have devoted many hours providing services, such as teaching leadership skills, to male youth in the Boy Scouts. In the photograph below, Bethel AME Cub Scouts, Boy Scouts, and Explorers leaders are receiving a leadership award. Pictured are, from left to right, Tommy Wilson (seated), the Explorer advisor for Troop 102; scoutmaster Timothy Hurdle; unidentified; Joseph Boxley, holding a paper; and unidentified. (Both, courtesy of Bethel AME Church.)

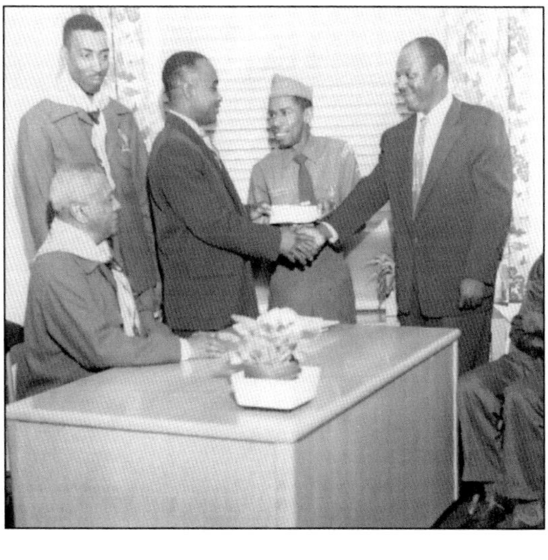

Providing leadership for girls and boys through other service groups was also promoted in the African American churches of San Francisco. Third Baptist Church of San Francisco formed a courtesy committee that allowed boys and girls to serve as junior ushers and church helpers. In this 1950 photograph are, from left to right, (standing) Joan Coleman, Gloria Hardy, and Lucille W. Valentine; (seated) Lois C. Winder and Mary Ellen W. Carr. The courtesy committee began training girls at 10 years old for the junior usher board. (Courtesy of Third Baptist Church of San Francisco Inc.)

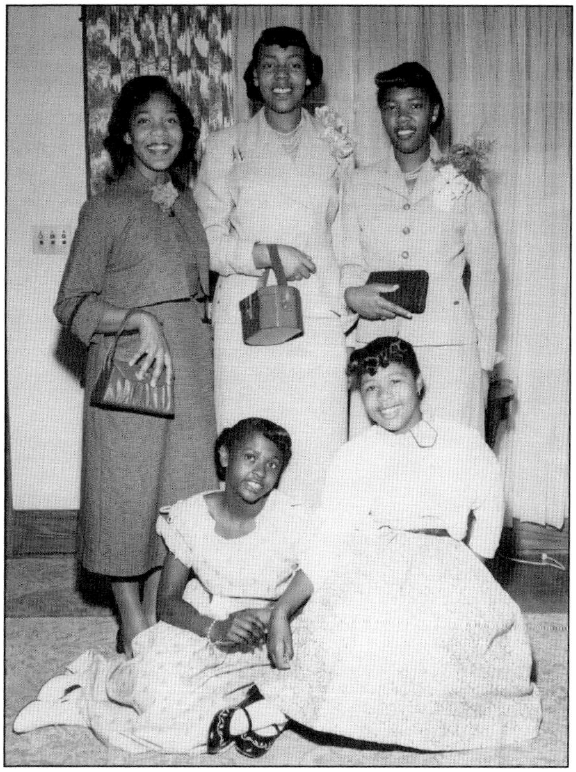

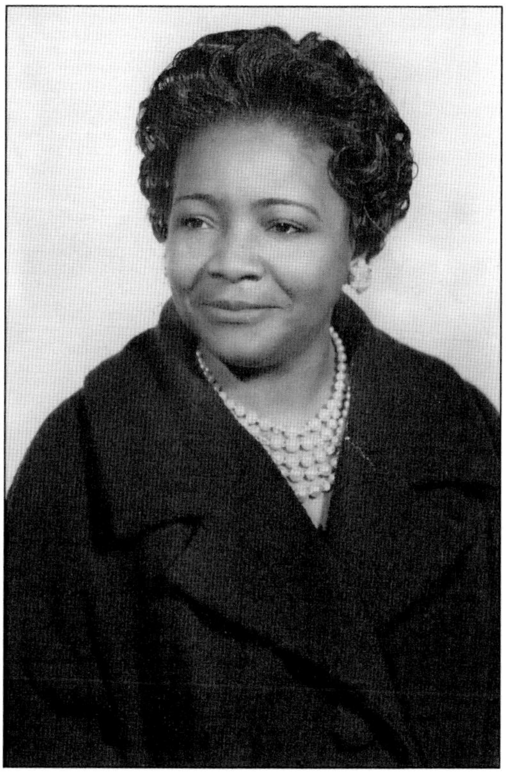

Community leadership for women often took place within the church. Roberta G. Garner, pictured here, was a member of Third Baptist Church after arriving in the area in the 1940s. She became a resident of San Francisco in 1942. According to church records, Garner promoted race relations by giving free lodging, with breakfast and evening meals, in her home for five days and nights to three visiting male missionaries—one white, one Indian, and one Spanish. Garner continued working in a leadership capacity at the church for over 20 years. She was involved in fundraising activities and helped to raise money for a church parking lot at 1400 McAllister Street. (Courtesy of Third Baptist Church of San Francisco Inc.)

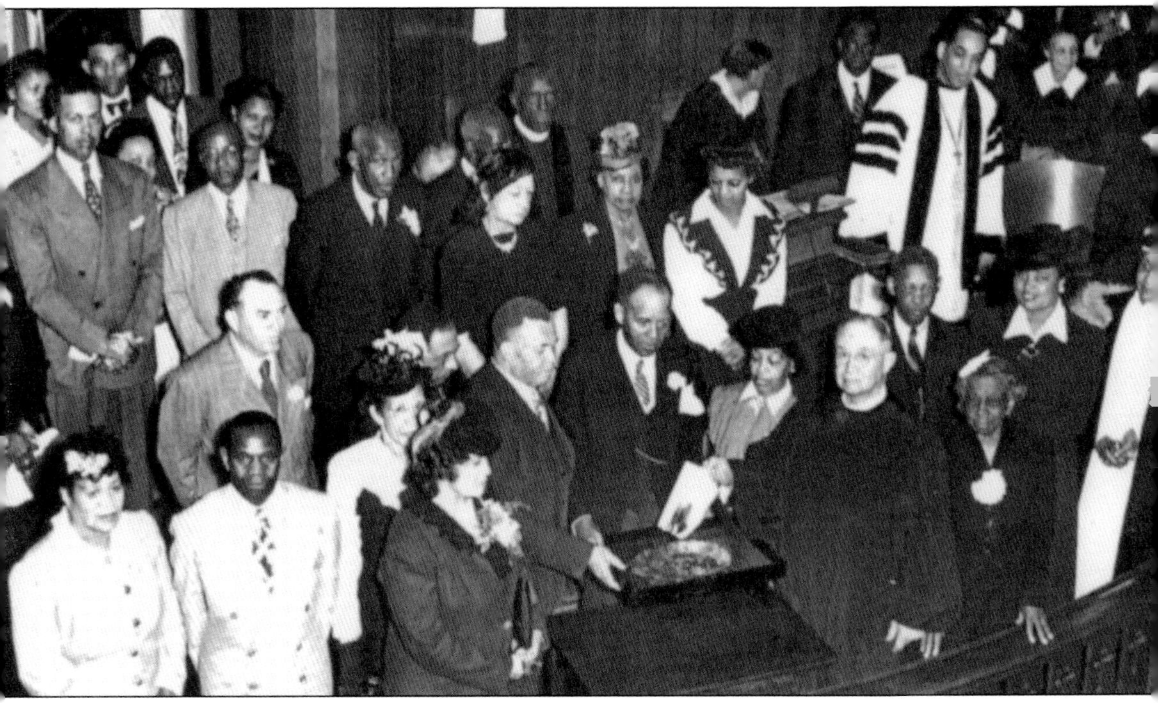

In 1945, Dr. H.B. Gantt was a local civil rights activist and pastor of First AME Zion Church. In this 1945 photograph, community leaders and church members are gathered at First Zion Church AME on Geary Street for a mortgage-burning ceremony. After 30 years, the congregation was able to pay the mortgage owed on the church property on Geary Street between Webster Street and Buckingham Way. Gantt is in the middle of the photograph and is holding the mortgage. Bishop W.C. William Brown Cornelius is standing next to him. Also surrounding Gantt are the parishioners of First AME Zion Church. Gantt served as pastor from 1941 to 1946. He was also active in the Black Ministerial Alliance, which advocated equality in employment, housing, and public accommodations for African Americans. (Courtesy of the First AME Zion Church.)

Dr. Howard Thurman and wife, Sue Bailey Thurman, moved to San Francisco from Atlanta, Georgia, in 1944. Dr. Thurman, one of the most distinguished church leaders in San Francisco, was pastor of the Church for the Fellowship of All People. He had authored more than two-dozen books and was designated by *Life* magazine as one of the most influential ministers in America. Dr. Thurman was born in 1899 and died in 1981. (Courtesy of the Church for the Fellowship of All People, San Francisco.)

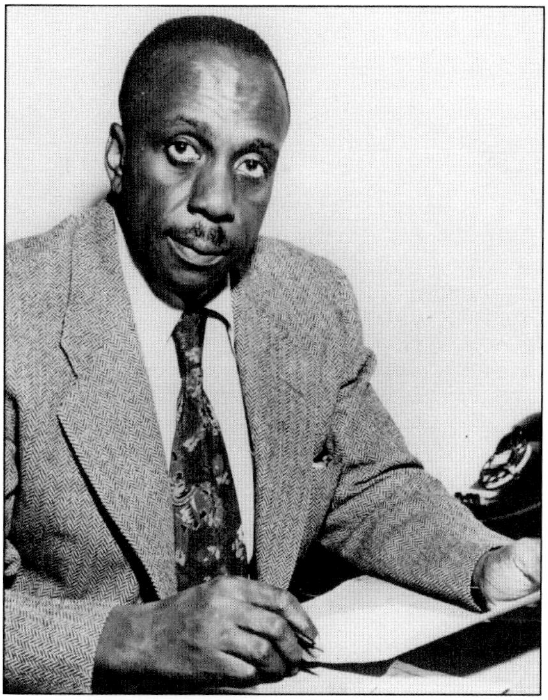

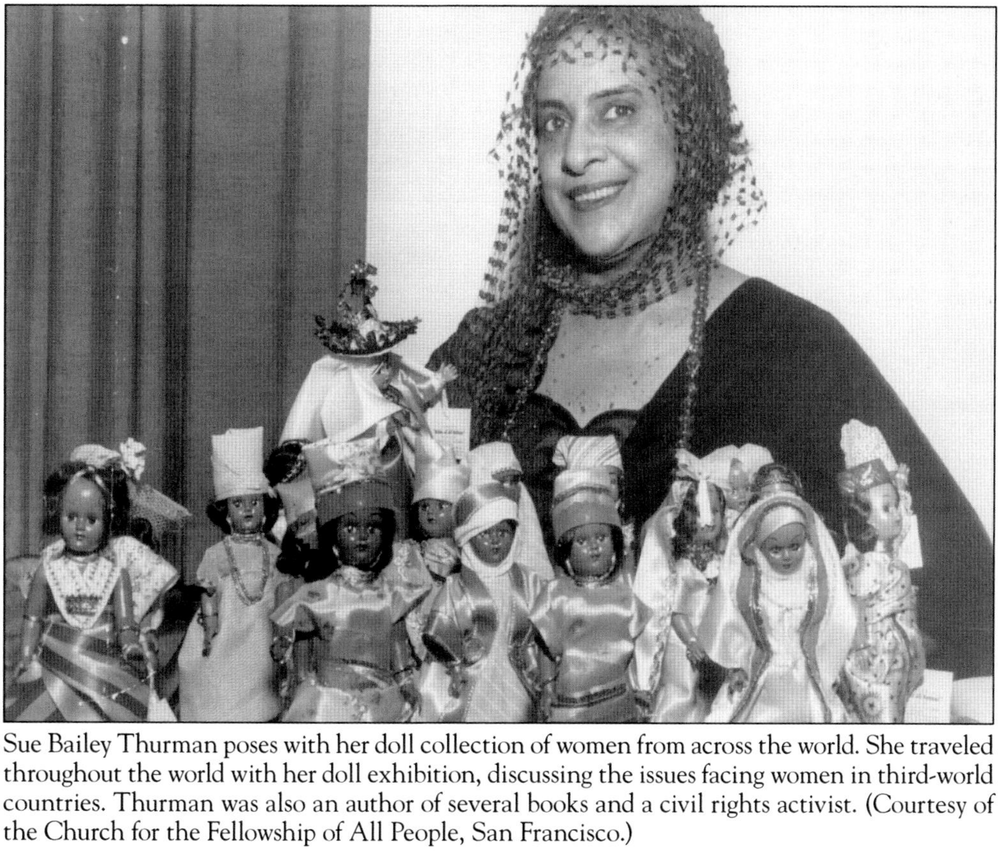

Sue Bailey Thurman poses with her doll collection of women from across the world. She traveled throughout the world with her doll exhibition, discussing the issues facing women in third-world countries. Thurman was also an author of several books and a civil rights activist. (Courtesy of the Church for the Fellowship of All People, San Francisco.)

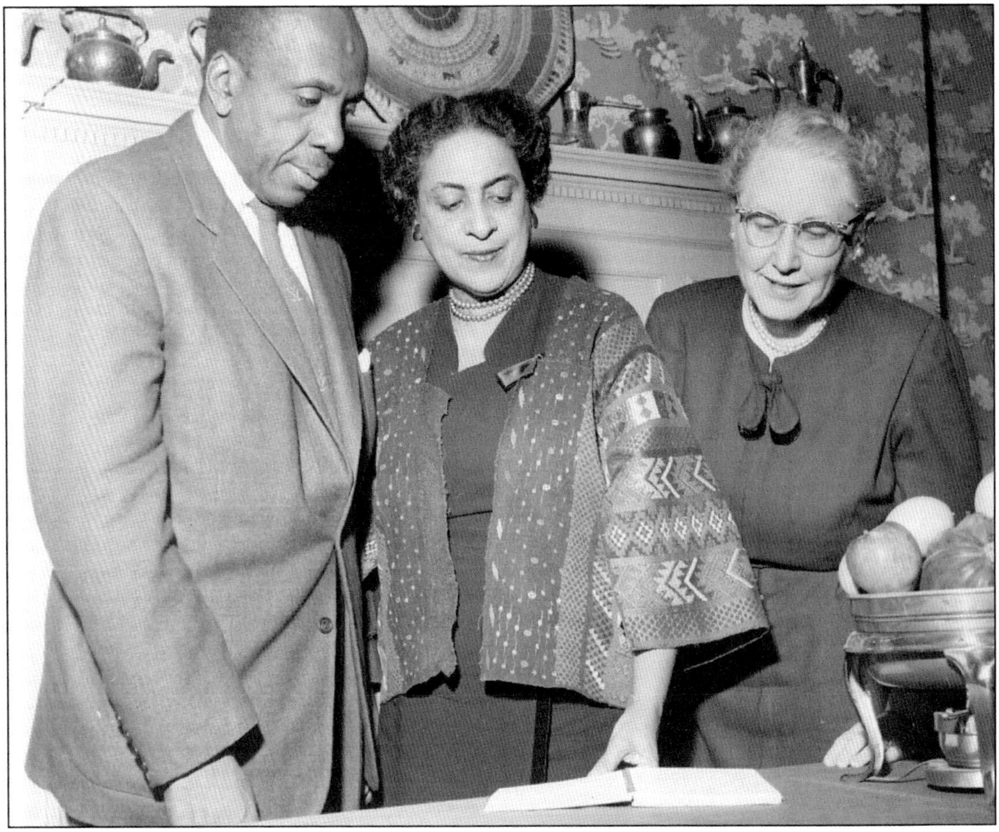

Dr. Howard and Sue Bailey Thurman were leaders at the nation's first interracial church, the Church of All Peoples. They promoted understanding between all races and applied this understanding to Christian traditions of spirituality. They are shown at left in both images, with other church members. (Both, courtesy of the Church for the Fellowship of All People, San Francisco.)

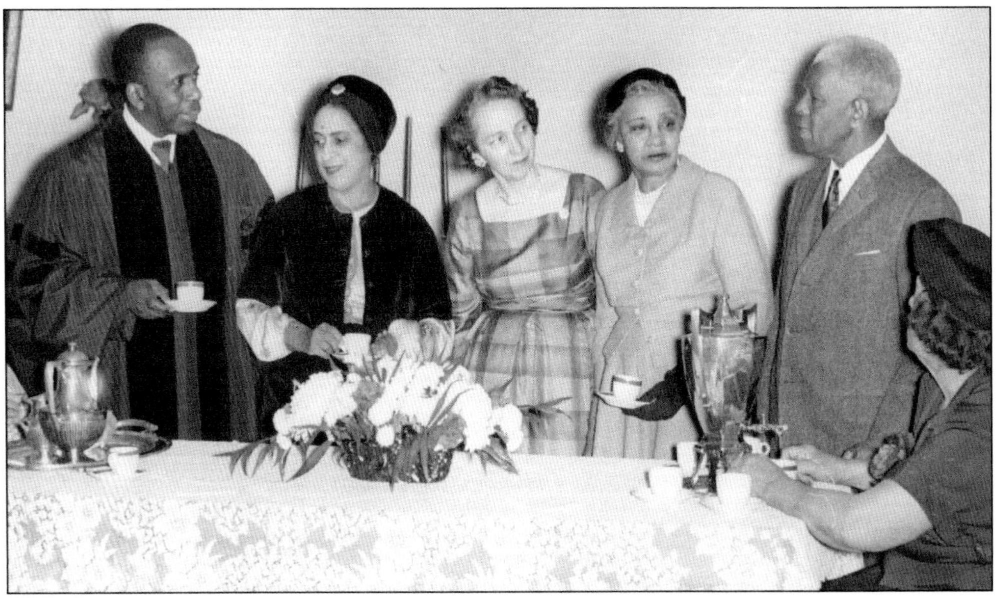

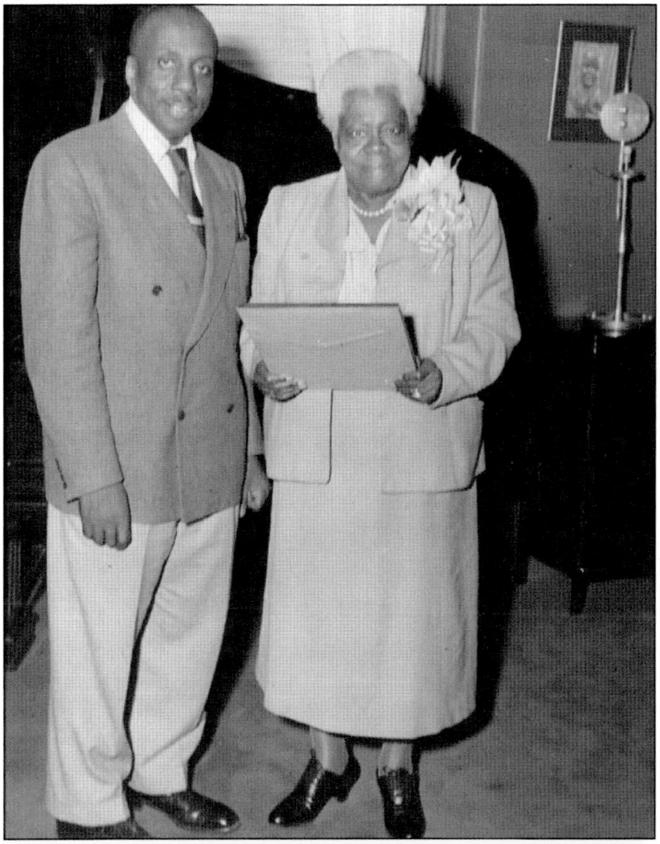

Dr. Thurman was well respected by African American leaders from all over the country. At right, Thurman is receiving an award from civil rights activist Mary McLeod Bethune. Below, he is standing with Coretta Scott King after the death of Dr. Martin Luther King Jr. Thurman was a spiritual advisor to Dr. King. (Both, courtesy of the Church for the Fellowship of All People, San Francisco.)

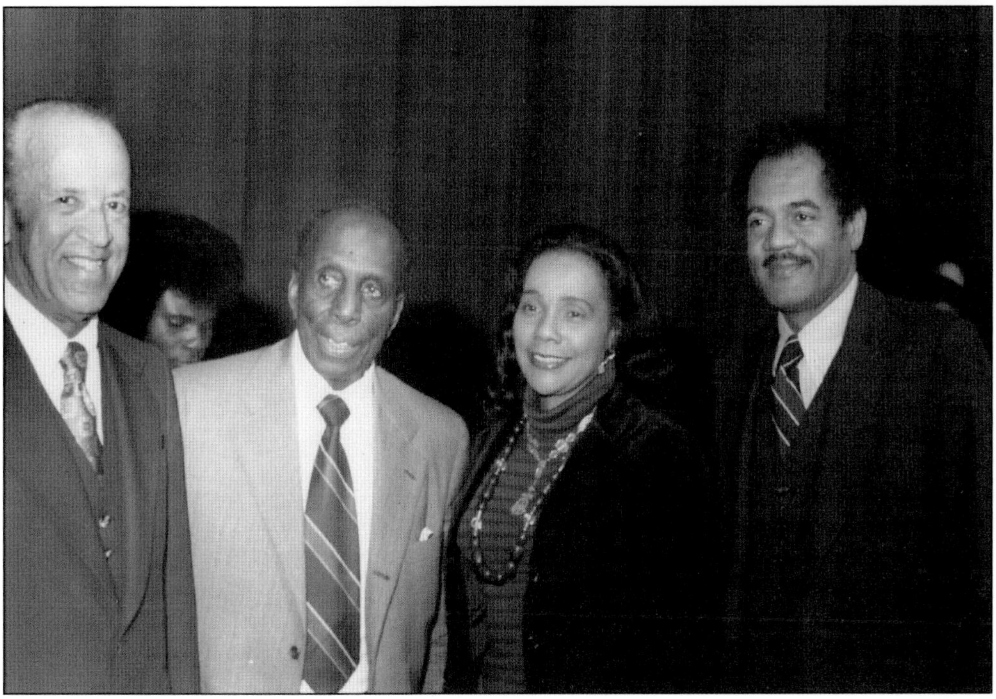

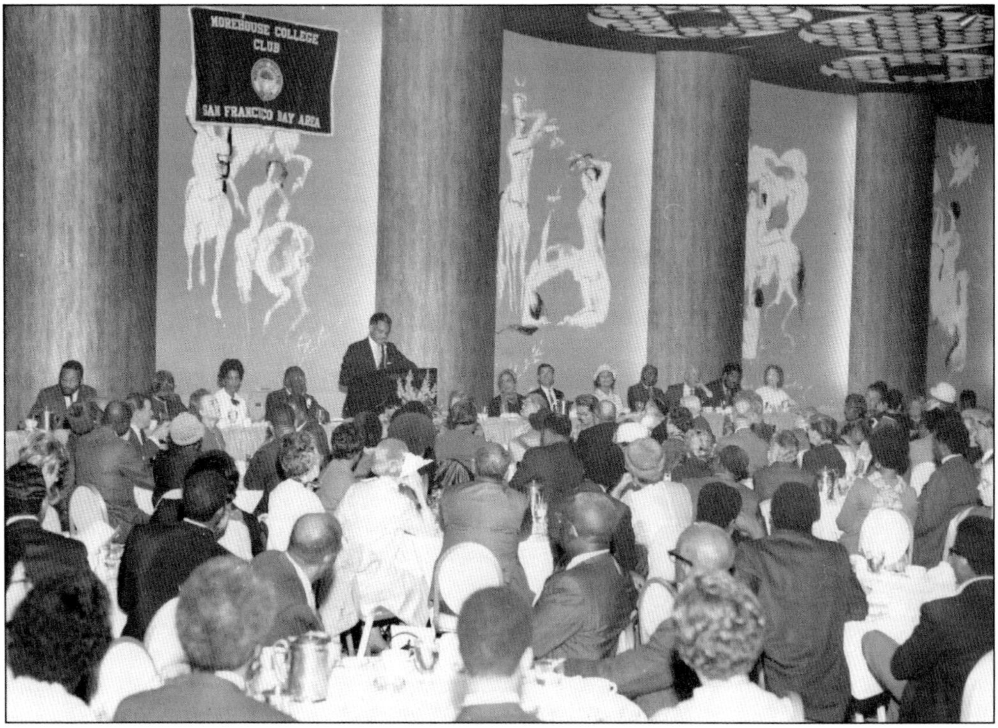

Dr. Thurman was honored at a meeting of the Morehouse College Club of San Francisco Bay Area. In the photograph below, Thurman (second from left) is receiving an award from the club. Sue Bailey Thurman and two unidentified Morehouse College officials are also pictured. (Both, courtesy of the Church for the Fellowship of All People, San Francisco.)

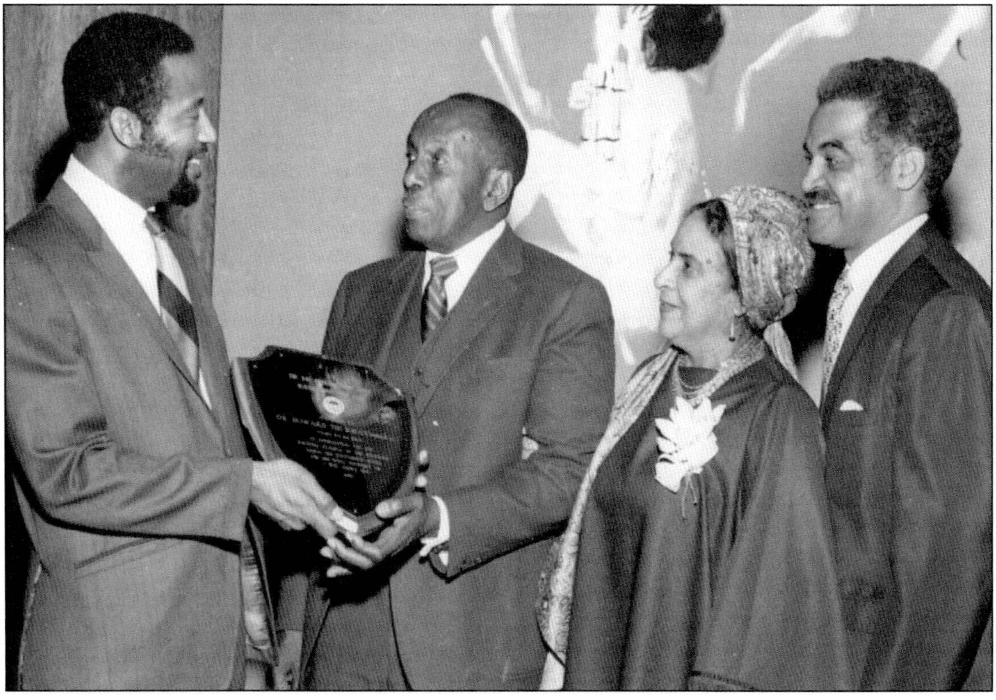

In 1935, from left to right, Howard Thurman, Sue Bailey Thurman, and other church members traveled to India. According to church records, Dr. and Mrs. Thurman visited Mohandas Gandhi to discuss the application of Gandhi's nonviolence movement to the African American struggle for civil rights. (Courtesy of the Church for the Fellowship of All People, San Francisco.)

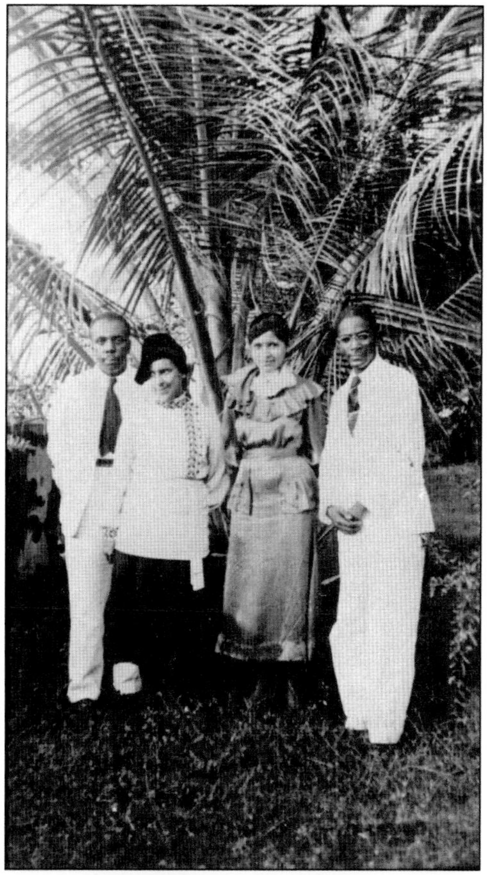

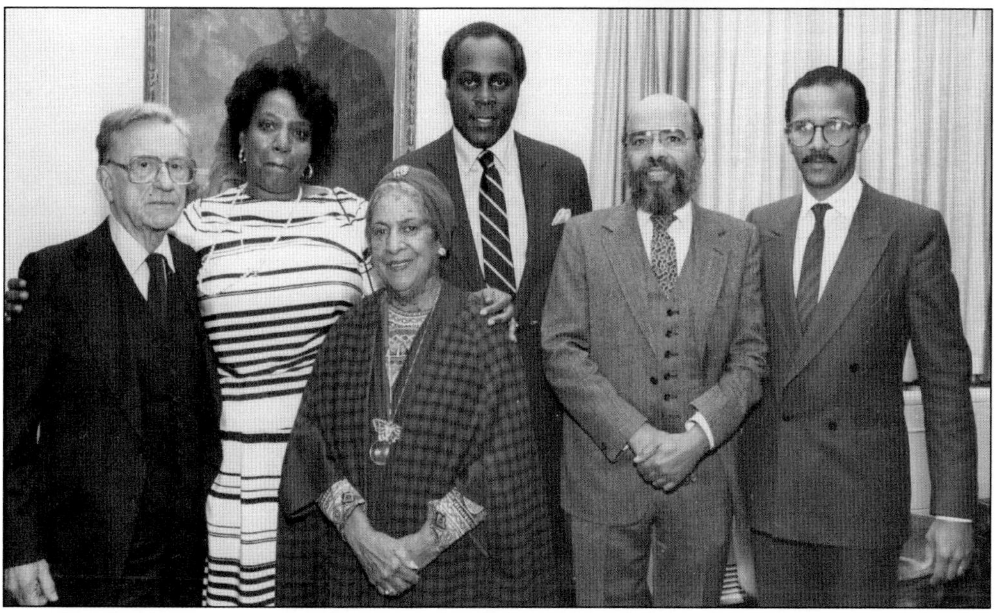

Sue Bailey Thurman, Benjamin Hooks, and others attend the funeral of Howard Thurman in 1981. (Courtesy of the Church for the Fellowship of All People, San Francisco.)

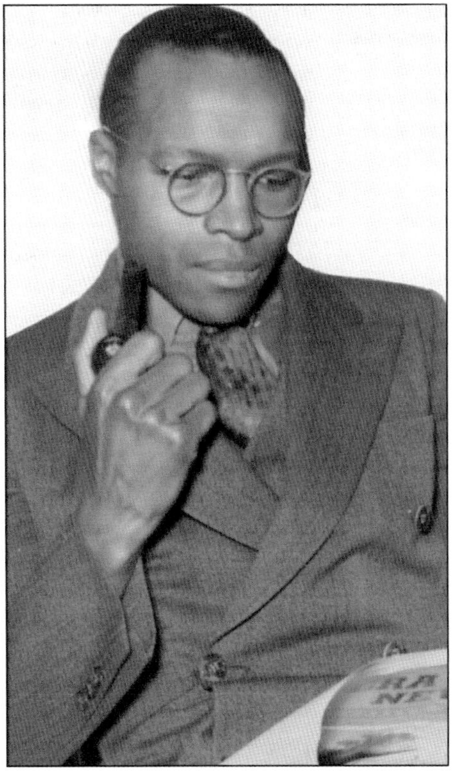

In the 1940s, Joseph James, a resident of the Fillmore District, was a prominent community leader who fought for equal rights on behalf of black workers during World War II. James was involved with the San Francisco branch of the NAACP and was elected president in 1944. Unlike many among San Francisco's black leadership, James was a blue-collar worker who worked in one of the Bay Area's largest shipyards, Marinship. In 1942, he was promoted from "welder's helper to journeyman" in a matter of months. In the fall of 1943, black workers stopped paying dues to the Boilmakers Union in protest of segregated auxiliaries. James helped organize the committee against segregation and discrimination as well as an interracial committee opposed to union practices. As a result of their efforts, hundreds, including James, were fired from their jobs at Marinship. James filed multiple lawsuits against the Boilmakers Union in the attempt to bar segregated auxiliaries. In 1945, the California Supreme Court upheld a lower court's opinion to prohibit the practice in James v. Marinship. (Both, courtesy of Labor Archives and Research Center, San Francisco State University.)

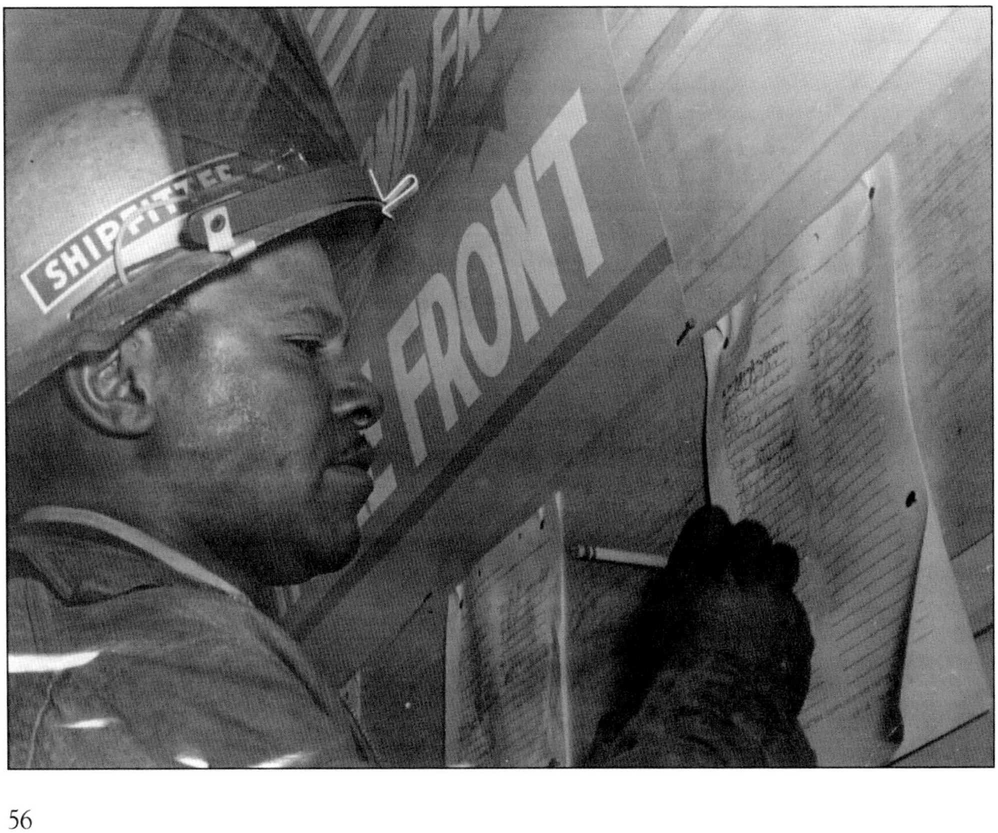

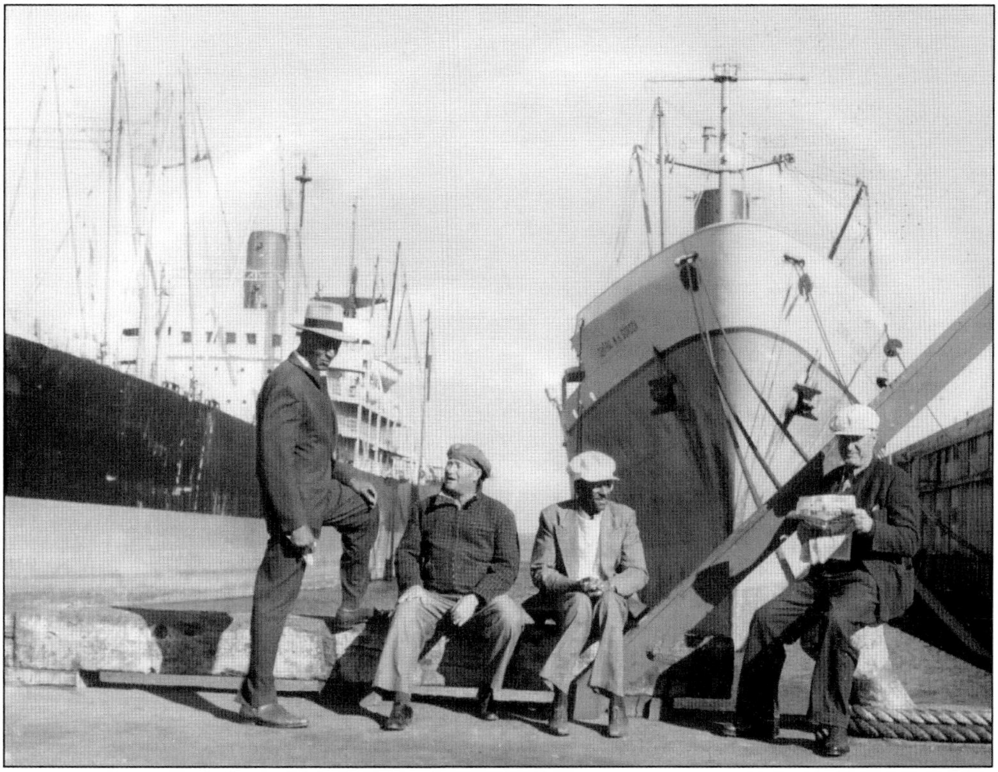

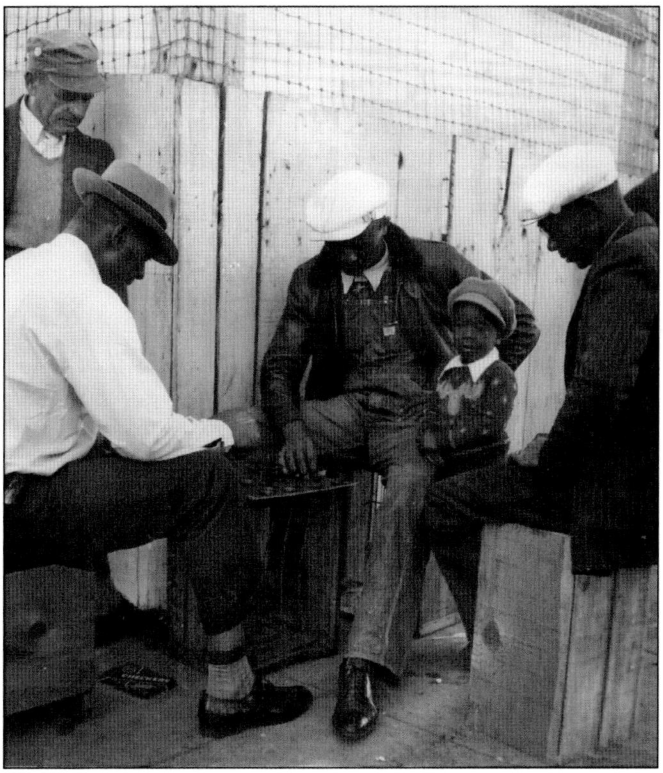

The labor movement under the leadership of Harry Bridges increased jobs opportunities for African Americans in the International Longshore and Warehouse Union (ILWU). After the strike of 1934, Bridges stated that "if only two long shore workers are left on the docks, one would be black and the other white." Black longshoremen were recruited into the ILWU after the 1934 strike. (Both, courtesy of Anne Rand Memorial Library and Archives, International Longshore and Warehouse Union.)

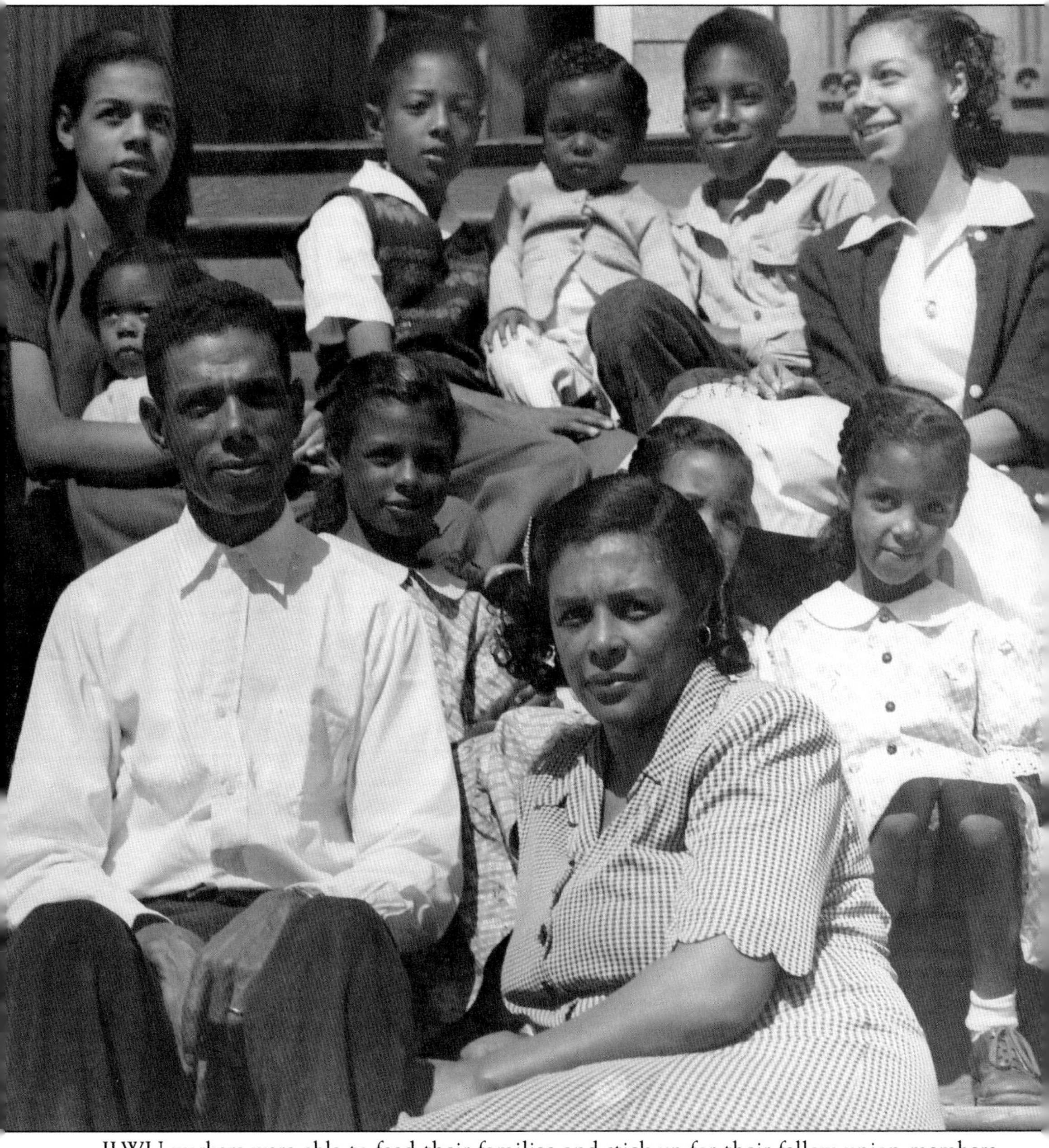

ILWU workers were able to feed their families and stick up for their fellow union members throughout the strikes of 1934 and 1948. After the strike of 1948, the union hired many black workers because of their support in the strike. Still, parity was not achieved, and black workers did not see improvement in the work force until the World War II mobilization. The economic status of many African American families improved during the war. (Courtesy of Anne Rand Memorial Library and Archives, International Longshore and Warehouse Union.)

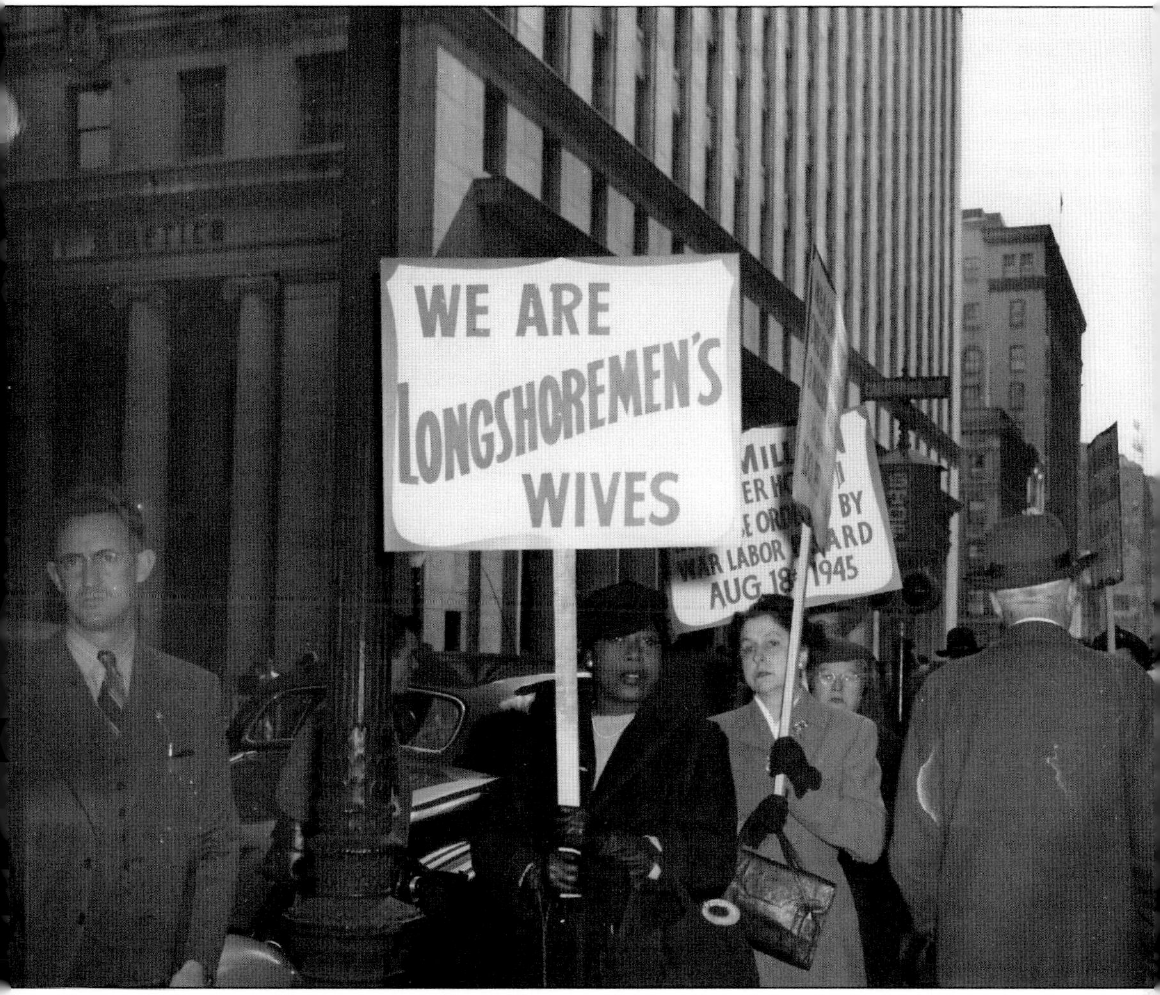

During 1946, wives of longshoremen also demonstrated in support of their husbands. (Courtesy of Anne Rand Memorial Library and Archives, International Longshore and Warehouse Union.)

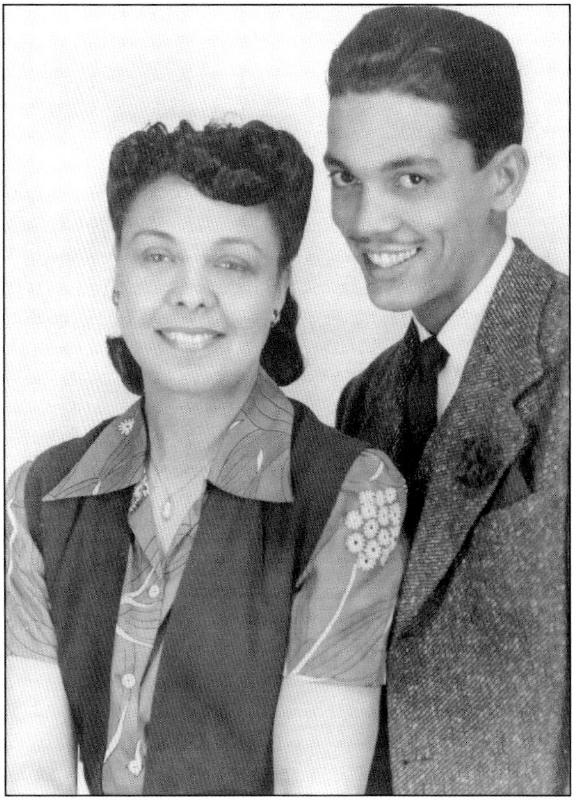

Audley and Josephine Cole were pioneers in their own right. Born in San Francisco in 1913, Josephine became, in 1942, the first black teacher hired by the San Francisco Unified School District. She worked at Balboa High School and later served as director of community relations at San Francisco City College. In 1944, Audley, at 23, became San Francisco Municipal Railway's first black motorman. Although he passed the physical and civil service exams, he was refused formal training by the Carmen's Union. The union threatened any member willing to train Audley with a $100 fine. As a result of the ban, several members were suspended for defying it, and one was physically assaulted. Audley was eventually accepted into the union, and San Francisco Municipal Transportation Agency hired hundreds of black workers by 1945. (Both, courtesy of Labor Archives and Research Center, San Francisco State University.)

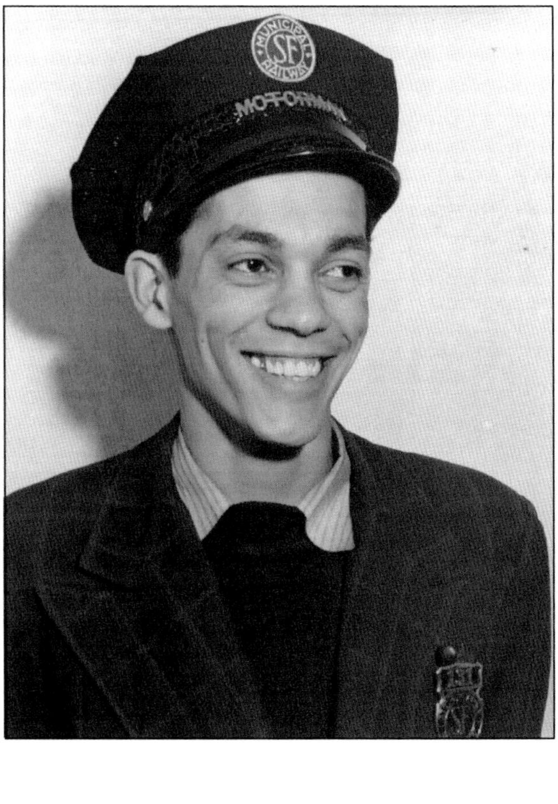

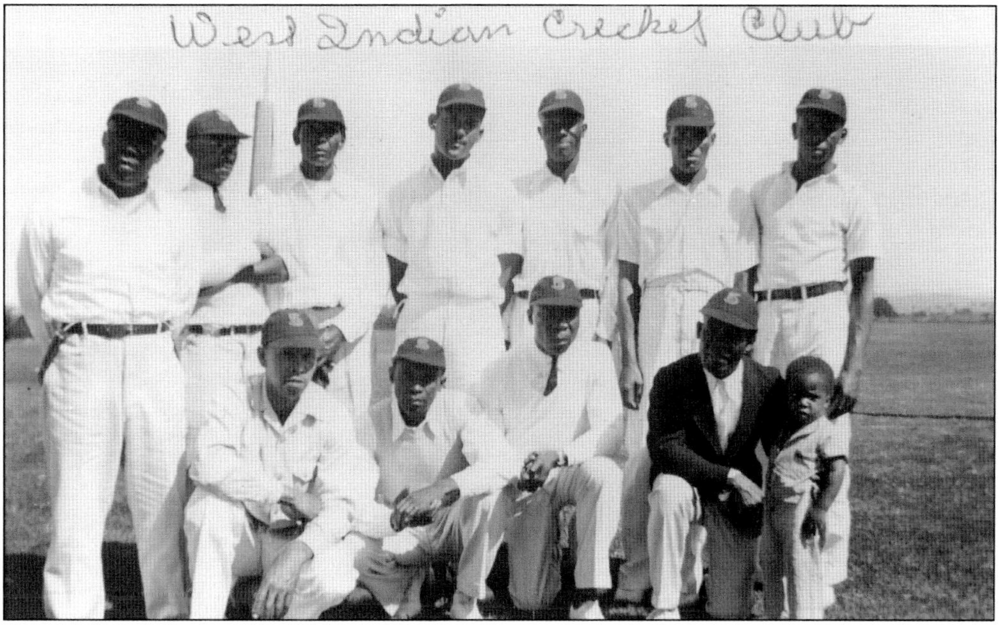

Local sports events were common in the Western Addition. This photograph is from a family in the neighborhood and shows members of the West Indian Cricket Club in 1940 before a match at Hans Park. (Courtesy of Shades of San Francisco, San Francisco Public Library.)

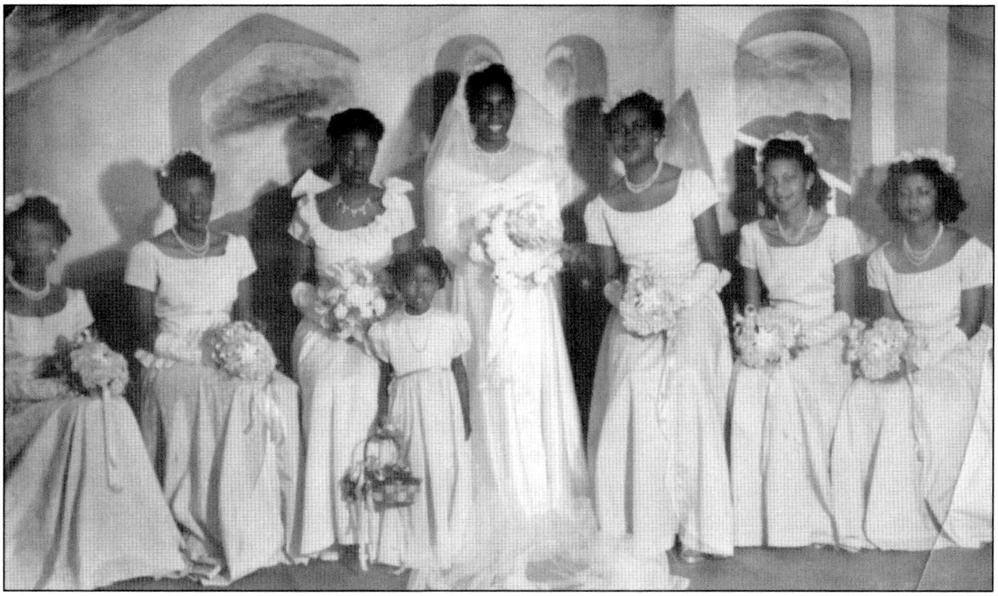

According to several women, weddings were elaborate in 1949. The bride is surrounded with six bridesmaids and a flower girl. From left to right are Pearl Thomas, Pealie Jones, Willie Jo Smith, flower girl Dorothy Johns, bride Imogene Smith (who married Charlie Hollins), Dorothy Washington, and Velma Webster. At Third Baptist Church, it was common for weddings to be held after Sunday church service, and the reception was held in the church's basement. Refreshments would have consisted of finger sandwiches, cake, and punch. Often, the brides' parents opened their homes after the reception so that guests could view the gifts. (Photograph by Wardell Bright, courtesy of LaZelle Westbrook.)

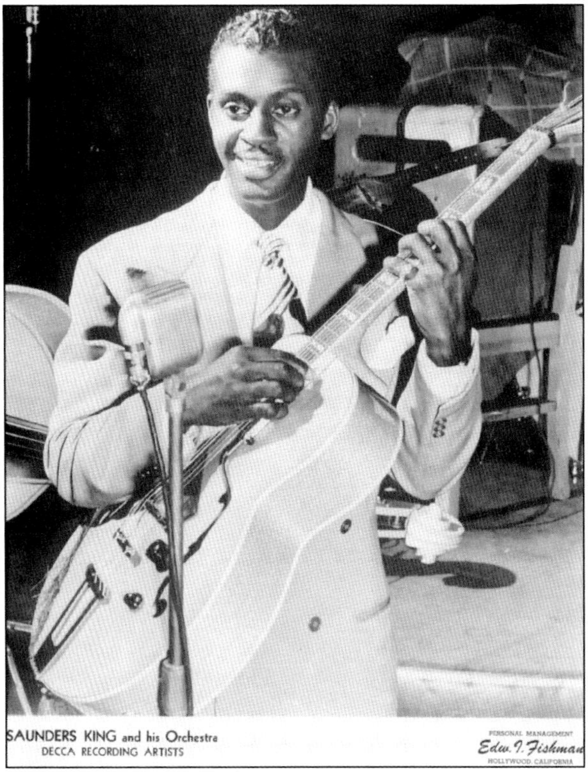

Saunders King's career started during World War II when his double-sided recording of S.K. Blues became a million-seller for the independent West Coast record company Rhythm. Throughout the 1940s, King worked with his own swinging six-piece band in many San Francisco and Los Angeles clubs and theaters. In San Francisco, King worked at the following venues: Jack's Tavern on Sutter Street, Backstage, Savoy, Blackhawk, Fairmont Hotel, Downbeat, and New Orleans Swing Club & Café Society. (Courtesy of the King family.)

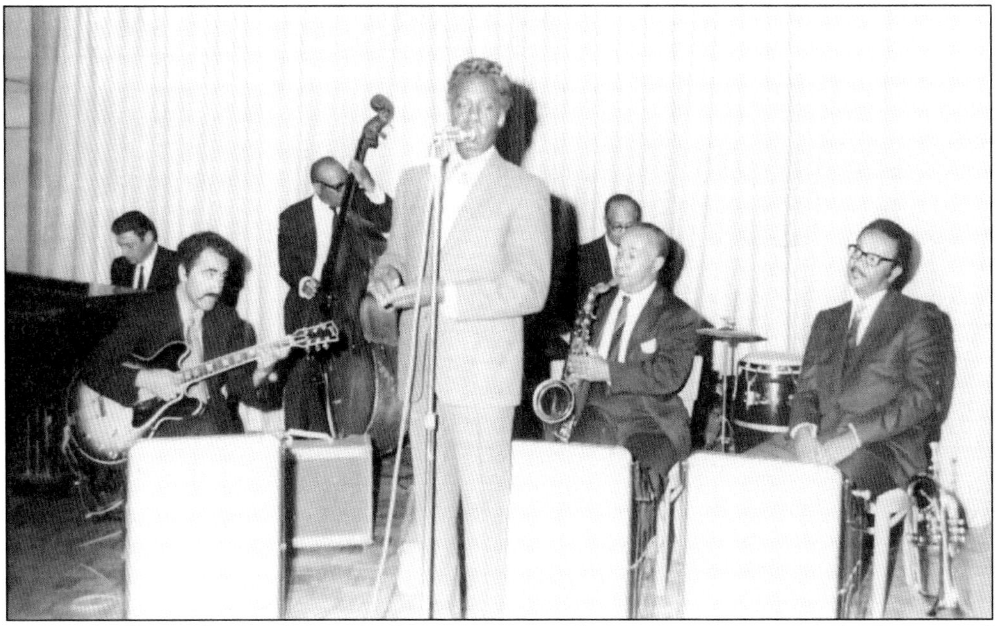

King said of himself, "I was born March 13, 1909 in Staple, Louisiana. My parents both sang, and from listening to them sing, I was always interested in music. My mother told me that she prayed for a singer when she was carrying me, and the Lord gave her a singer." King played piano, banjo, and ukulele in church. In 1938, King began working for the National Broadcasting Company (NBC) in San Francisco. (Courtesy of the King family.)

Three

1950–1980

Reshaping African American Communities, Leadership, Civil Rights, Students Rights, and Redevelopment

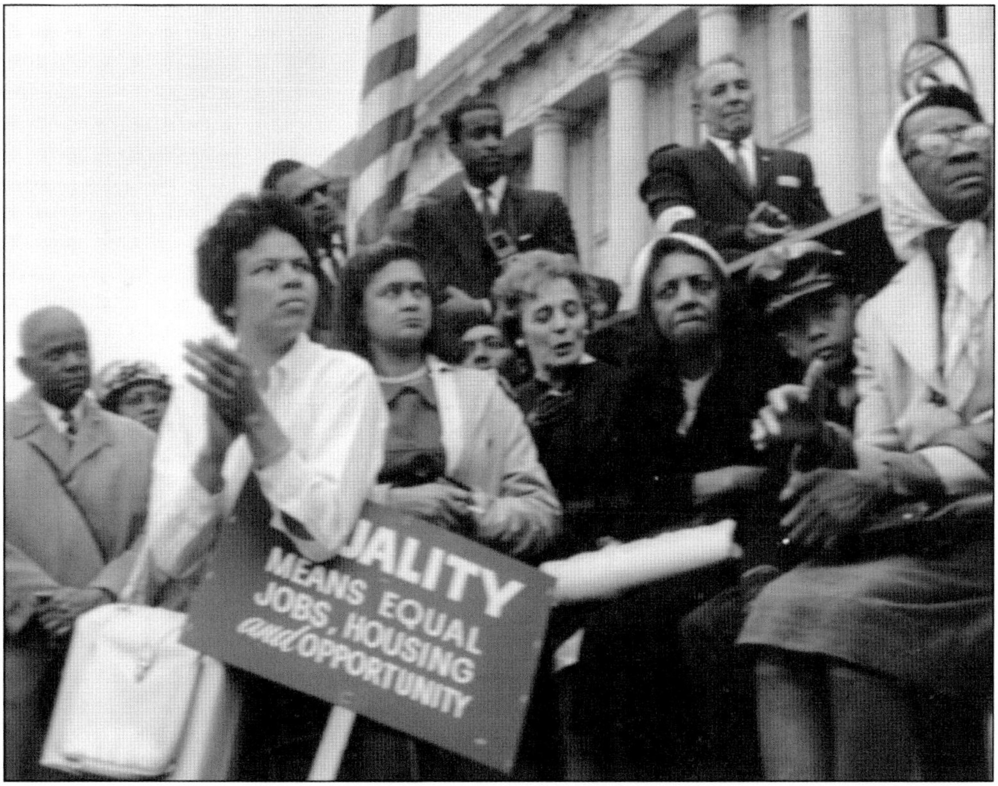

According to US Census reports, the black population in San Francisco increased tremendously between 1940 and 1970. In 1940, the black population was 4,846. In 1950, it increased to 43,460 and reached 74,383 in 1960. In 1970, it increased to 96,078. Many African Americans migrated to San Francisco from all over America for defense industry jobs. This increased population concentrated in neighborhoods accessible to shipyards and other centers of employment for unskilled and semiskilled workers. (Courtesy of David Johnson.)

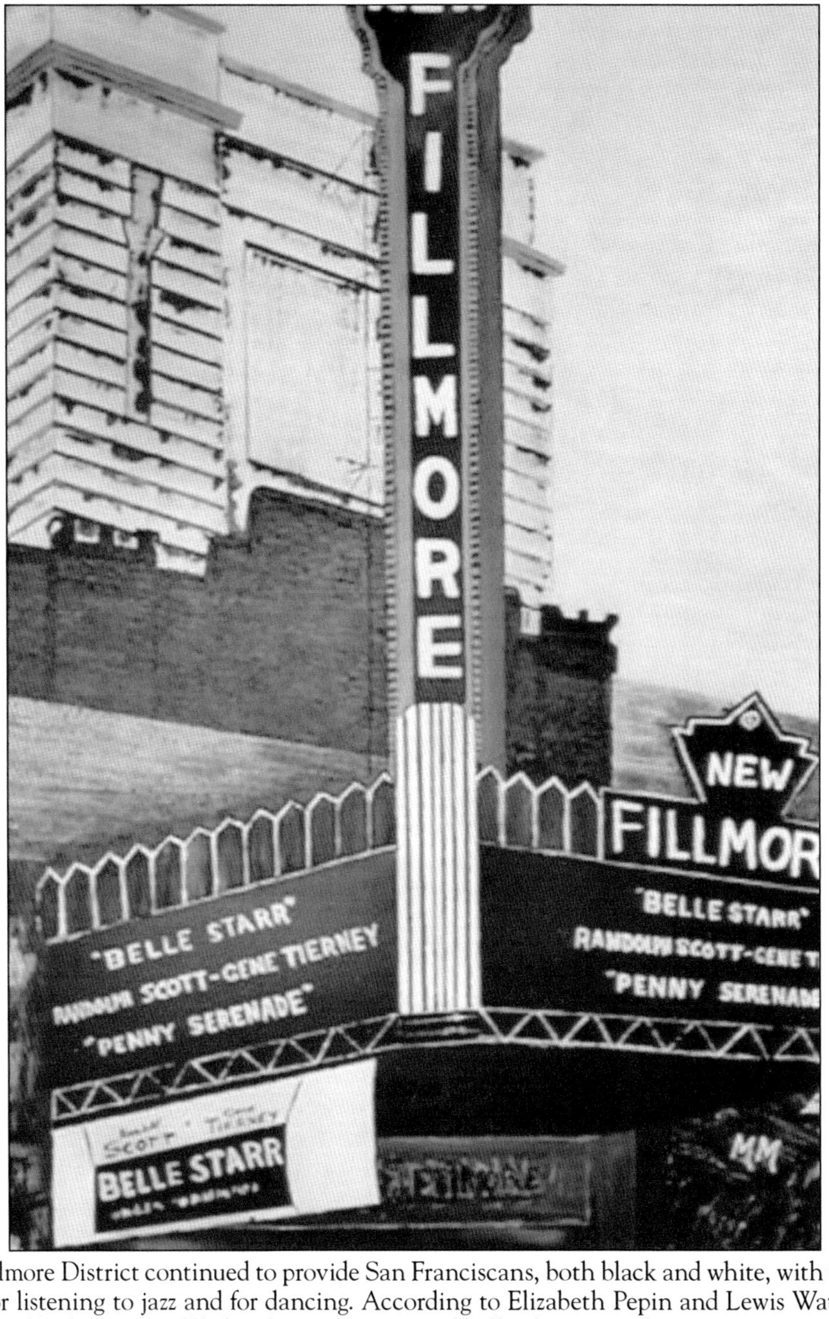

The Fillmore District continued to provide San Franciscans, both black and white, with the best clubs for listening to jazz and for dancing. According to Elizabeth Pepin and Lewis Watts, "the 10-square-block area was filled with restaurants, pool halls, theatre, and stores. Many were owned and run by African Americans." Given racial discrimination in San Francisco, African Americans in the 1940s and 1950s were limited to patronizing black clubs, hotels, and rooming houses. Even African American celebrities could not find a hotel room in downtown San Francisco, so they stayed in the Fillmore District, which was where they could eat and sleep. For musicians, the Fillmore became a place to entertain black fans as well as whites who appreciated good jazz. In their book, Pepin and Watts call the Fillmore District of the 1940s and 1950s the "Harlem of the West." (Courtesy of the Jazz Heritage Center of San Francisco.)

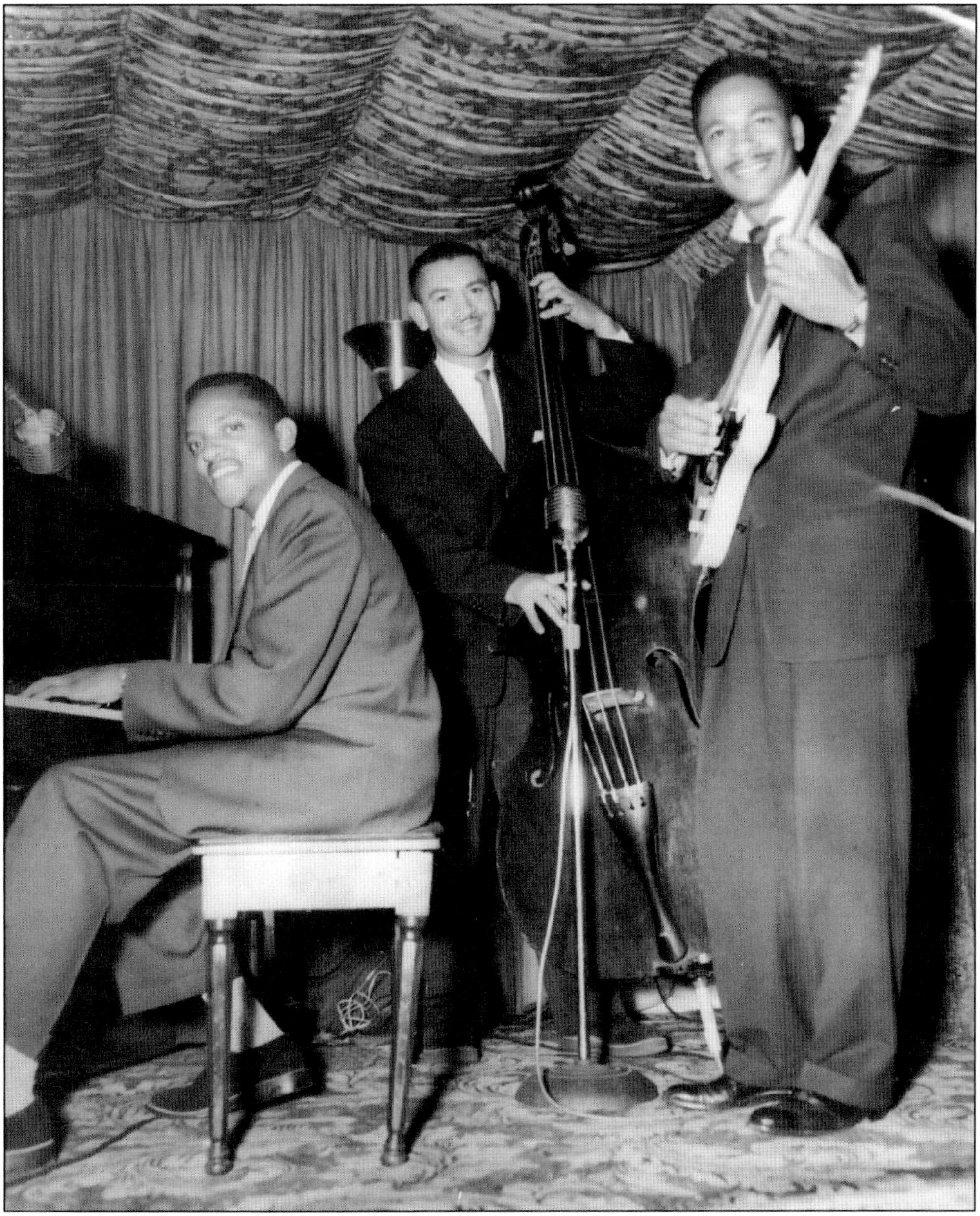

Led by Frank Jackson, the Frank Jackson Trio performed in many clubs throughout the Fillmore during the 1950s. The group consisted of Jackson on piano, Walter Sanford on bass, and Junius Simmons on guitar. As a teenager, Jackson began performing in jazz clubs throughout the Fillmore District. He is considered a living legend who embodies the spirit of the Fillmore. A childhood friend of Maya Angelou, Jackson played in neighborhood clubs as a pianist and singer and later became a preeminent jazz pioneer. Today, he continues to perform in San Francisco at Yoshi's, Razz Room, or Castagnola's. Often, he mentors young jazz musicians at schools and in the clubs. He believes "musicians must encourage and help youth appreciate jazz music." (Courtesy of Frank Jackson Collection.)

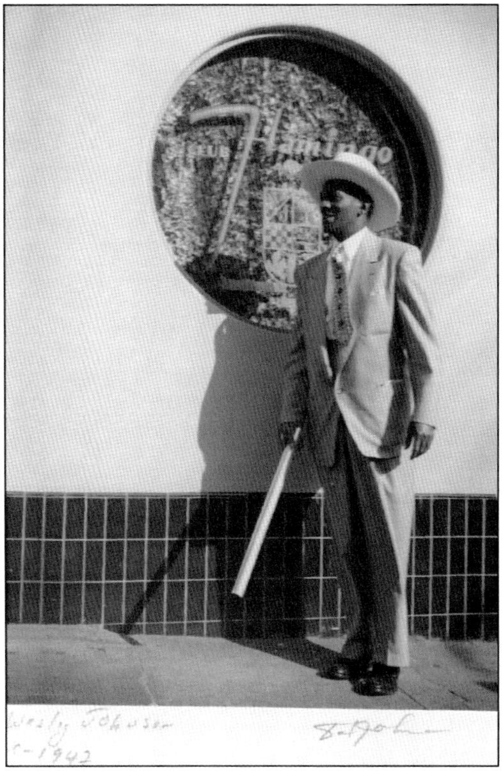

According to Pepin and Watts, Wesley Johnson Sr., a well-known nightclub owner, ran the popular Texas Playhouse/Club Flamingo. He provided a jovial ambience with his Texas-inspired style and personality. Johnson and other business owners in the thriving Fillmore District invested back into the community in forms of service and, in some cases, endowments. Johnson saved money to put his son Wesley Johnson Jr. through pharmacy school. When Johnson Jr. finished his education, he worked in the family-owned pharmacy, located in the Fillmore District. (Courtesy of David Johnson.)

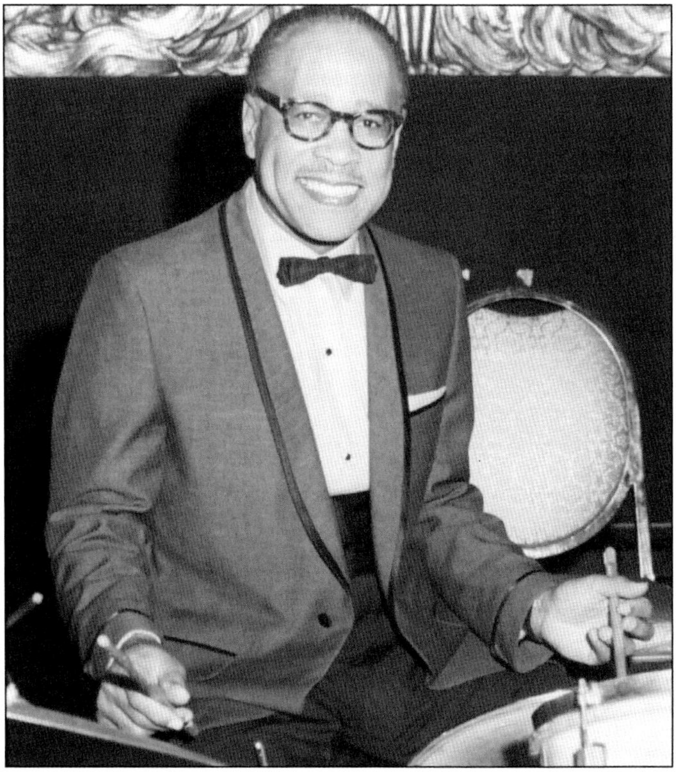

Information in *Harlem of the West* says that Eddie Alley, raised in San Francisco, began drumming in grade school. He got his start playing the drums at Topsy's Roost, where he was a busboy. A highly respected professional musician, Alley is known for his professional demeanor and love of music. He was the leader of several bands, and he and his brother Vernon established their family as a music-playing dynasty. (Courtesy of the Jazz Heritage Center of San Francisco.)

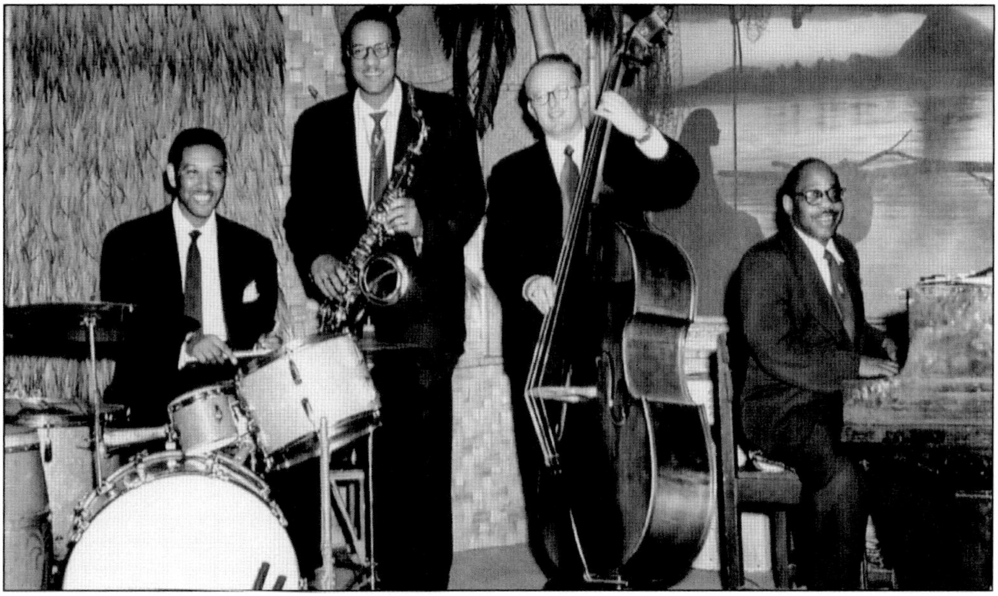

Pepin and Watts write that Earl Watkins, a longtime resident of the Fillmore, got his start drumming as a curious kid. His mother, a classically trained pianist, and father, a vocalist and ukulele player, encouraged his interest in music. The family would play music together, developing Watkins's desire to become a professional. Watkins became enthralled with the drums, eventually becoming a regular at local clubs and bars. Eventually, he played and recorded with Earl Hines and Dizzy Gillespie. (Courtesy of the Jazz Heritage Center of San Francisco.)

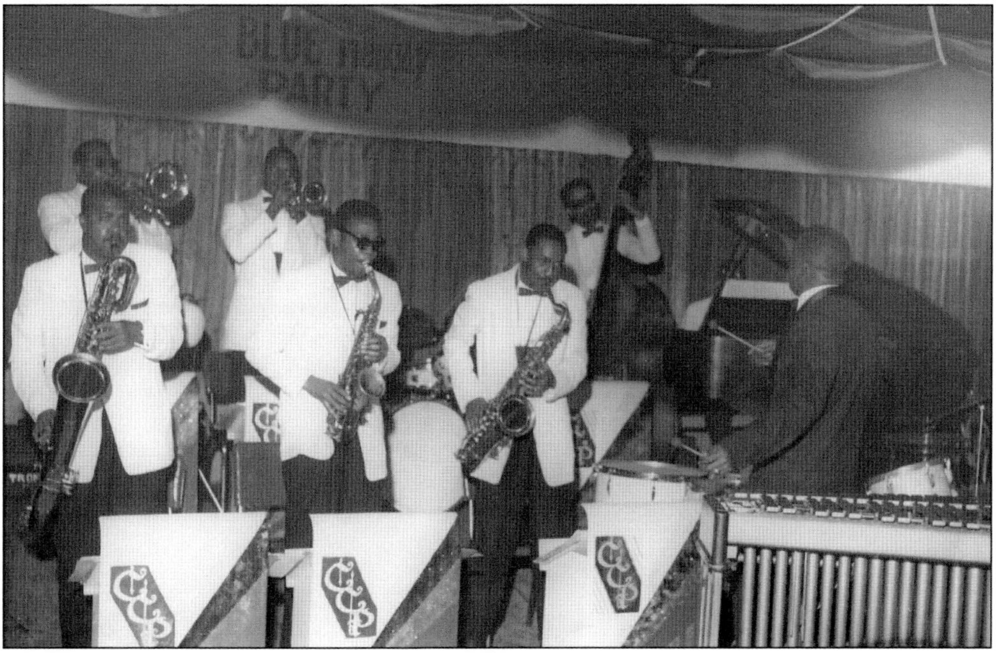

In the 1950s, Frank Fisher and his band played at various clubs around the Bay Area, and then they went to Jimbo's Bob City and played from 1:00 a.m. until 10:00 a.m. in the morning. Fisher started playing music as an elementary school student and continues performing today. (Courtesy of Frank Fisher.)

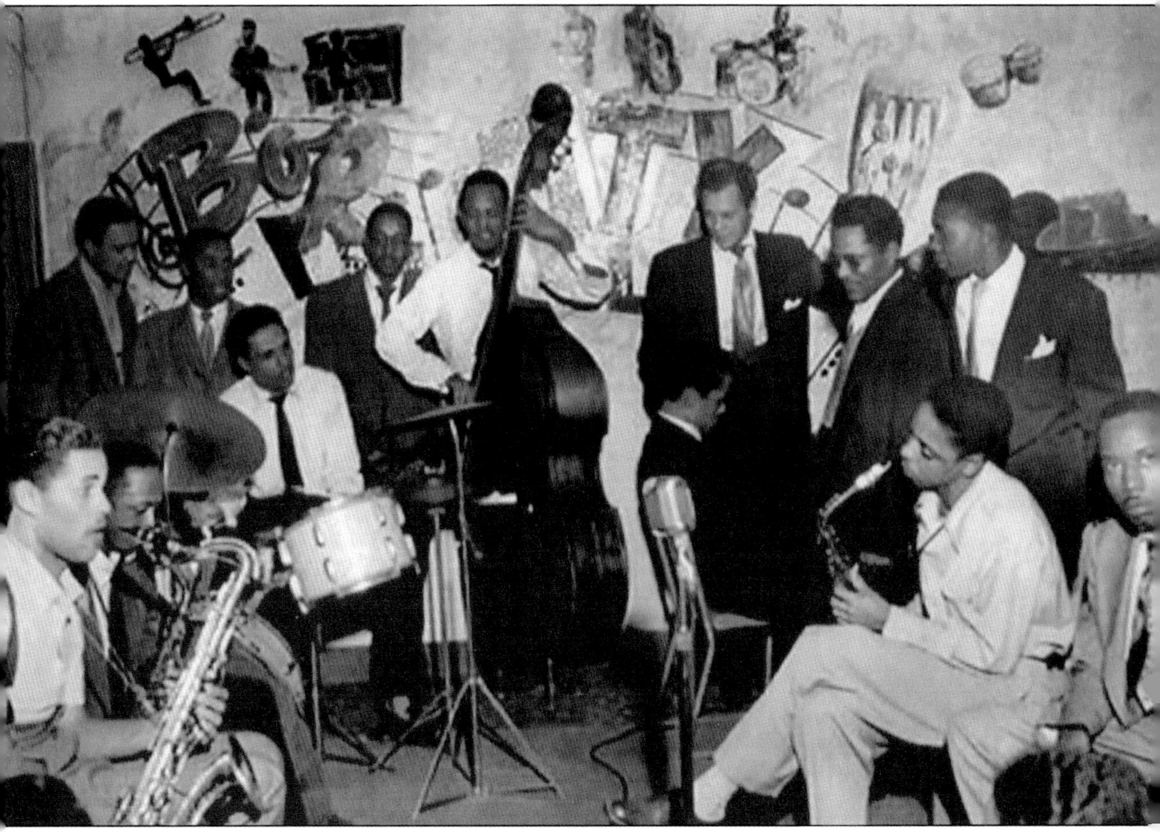

According to Frank Fisher, Jimbo's Bop City did many things to help integrate races and bring them together. Jam sessions were held nightly. During the height of the Fillmore District's jazz days, Jimbo's Bop City had been an essential club, a legendary after-hours establishment that played host to names like Count Basie, Charlie Parker, John Coltrane, Miles Davis, Ella Fitzgerald, and more. Frank Jackson calls it a place for learning: "You got a chance to play with the good, bad, and the ugly!" (Courtesy of the Jazz Heritage Center of San Francisco.)

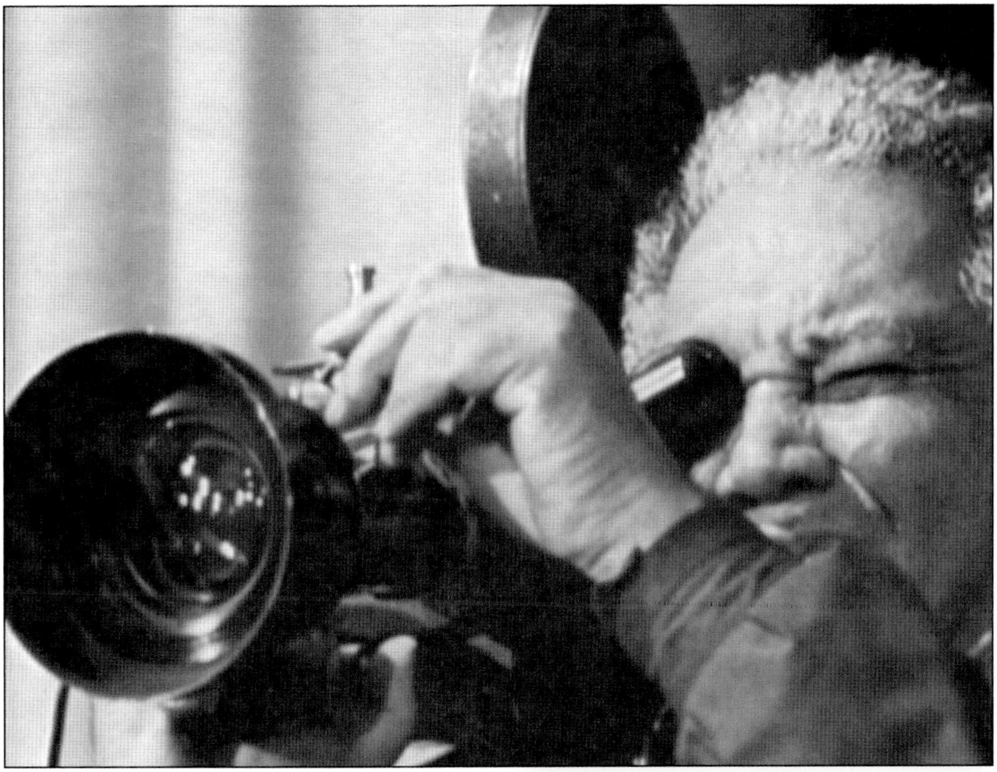

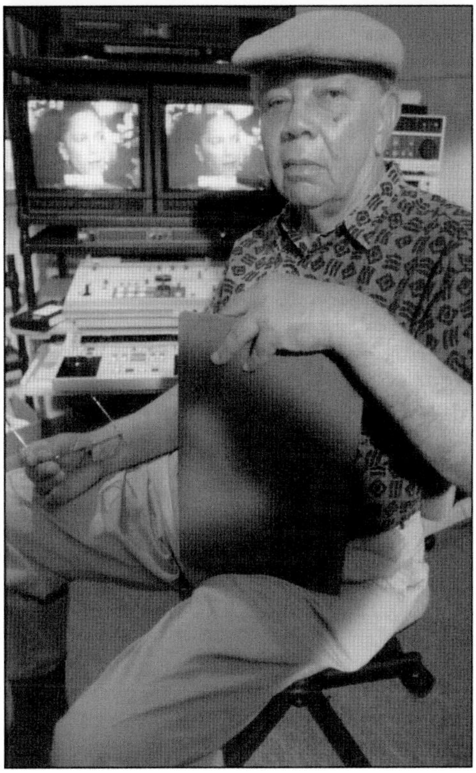

Allen Willis, born in 1916 in Washington, DC, moved to San Francisco with his wife, Lillian, in the 1950s. He had a distinguished career as a filmmaker and writer. As the first black electronic broadcast journalist in the state of California, Willis was considered the dean of African American filmmakers in the Bay Area. In the 1950s, Willis studied with photographers Ansel Adams, Minor White, and David Johnson. Willis was a founder of the independent filmmaking community. From 1963 to 1983, he worked for PBS station KQED–TV in San Francisco as a news and documentary cinematographer. Willis created many award-winning films, such as *The Other America*, a documentary on a speech by Dr. Martin Luther King Jr. at Stanford University in 1967. From 1970 to 2008, Willis wrote a column under the name John Alan for the Marxist-humanist publication *News and Letters*. According to the East Bay Media Center of Berkeley, which houses Willis's archives, he was devoted to Marxist-humanist values. Willis died at 94 in February 2011. (Both, courtesy of Allen Willis and KQED.)

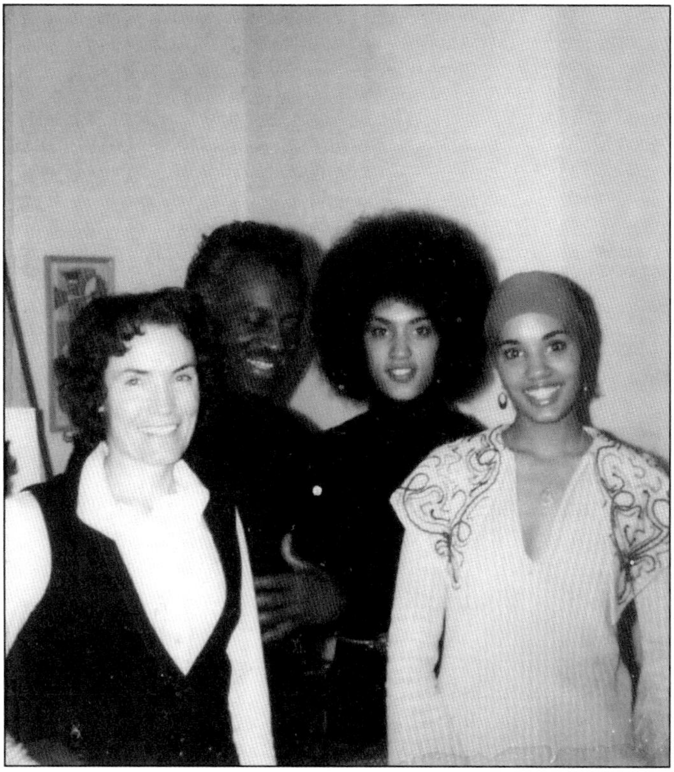

Seen in this 1960s image, Saunders King, a musician from the Fillmore District in the 1940s and 1950s, and his family lived in San Francisco on Majestic Avenue. He is pictured with his wife, Jo Frances, and their daughters, Kitsaun (left) and Deborah. Both Deborah and Kitsaun completed elementary and high schools in San Francisco. (Courtesy of the King family.)

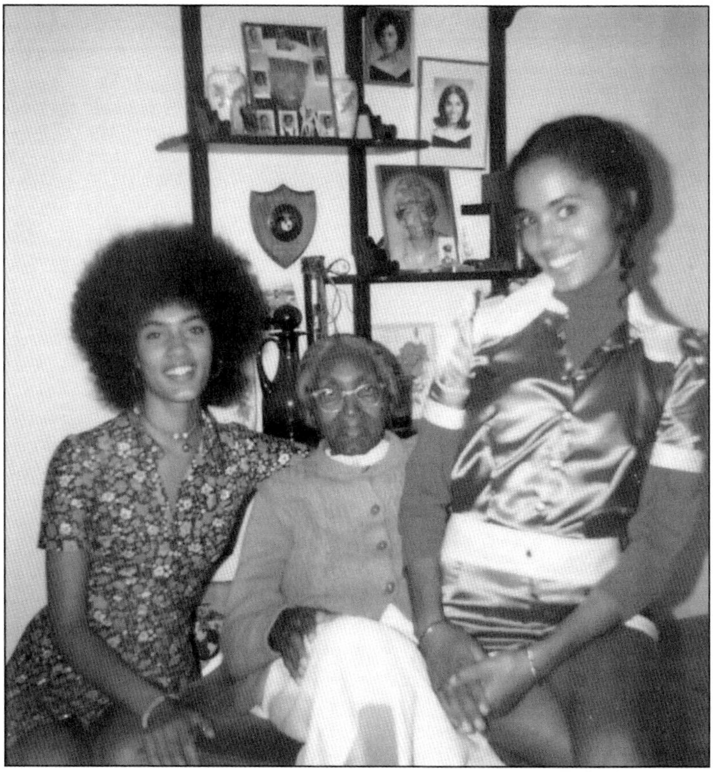

The Kings' two daughters, Kitsaun (left) and Deborah, are seen here with their grandmother. Her visits were an annual summertime event. As adults, both daughters returned to the Bay Area to raise their children. Today, the neighborhood streets hold many memories for the family. (Courtesy of the King family.)

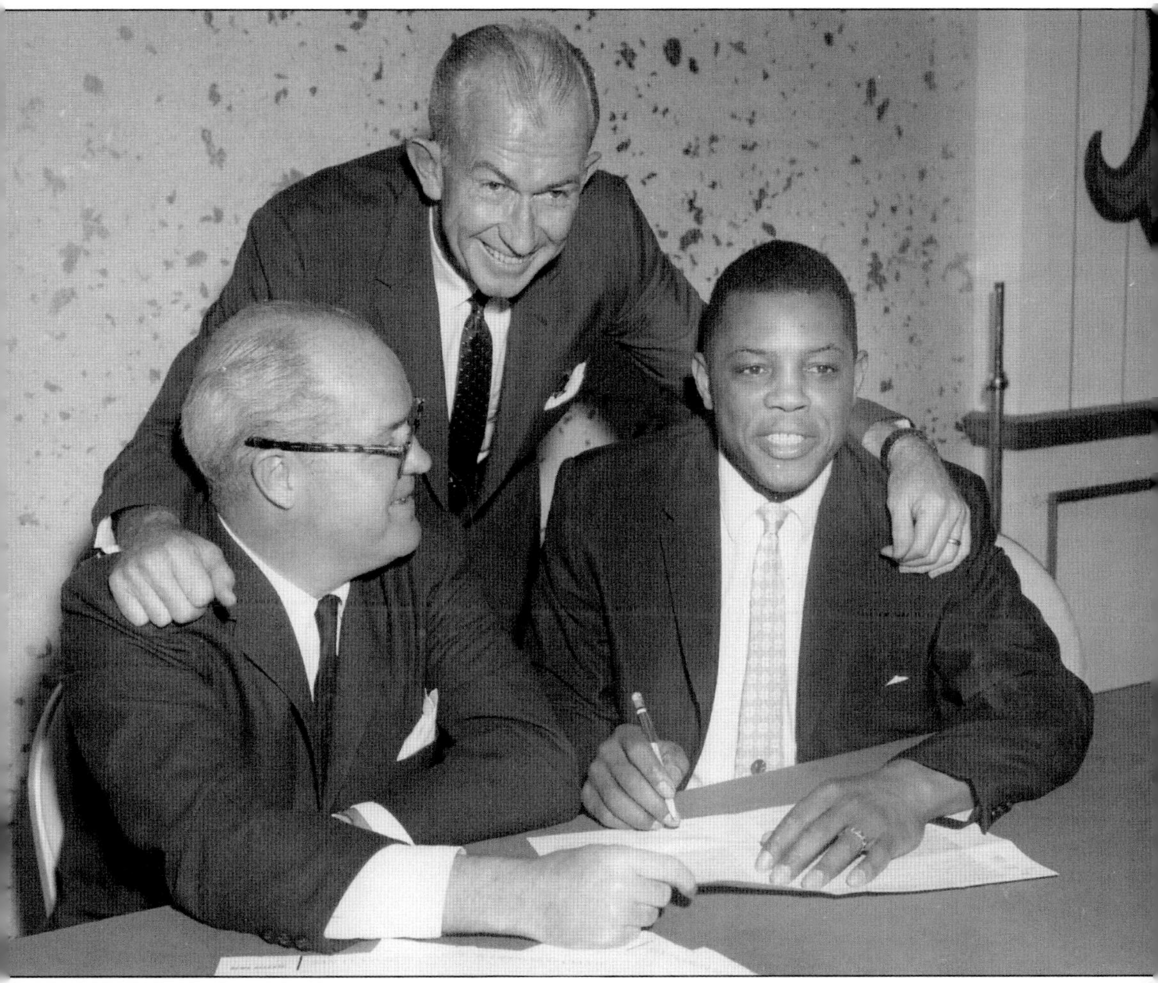

Born on May 6, 1931, Willie Howard Mays Jr. had an illustrious career with the New York and San Francisco Giants, eventually retiring from the New York Mets. Mays was born in Westfield, Alabama, to William Howard Mays Sr. and Annie Satterwhite. As a young man, Mays was introduced to baseball watching his father play in the Negro Leagues. Ernest Withers writes that, for Mays Sr., the Negro Leagues was a way to "make a little money doing something I was good at." Considered the first African American superstar of Major League Baseball, Mays is known for his ability to transcend race and color lines. In 1950, he played for the Giants' Class B farm team in the Interstate League. Freedman writes, "During his first years with the Giants, racism was common, but Mays maintained his dignity and demanded respect." Mays is a legendary San Francisco Giant and member of the exclusive 600 Home Run Club, hitting his 600th home run in the summer of 1969, eventually retiring in 1973 with 660 home runs. (Courtesy of San Francisco History Center, San Francisco Public Library.)

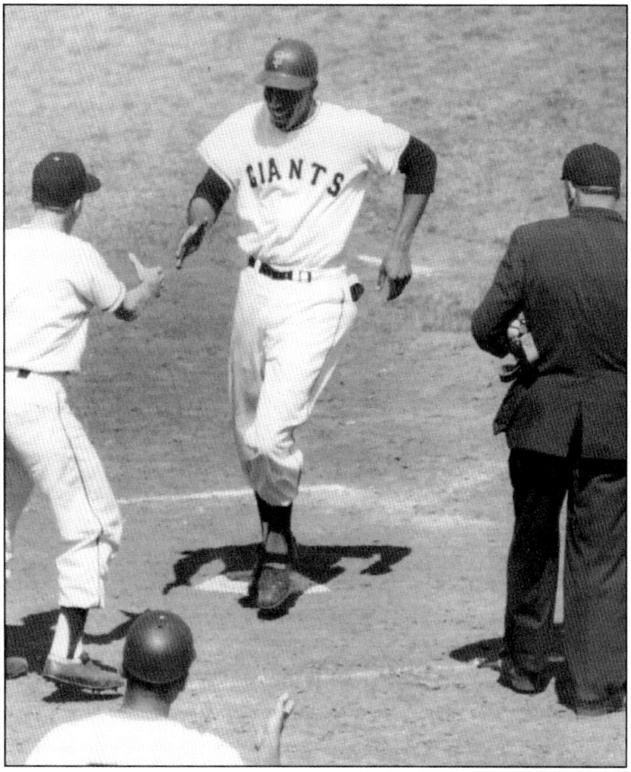

Willie McCovey was born on January 10, 1938, in Mobile, Alabama. McCovey signed with the New York Giants as a free agent in 1955 and played 19 seasons for the San Francisco Giants. McCovey was considered one of the most intimidating power-hitters in his time. He batted and threw the baseball with his left hand. His powerful swing generated 521 home runs, of which 231 were hit in Candlestick Park. McCovey was inducted into the Baseball Hall of Fame in 1986 and the Afro Sports Hall of Fame in Oakland in February 2009. The inlet of San Francisco Bay has been renamed McCovey Cove, and a statue has been erected in his honor at McCovey Point. (Courtesy of San Francisco History Center, San Francisco Public Library.)

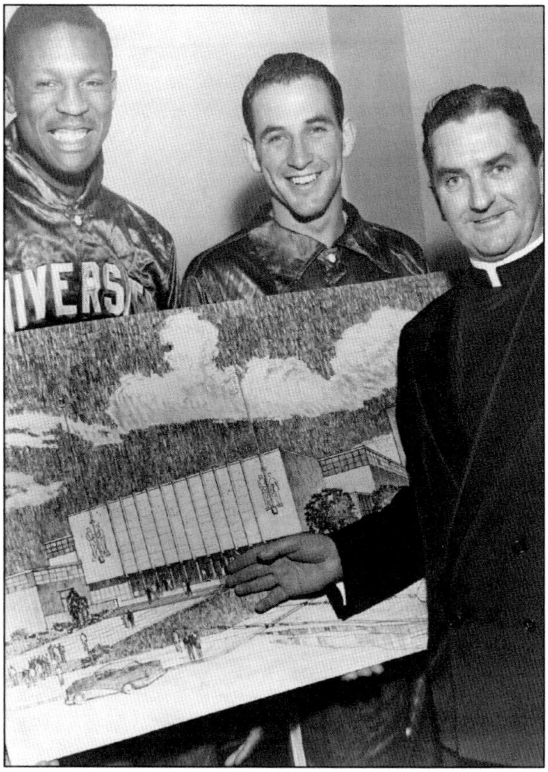

Eleven-time NBA Champion Bill Russell (left) was born on February 12, 1934. He attended McClymonds High School in Oakland, enrolled at the University of San Francisco (USF) in 1953, and led USF to two national championships. Russell entered the 1956 NBA draft and became a first-round pick by the St. Louis Hawks. Originally from Monroe, Louisiana, Russell established his career with the Boston Celtics, becoming one of the best players in NBA history. In total, Russell totaled 21,620 rebounds and 14,522 career points. Considered by many to be the first African American player to be considered an NBA superstar, he is shown here with USF teammate Jerry Mullen (center) and USF president John F. X. Connolly. (Courtesy of San Francisco History Center, San Francisco Public Library.)

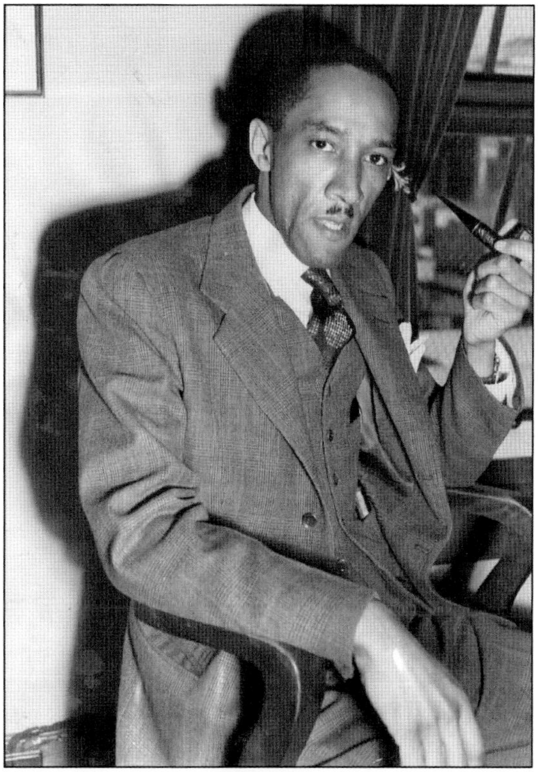

Cecil Francis Poole, born in Birmingham, Alabama, on July 14, 1914, was the first African American US attorney and the first African American federal judge in Northern California. He received his Juris Doctor from Harvard University in 1939. In 1942, Poole married Charlotte Crump and was drafted into the US Army. He was assigned to an all-black unit used primarily for manual labor. After being promoted to staff sergeant, he later became lieutenant in the judge advocate general's office. After an honorable discharged in 1946, Poole and his family moved to San Francisco where he took a job as a research attorney. In 1949, he accepted a job as assistant district attorney in the office of the San Francisco District under Gov. Edmund "Pat" Brown. (Both, courtesy of San Francisco History Center, San Francisco Public Library.)

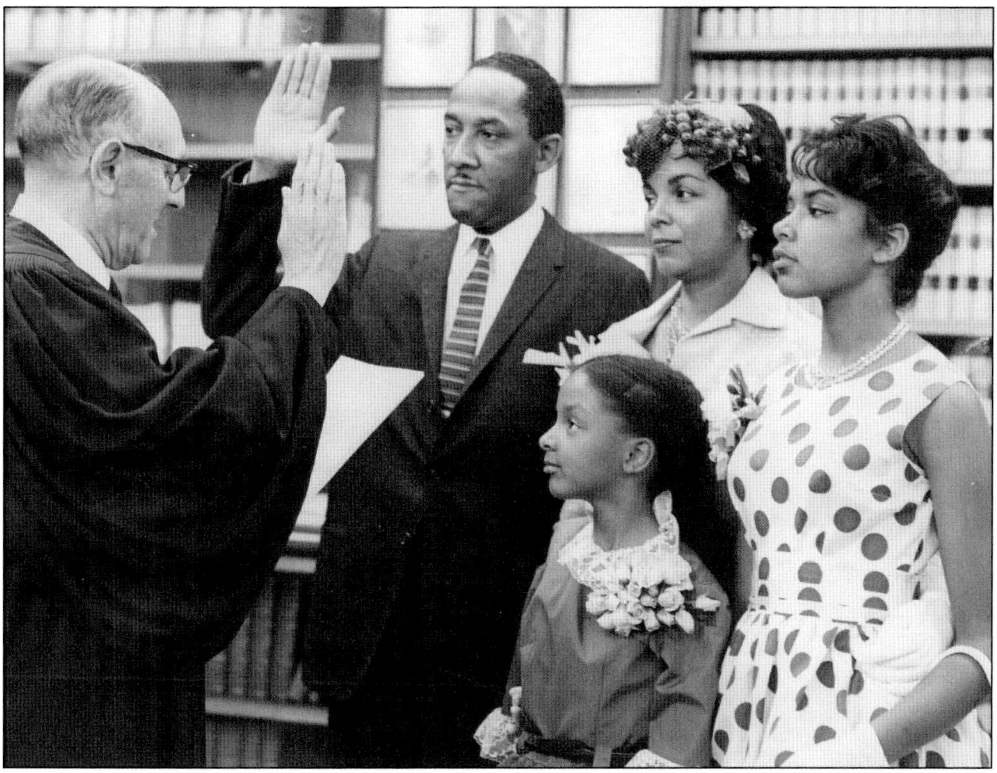

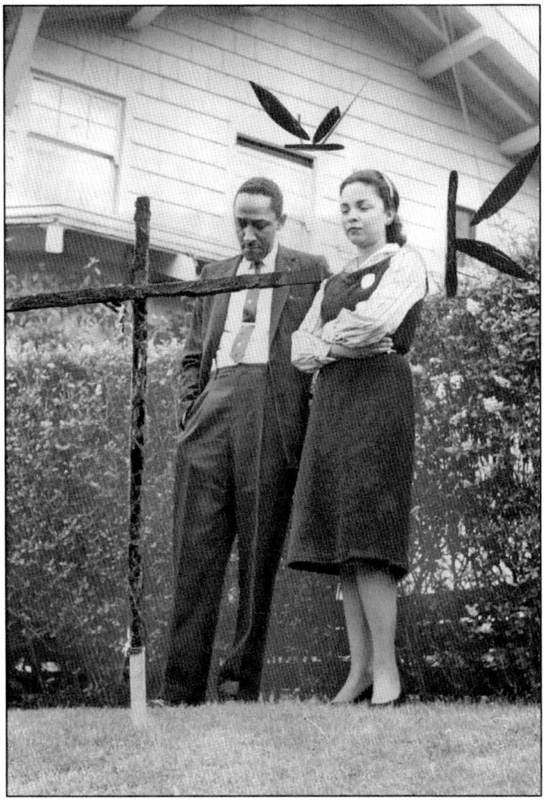

At left with his wife, Charlotte, Poole and his family faced racism and intimidation while serving the citizens of Northern California. A cross was burned on the front lawn of their home. In the 1961 photograph below, Poole is shown with US attorney general Robert Kennedy. In June 1960, Pres. John F. Kennedy appointed Poole as US attorney for the Northern District of California, making him the first African American federal attorney in the continental United States. (Both, courtesy of San Francisco History Center, San Francisco Public Library.)

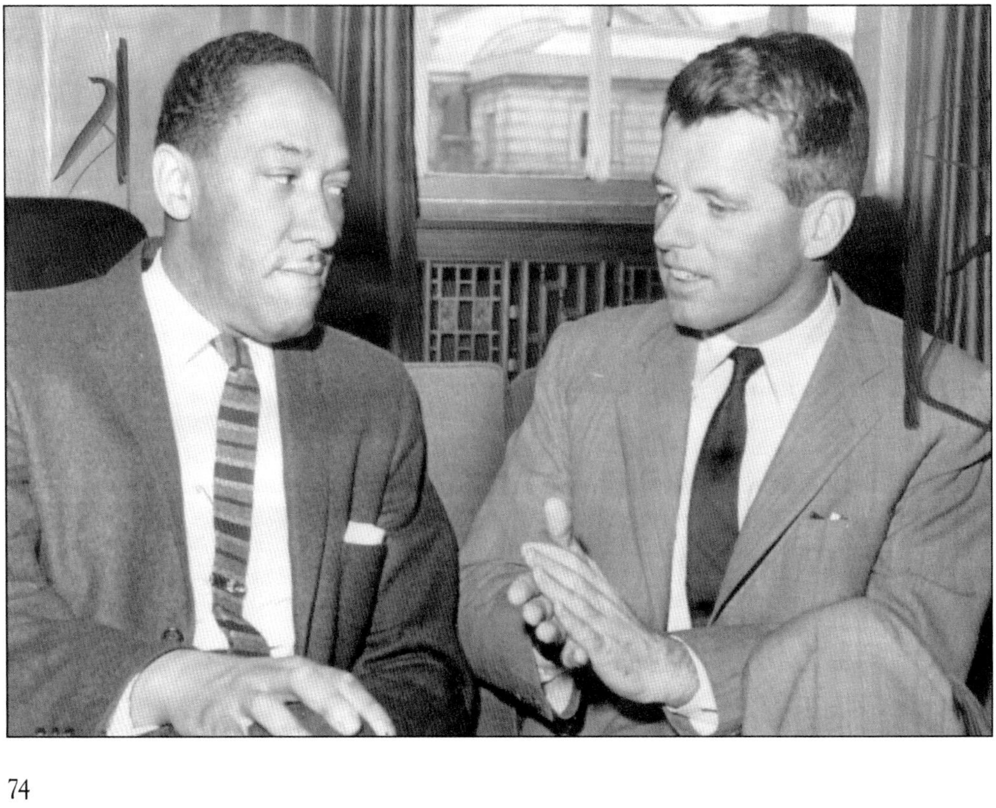

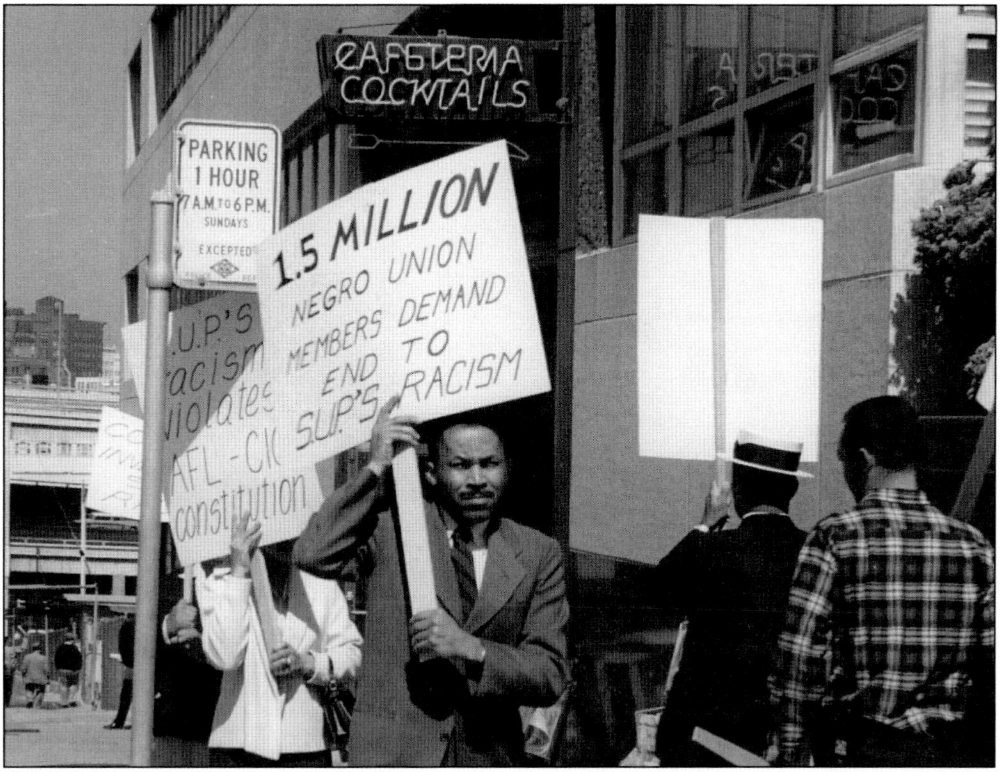

In 1955, James Herndon and Frances Miller cofounded the African American Historical and Cultural Society of San Francisco (AAHCS), which is a descendent of the San Francisco Athenaeum and Literary Association founded by blacks in San Francisco in 1853. Herndon, born in 1925 in Troy, Alabama, was the first black person to become a partner in a major San Francisco law firm at Garry Dreyfus & McTernan. He graduated from Morehouse College in Atlanta in 1948. There, he was a classmate of Martin Luther King Jr. and president of the campus NAACP chapter. Herndon earned his law degree in 1950s from Howard University in Washington, DC. Herndon move to San Francisco in 1956. In San Francisco, he was president of the Negro American Labor Council and led a campaign for hiring African American checkers at a major supermarket in the Bayview neighborhood. Herndon spent his 30-year legal career representing affordable housing groups in Bayview-Hunters Point and the Mission Tenants Union. He was also the lawyer for the United Farm Workers. (Both, courtesy of David Johnson.)

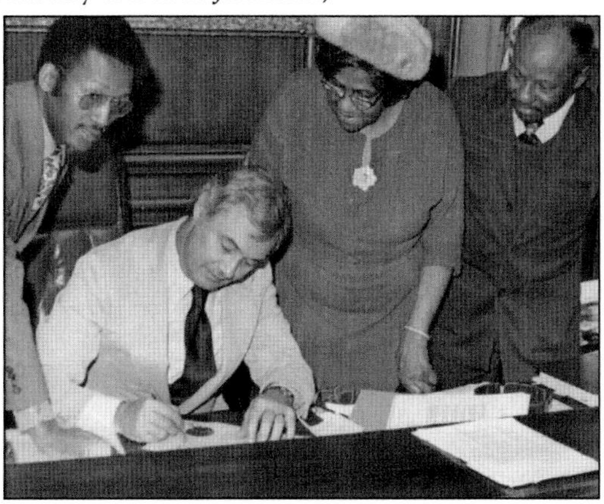

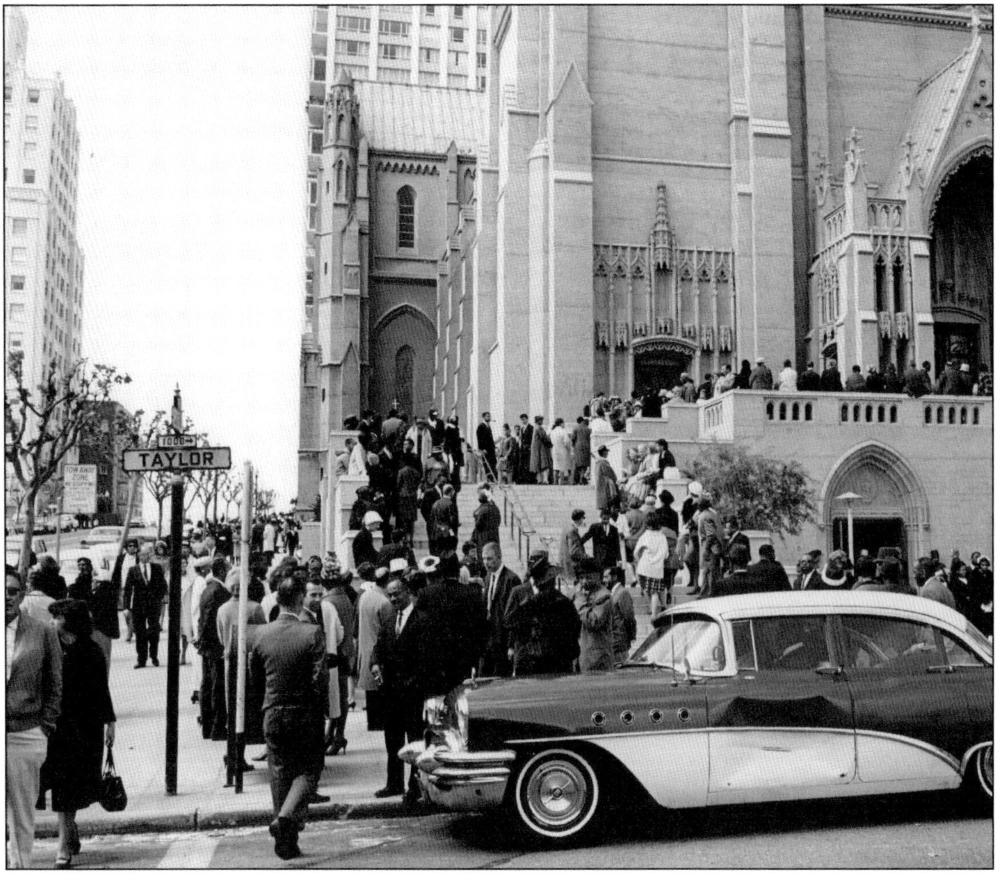

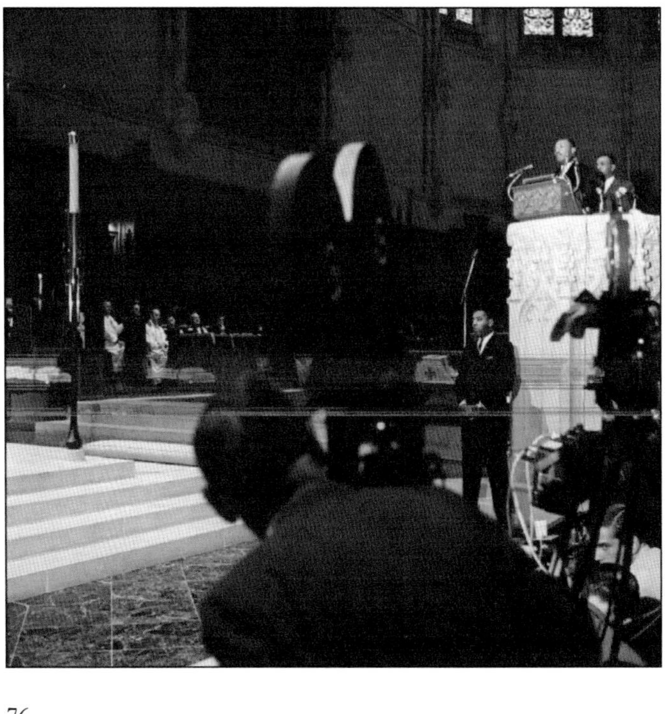

On March 28, 1965, the Reverend Dr. Martin Luther King Jr. preached at Grace Cathedral Catholic Church. There were 5,000 people, most of them African-Americans, in attendance at the 10:00 a.m. service on California Street. Invited as part of the cathedral's Festival of Grace, Dr. King applauded the efforts of Bay Area residents and their support for the Civil Rights Movement. In Dr. King's speech, he addressed issues of discrimination towards African Americans and the role of the church and clergy. (Both, courtesy of the Archives of the Archdiocese of San Francisco.)

In 1960, Drs. Raye (right) and Julian Richardson (below) established Marcus Books, located in a Victorian house at 1712 Fillmore Street, the former site of Jimbo's Bop City. In 2011, the San Francisco outpost of Marcus Books, the oldest independent black bookstore in the country, celebrated 50 years in business at the same location. The Richardsons recognized a need for the African American community to have an establishment devoted to selling and promoting books written by black people that dealt with the black experience. Both Raye and Julian were individuals who committed their life's work to nurturing literature and community. Julian passed away in 2000. (Both, courtesy of the Richardson family.)

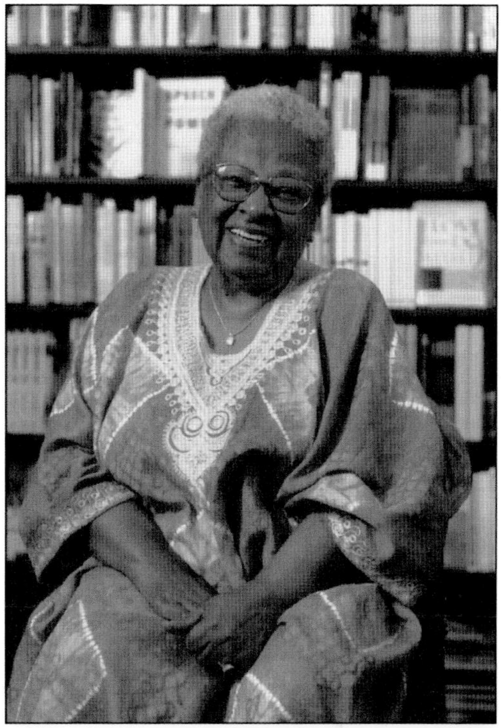

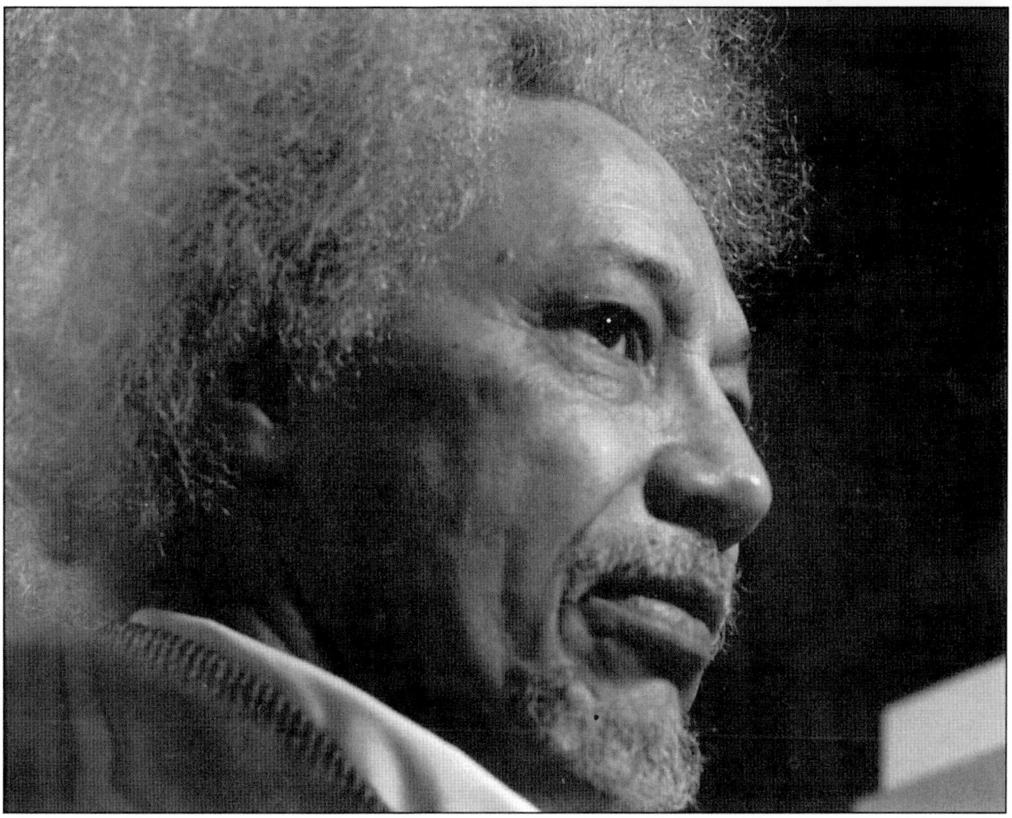

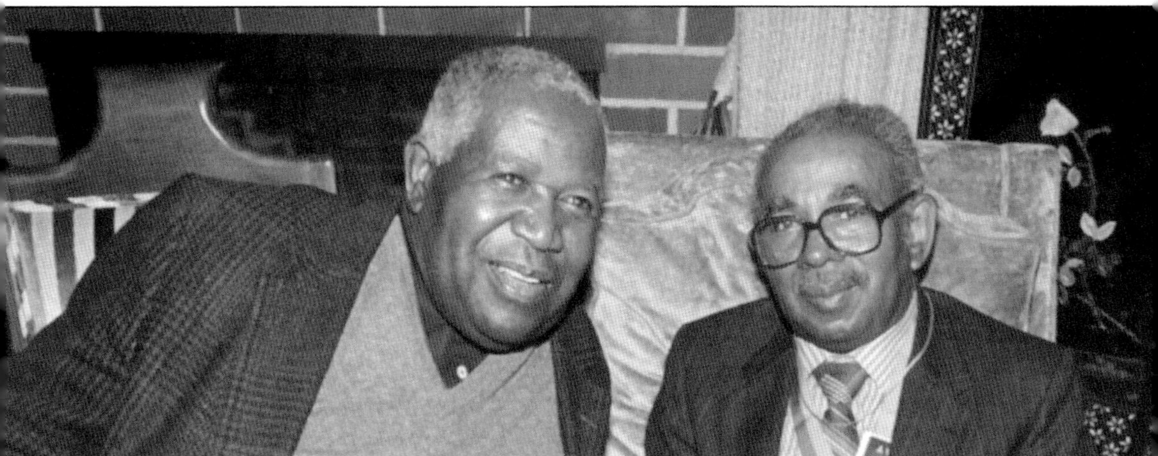

Thomas C. Fleming (left) and Dr. Carlton B. Goodlett had a friendship that lasted over 50 years. These two civil rights pioneers used their expertise and professional positions and combined their 100 years as activists to fight for the rights of San Francisco's African American community. Goodlett was a physician and the publisher of the *Sun-Reporter* newspaper. He was dedicated to both the newspaper and his medical practice. Both were housed in the same building so that he could work at both sites at the same time. In an interview, Fleming stated that Goodlett was an important figure in San Francisco: "It was Carlton Goodlett who used to go downtown and argue with the politicians." Goodlett died in 1997. In January 1999, Mayor Willie Brown led a ceremony to rename city hall's address as Dr. Carlton B. Goodlett Place. (Courtesy of George Kruse.)

Terry Francois (right), seen here with judge James J. Welsh, was born in 1921 in Louisiana, moved to San Francisco in the 1940s and graduated from Hastings School of Law in 1949. In 1952, Francois helped to win a major case against the San Francisco Housing Authority. In 1964, Mayor John Shelley appointed Francois to the San Francisco Board of Supervisors. Francois was a leading force on the board and led the fight in 1965 against the construction of a proposed freeway through Golden Gate Park. He also championed the urban renewal project in the Western Addition, which earned him the distrust of the African American community as well as its leaders, such as Willie Brown Jr. and Carlton Goodlett. Brown Jr. and Goodlett opposed the Western Addition project because of issues of displacement of black residents. (Courtesy of San Francisco History Center, San Francisco Public Library.)

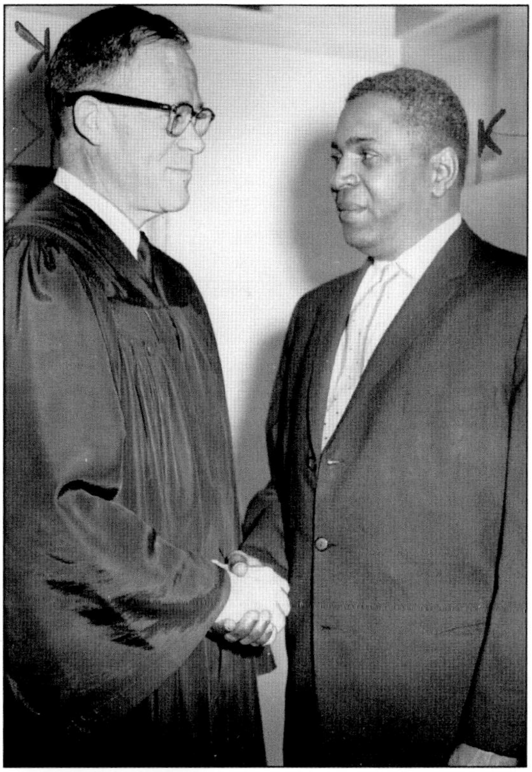

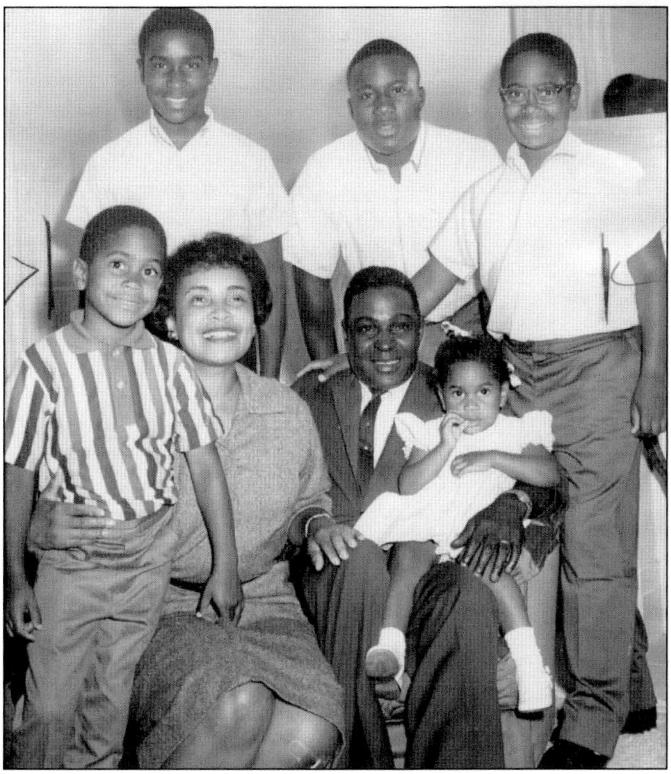

The Francois family is shown here. They are, from left to right, (first row) Eric, Marion, Terry, and Carol; (second row) Gary, Wade, and Brian. Terry retired from his supervisor seat in 1977. He continued practicing law until his death on June 12, 1989. (Courtesy of San Francisco History Center, San Francisco Public Library.)

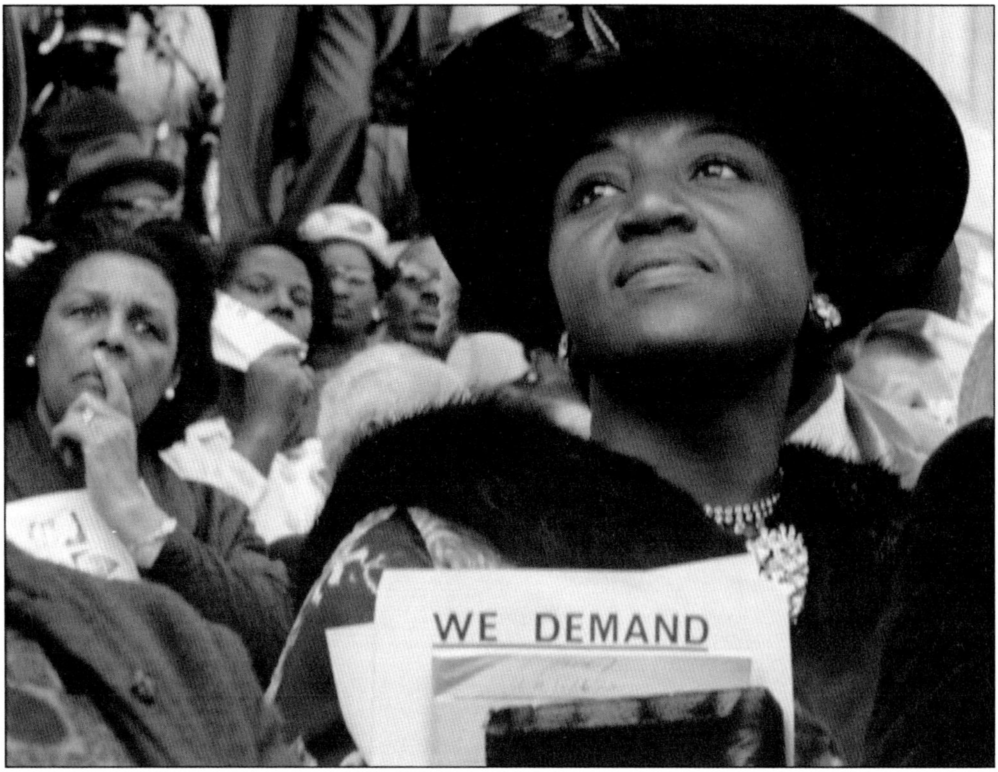

San Francisco experienced the civil rights movement in the 1950s and 1960s. After World War II ended, African Americans found themselves out of jobs all over the city. Thousands migrated from the city to look for work elsewhere, while others went to work in service industries engaged in menial labor. Local branches of civil rights organizations, such as San Francisco's NAACP, the Congress on Racial Equality (CORE), and the Student Nonviolent Coordinating Committee (SNCC), began to target local businesses as a means of highlighting employment discrimination in San Francisco. Downtown hotels, car dealerships, and banks were boycotted until fair hiring practices were implemented. These groups also targeted retailers like Woolworth and Kress department stores in solidarity with those marching for freedom in the South. San Francisco residents of all ethnicities participated in these demonstrations, expressing their concern for discriminatory practices in housing and employment. (Both, courtesy of David Johnson.)

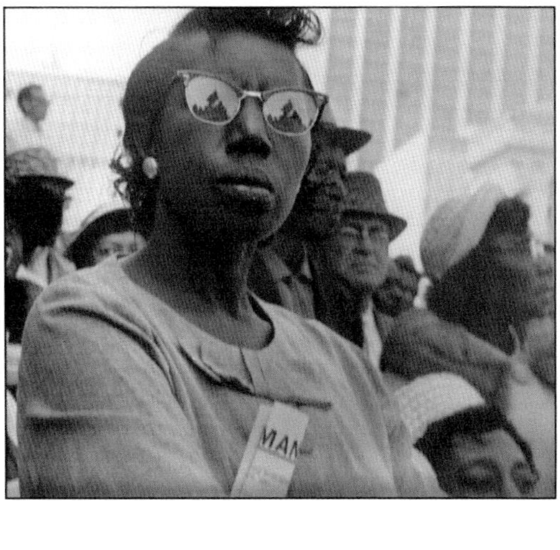

In 1959, Bill Chester served as the Northern California regional director for the ILWU. Chester fought for the rights of all members of the union. He brought the ILWU's tradition of antidiscrimination center stage and was a member of many civil rights organizations and coalitions, including the National Negro Labor Council in the 1950s. African Americans rose from the rank and file to assume leadership positions within the ILWU. African American leaders of the union in the San Francisco Bay Area often met with civil rights leaders to promote antidiscrimination strategies. (Both, courtesy of the Anne Rand Memorial Library and Archives, ILWU.)

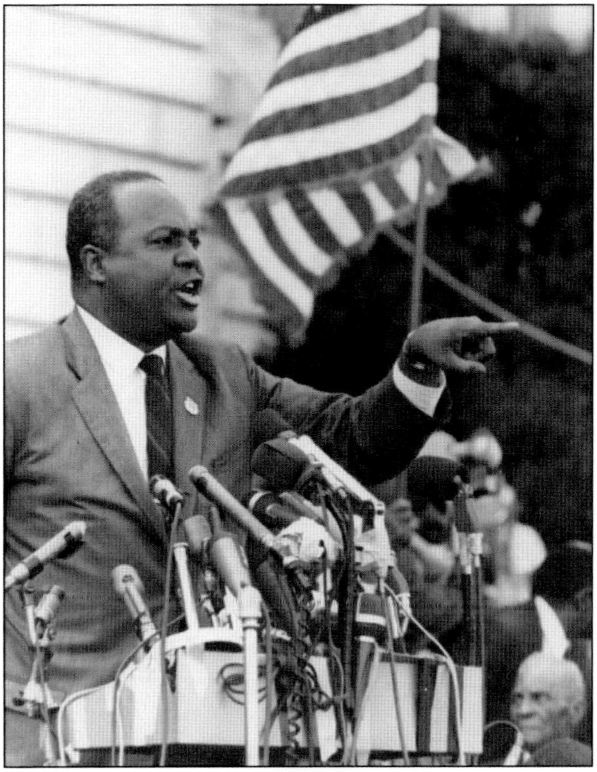

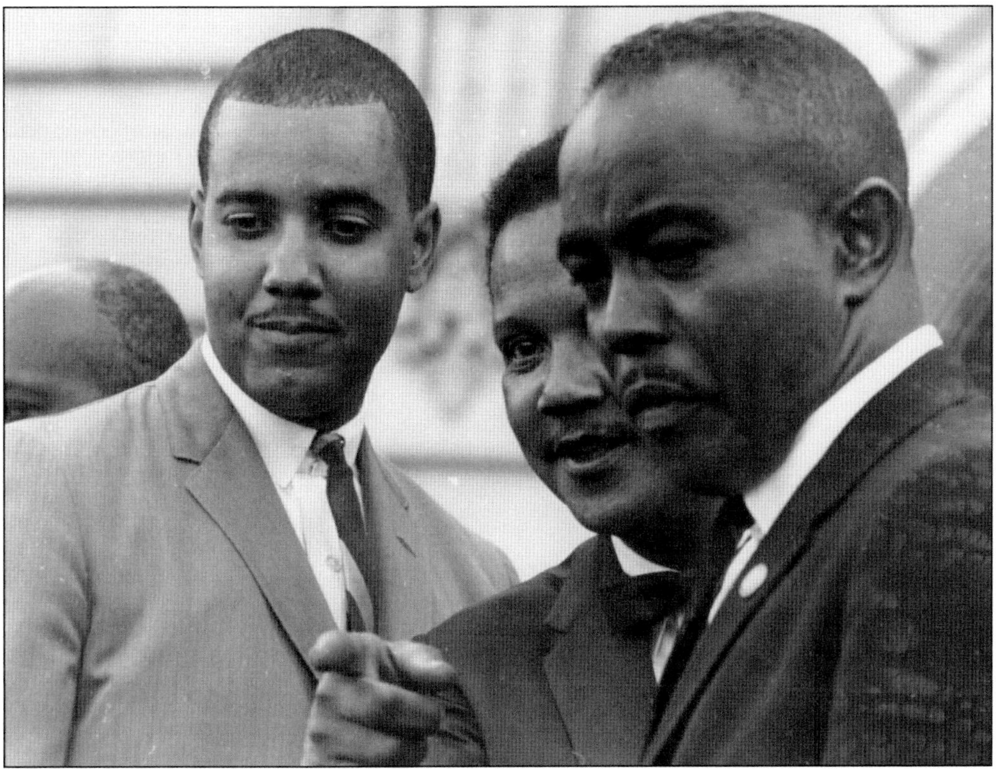

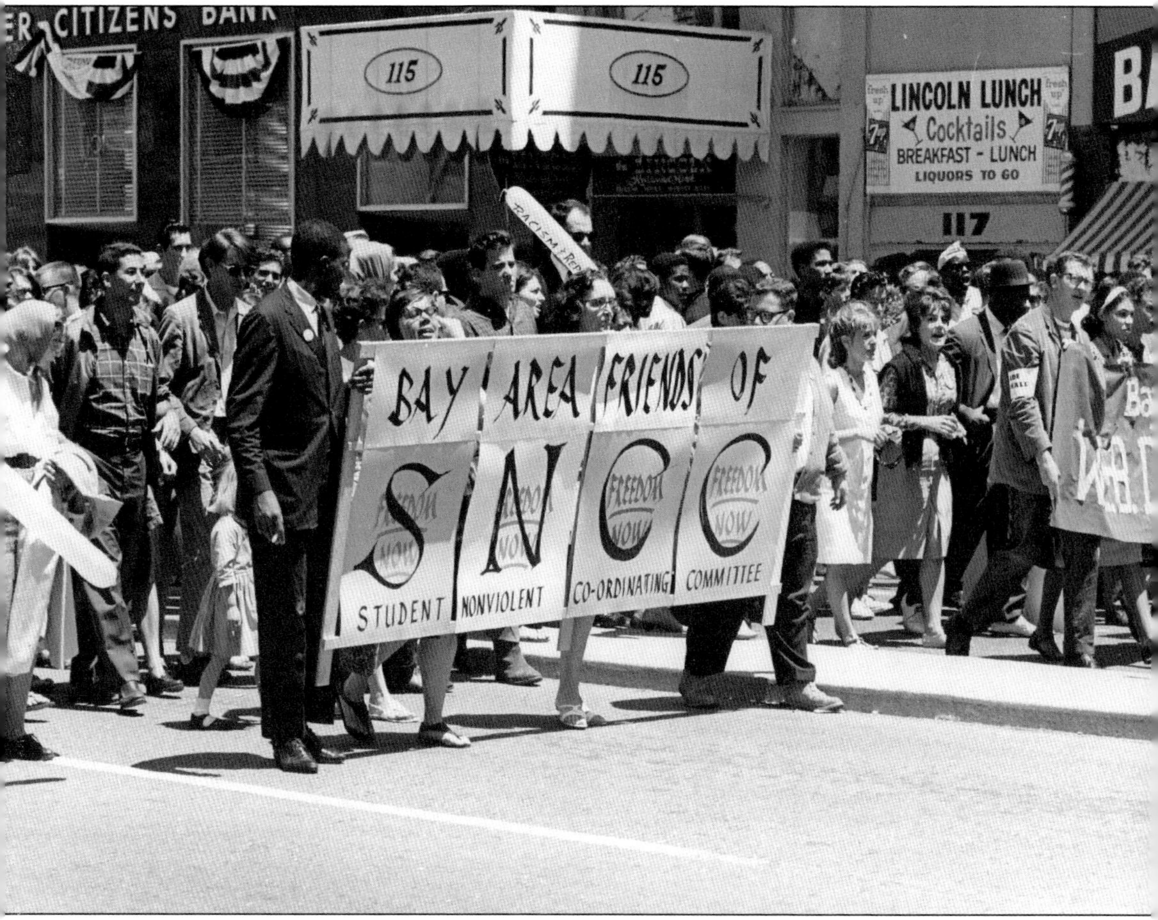

The Student Nonviolent Coordinating Committee was active in San Francisco in the 1960s. It became involved in the fight to end employment discrimination in the retail industry. (Courtesy of the Archives of the Archdiocese of San Francisco.)

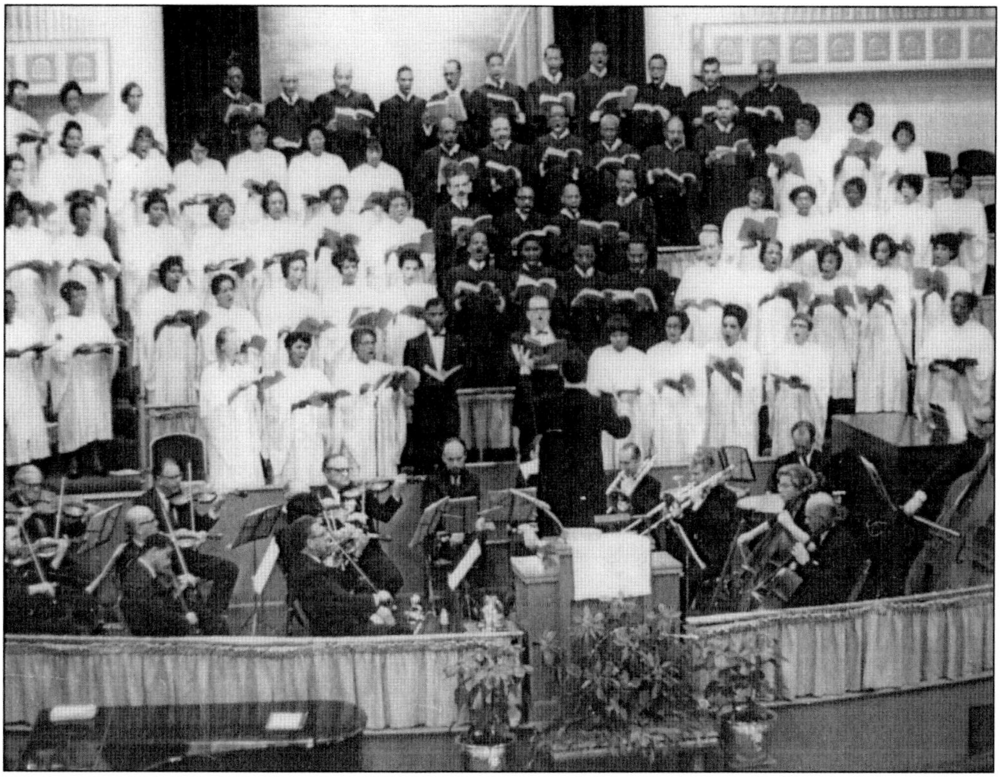

In the 1967, the San Francisco Symphony Orchestra performed Handel's *Messiah* with members of Third Baptist Church. In the photograph above, Herman F. Johnson Sr. (third row, far right) is a member of the church choir. To Johnson's immediate left are Bill Morgan Tenor and Reginald Alexis. Johnson sang with the choir for 20 to 30 years. He performed in Handel's *Messiah* every year for several years with the San Francisco Symphony Orchestra. Ray Taliaferro is the conductor in this photograph. Johnson was a World War II veteran who served in combat in the Pacific. In 1946, he migrated to San Francisco from New Orleans to work in the shipyards. Johnson died in September 2010. In the photograph below, members of the church perform Handel's *Messiah*. The conductor, Sir Jules Haywood, is a member of Third Baptist Church. (Above, courtesy of the personal archives of the Herman F. Johnson Sr. estate; below, courtesy of Clarence Santee.)

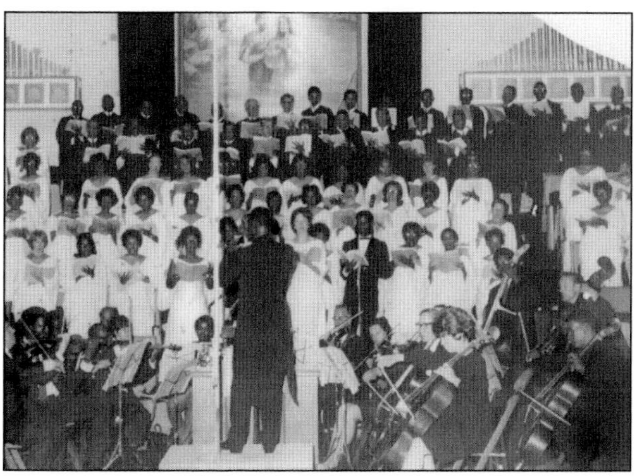

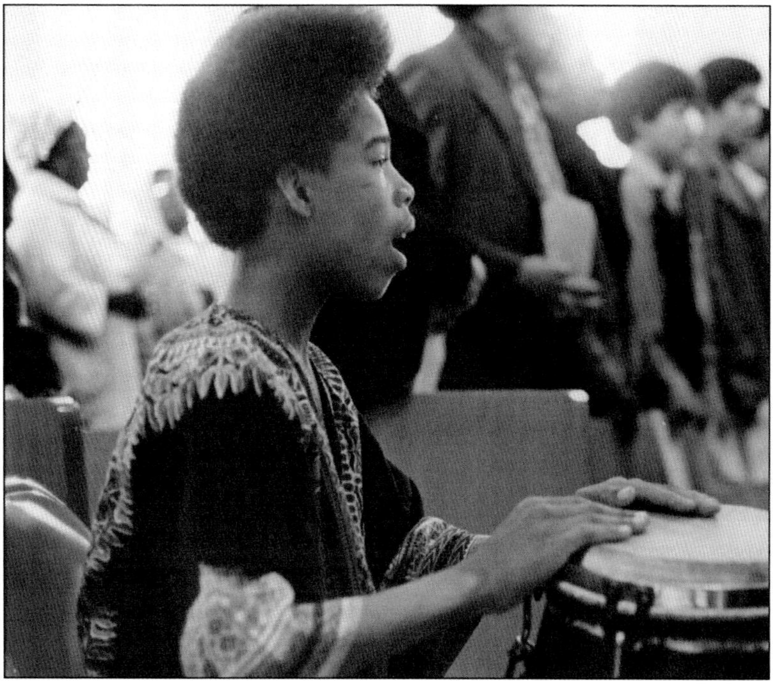

By the 1970s, even traditional forms of music performed in Catholic masses changed. This student plays drums in his dashiki during mass. (Courtesy of the Archives of the Archdiocese of San Francisco.)

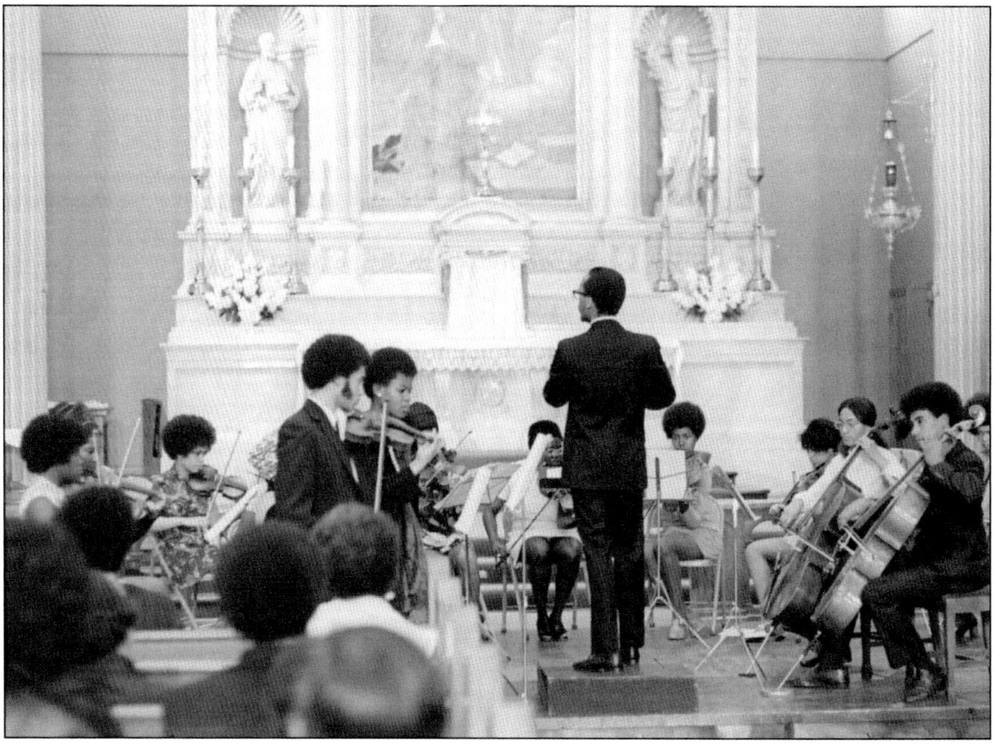

In spite of the turmoil caused by the city's urban renewal and efforts to overcome employment discrimination in 1971, many African American youth performed in the Afro-American Chamber Symphony in a performance at Sacred Heart Church. Randall Horton is the conductor and founder of the symphony. (Courtesy of the Archives of the Archdiocese of San Francisco.)

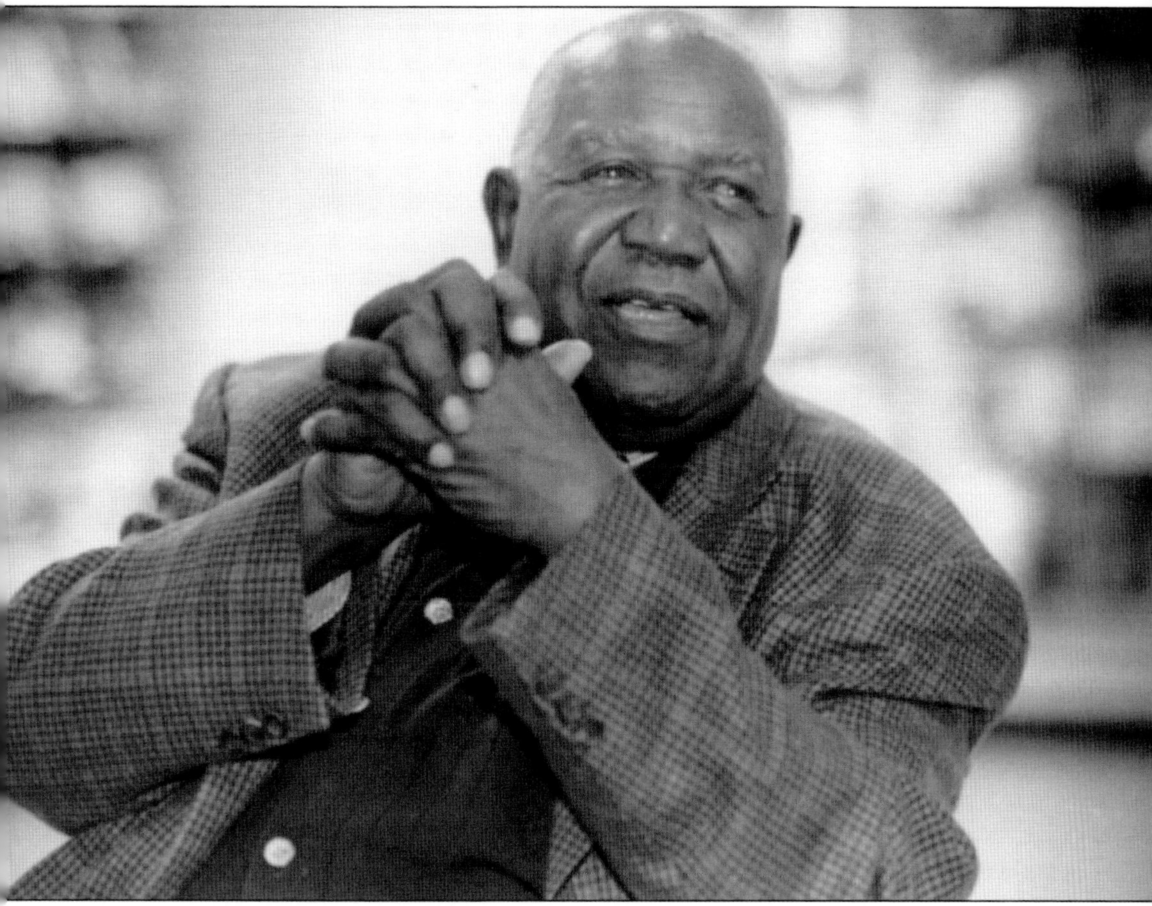

Born in Jacksonville, Florida, in 1907, Thomas Fleming was the nation's oldest and longest-running black journalist. In 1919, Fleming moved to Chico, California, where he attended Chico State University. He moved to San Francisco in 1934. In 1944, Fleming was hired as the founding editor of the *Reporter*, San Francisco's only black newspaper, which later merged with the *Sun* to become the *Sun-Reporter*. As a journalist, Fleming covered the workers strike of 1945 and continued reporting about events in the black community until he retired at age 89. He died in 2006. (Courtesy of George Kruse.)

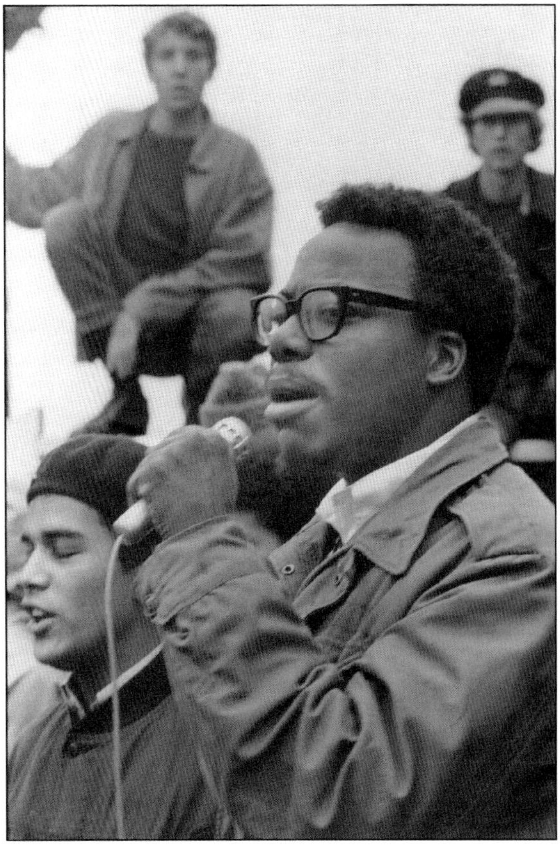

According to Anne Burke, in 1968, Nesbit Crutchfield, a student activist, and a female student were arrested for protesting at San Francisco State College. Crutchfield was jailed for 16 months for his role in the incident. In 1968, the Black Student Union, along with other student organizations, led the San Francisco strikes. The strikes, which began November 6 and lasted until March 20, 1969, were the longest student-run strikes in US history. It began after George Murray, minister of education in the Black Panther Party, was fired from his position as a teaching assistant. Students, faculty, and community activists came together to demand access to higher education for people of color, more tenured positions for faculty of color, and classes that focused on the histories of ethnic minorities. The strikes led to the creation of the School of Ethnic Studies, and as a result, other colleges created similar programs. (Both, courtesy of Phiz Mezey.)

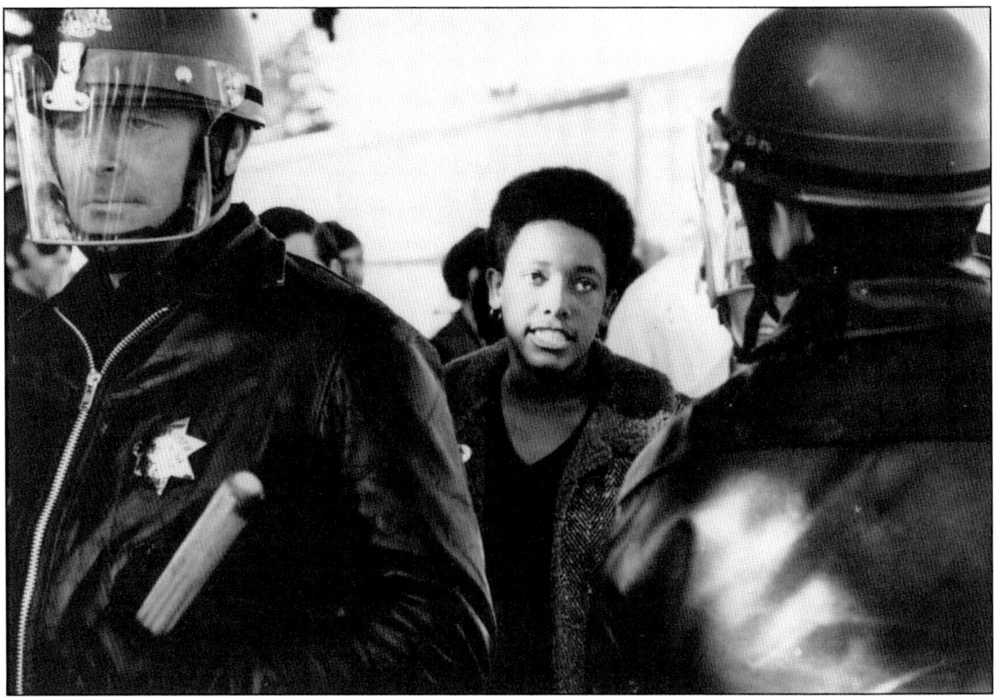

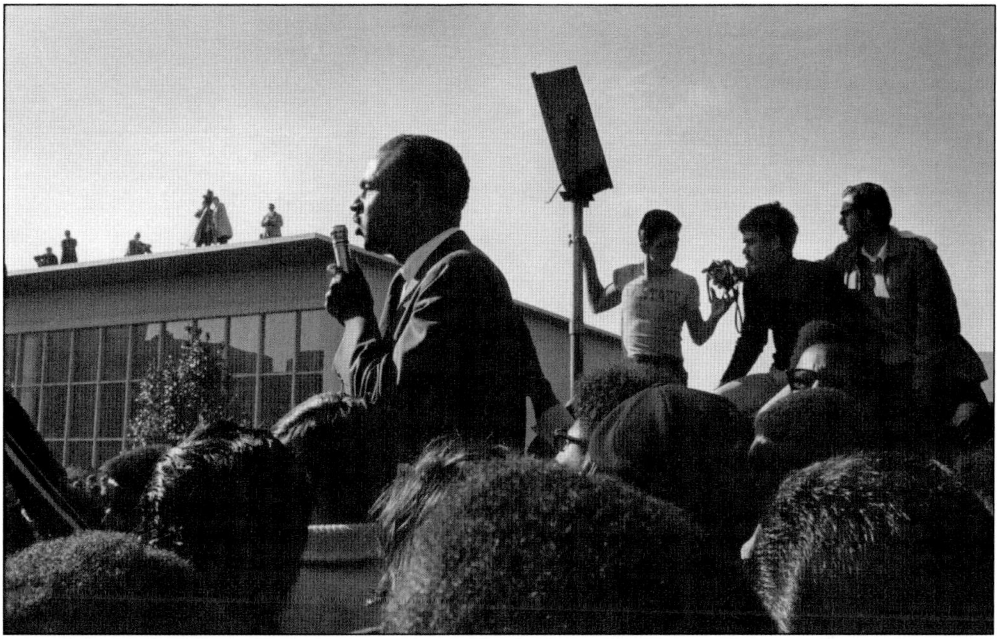

Dr. Carleton Goodlett, owner of the *Sun-Reporter* and community activist, addresses students during the San Francisco strikes in 1968. Goodlett was arrested as a result of his participation in the strike. (Courtesy of Phiz Mezey.)

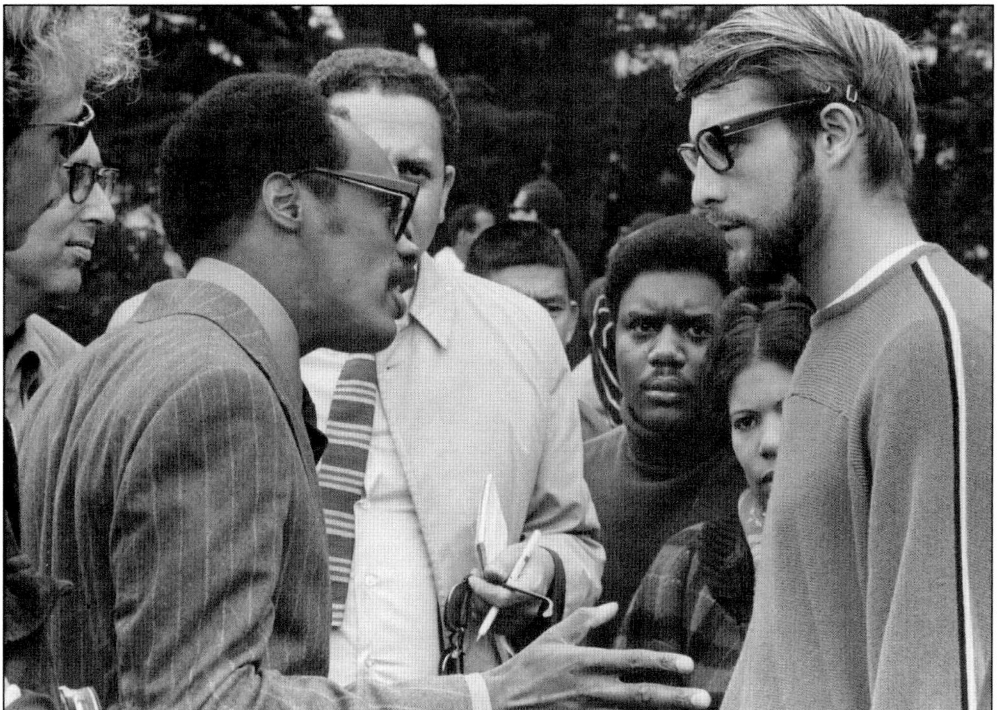

In 1968, attorney Willie Brown talks to students at San Francisco State College. As a former student at the college and a lawyer, Brown took an active role by representing jailed students. (Courtesy of Phiz Mezey.)

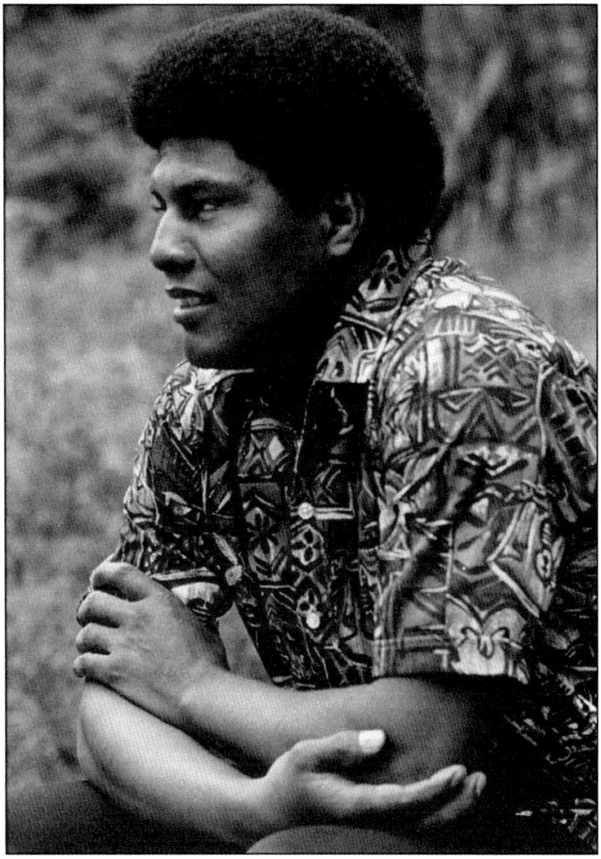

In early 1968, Dr. Nathan Hare was recruited by Black Student Union (BSU) members and San Francisco State College president John Summerskill to write a proposal for a possible black studies department. Hare responded with "A Conceptual Proposal for a Department of Black Studies" and was eventually hired as the program's first coordinator. He was later chair of the Department of Black Studies. When the student strikes began in November 1968, Hare participated as both a faculty member and as a de facto member of the BSU's central committee and worked alongside various black activists and cultural icons. The following year, San Francisco State College's president, S.I. Hayakawa, declined to renew Hare's contract as a result of his participation. Pictured in the 1968 photograph below are, from left to right, actor Ozzie Davis, Hare, Black Panther leader Bobby Seale, and an unidentified man. (Both, courtesy of Nathan Hare.)

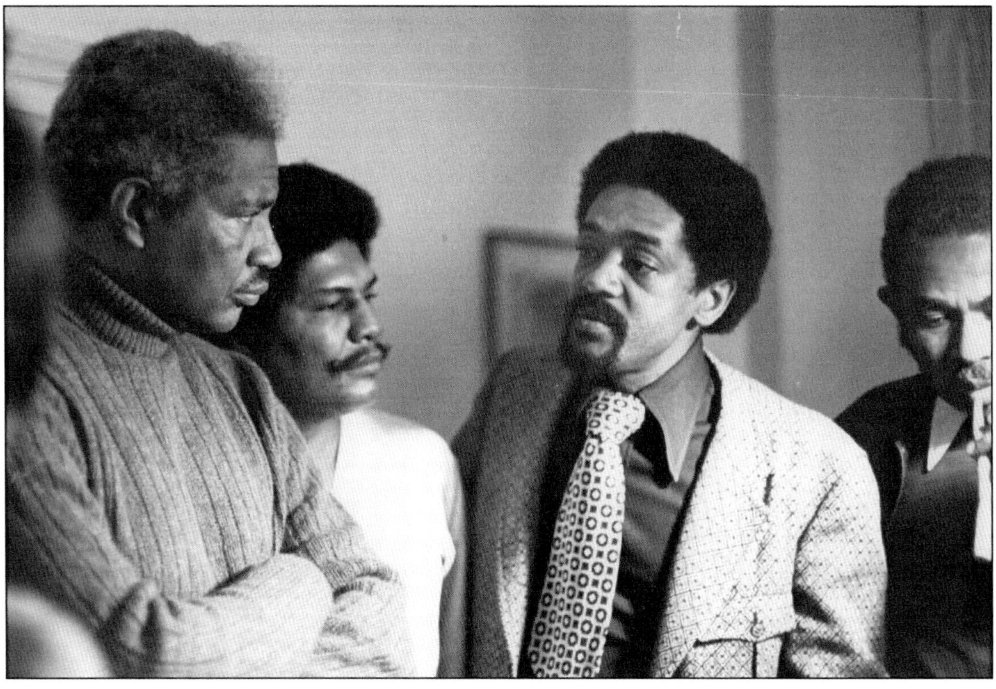

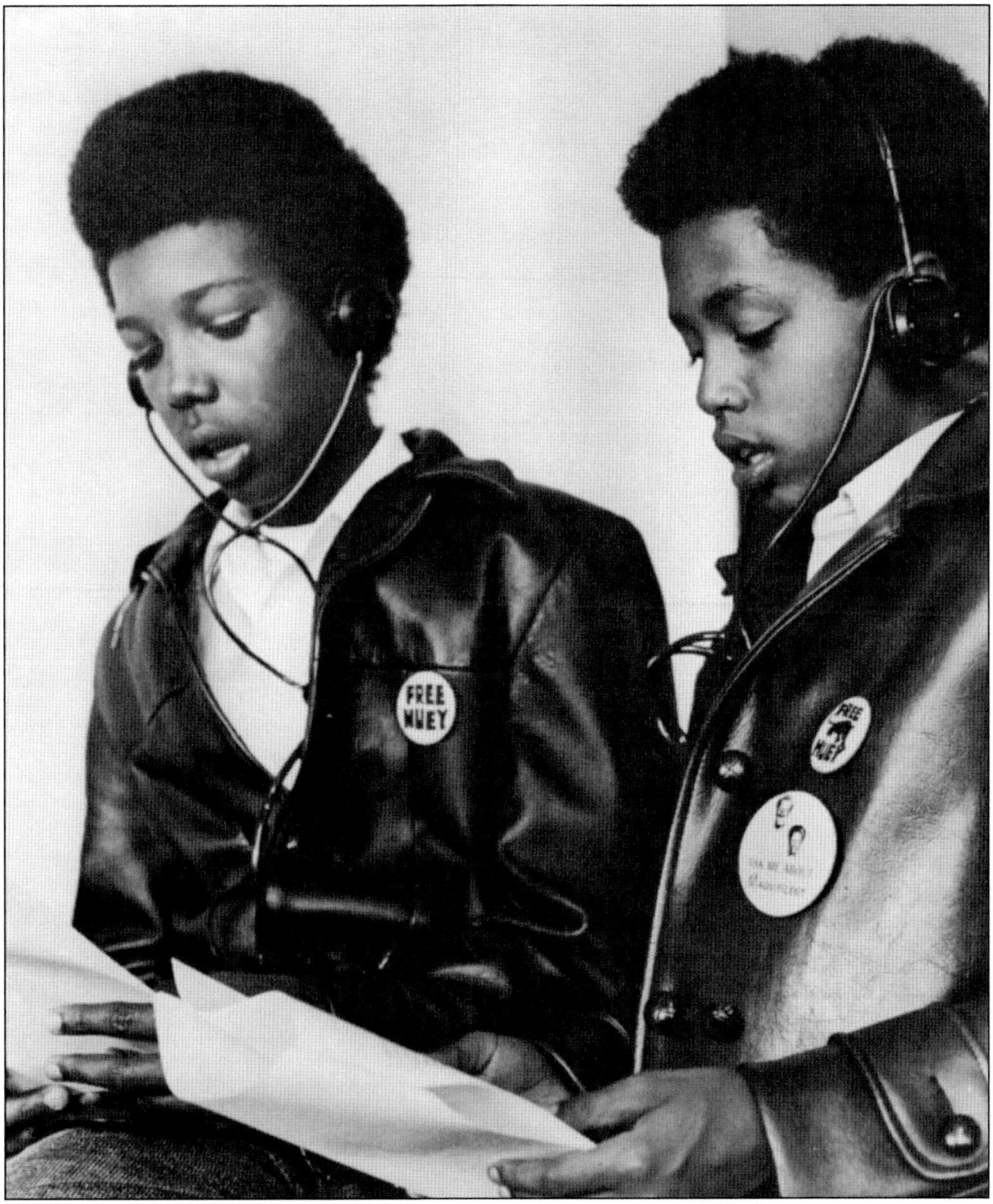

From 1968 to 1970, "Free Huey Newton" rallies were held all over the Bay Area. Newton, cofounder of the Black Panther Party for self-defense, was arrested for the murder of a white policeman in Oakland and was on trial in Alameda County in 1968. Although he was convicted of murder, it was later overturned on an appeal. During that time, supporters began a "Free Huey" campaign, creating public awareness about his case. Pictured above are two African-American youths with "Free Huey" buttons. These boys are broadcasting the announcements at their school. Many young people and community groups identified with this movement. (Courtesy of the Archives of the Archdiocese of San Francisco.)

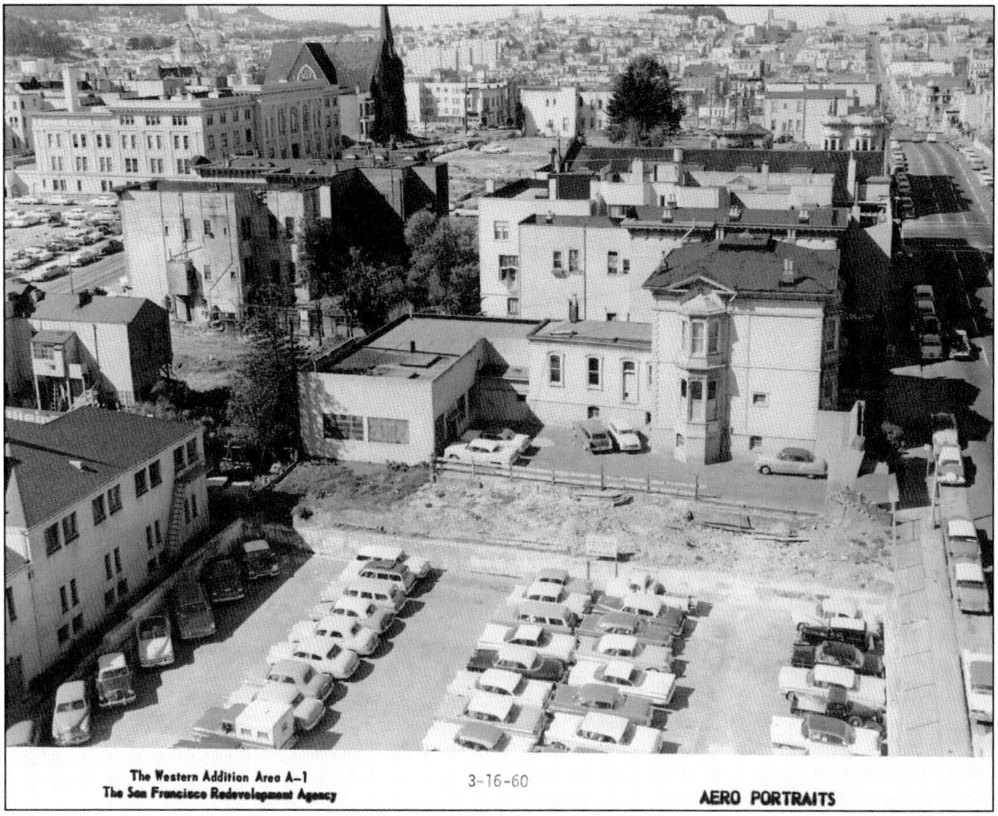

The Fillmore District's neighborhoods were forever changed by the city's urban renewal efforts. Redevelopment of the A-1 Western Addition area began in the 1950s. The March 1960 photograph above depicts a section of the neighborhood before redevelopment. The below photograph indicates the number of homes removed in an effort to build access through the Western Addition. Many residents were displaced and had to find housing in other neighborhoods in San Francisco or in surrounding cities. Local leadership from the Western Addition began to organize to fight the questionable policies by the city. (Both, courtesy of the San Francisco Redevelopment Agency.)

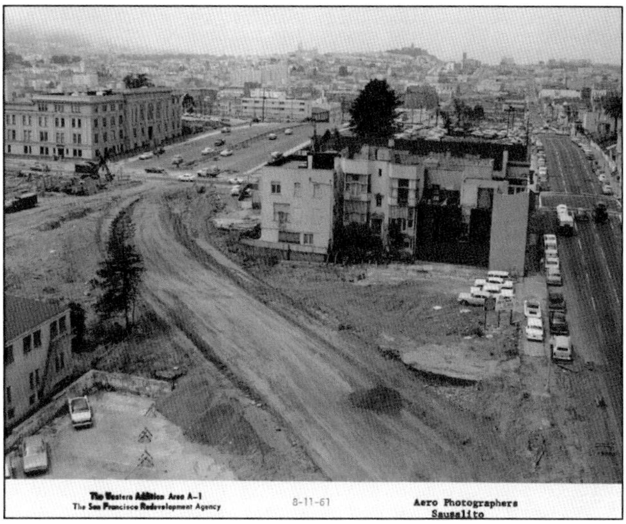

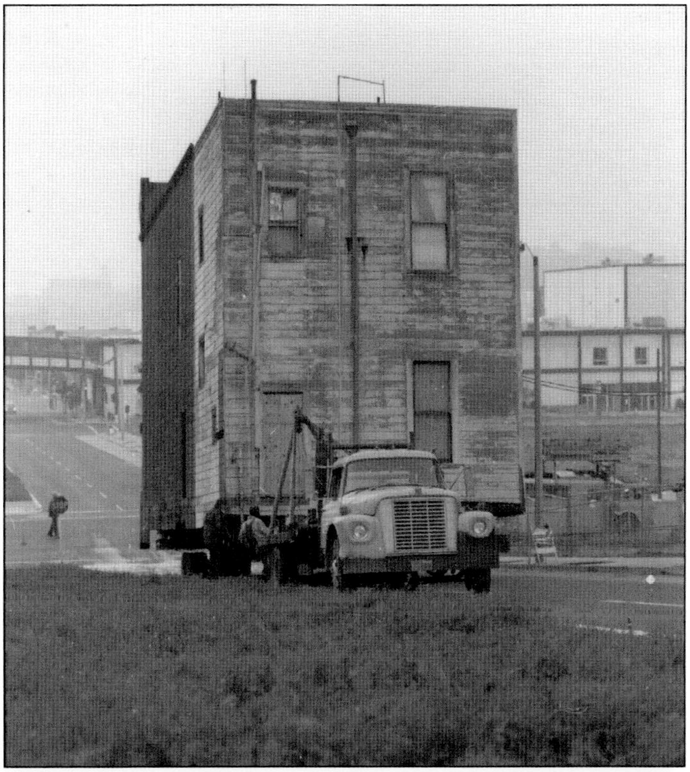

Entire blocks of homes were removed under the city's urban renewal. Gerri Sumner, a resident during the initial stages of the program in the 1960s, said, "I can remember as a child going to school and coming home and seeing a home on the site in the morning, and it was torn down or removed by the time I came home from school. It was quite unsettling for a child to see this in your own neighborhood." (Both, courtesy of the San Francisco Redevelopment Agency.)

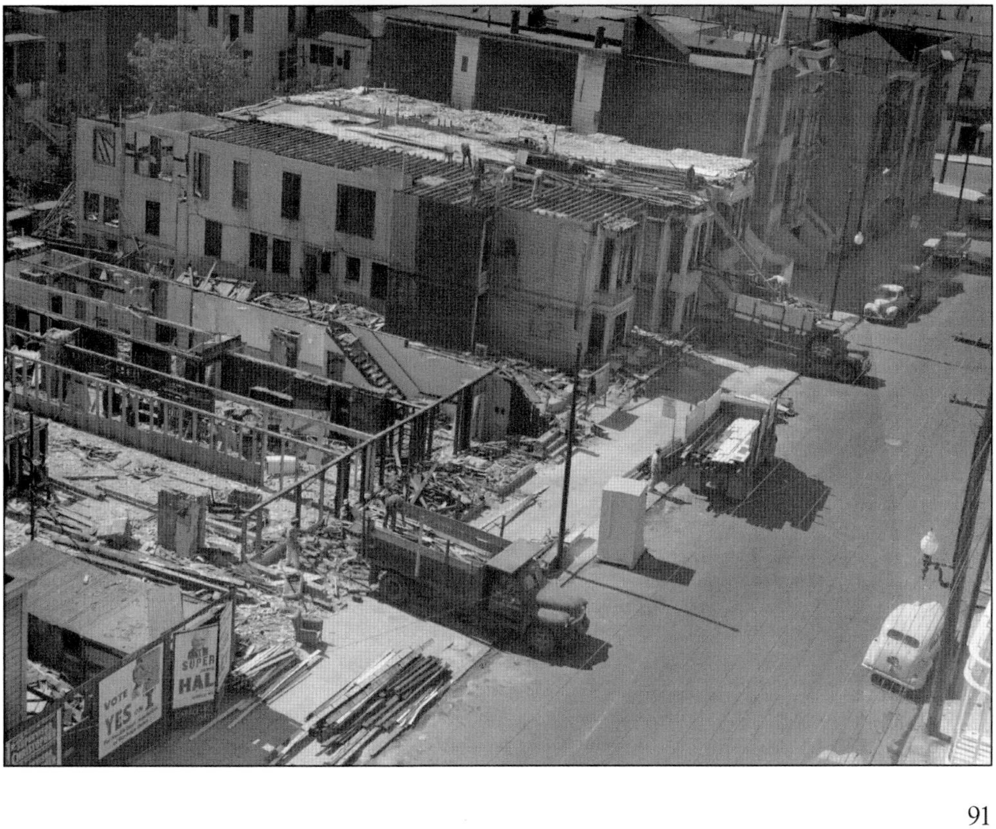

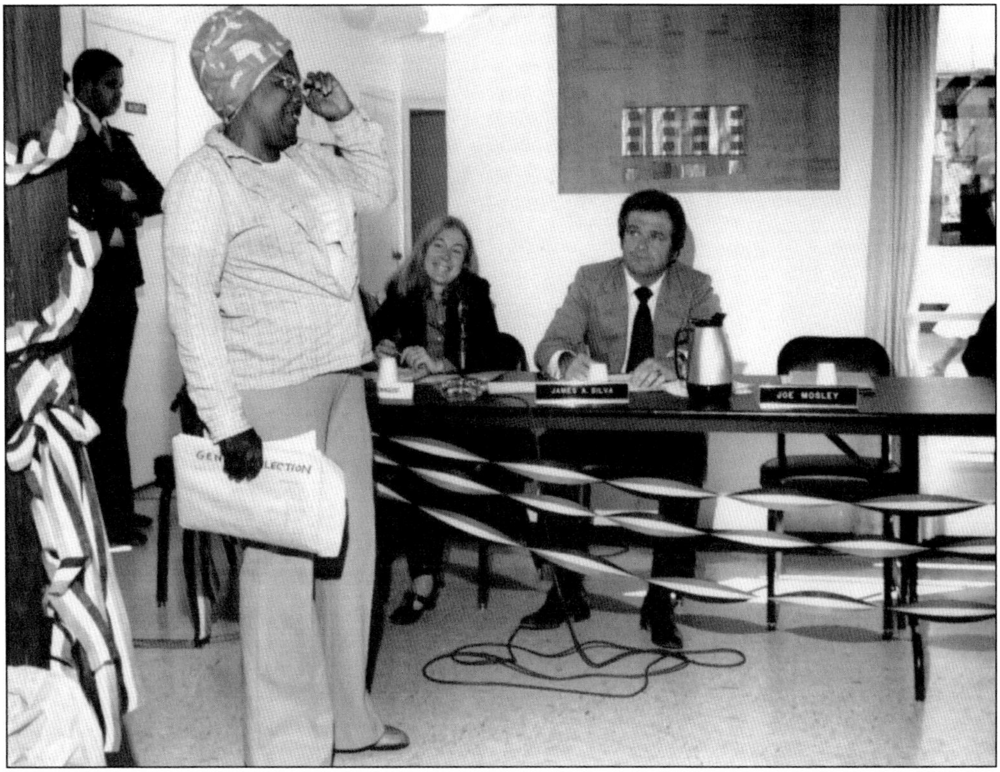

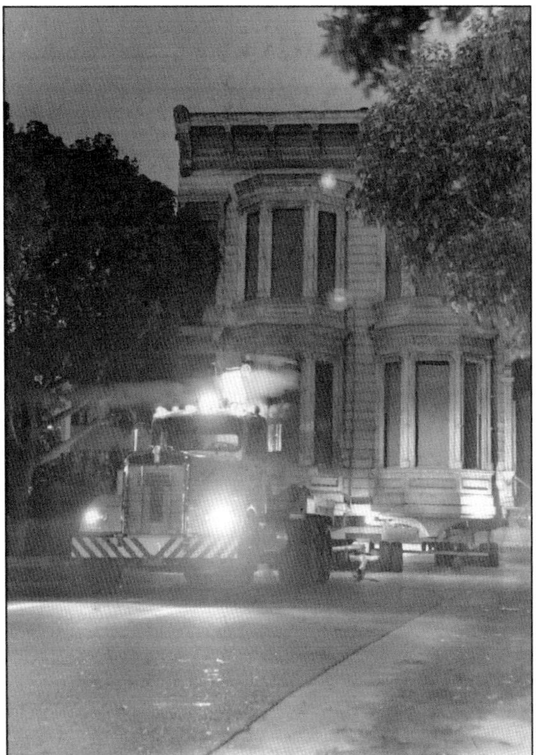

Mary Ellen Rogers moved to San Francisco's Fillmore District in 1965. She was a community activist who advocated for community participation in the redevelopment process. She helped start the Western Addition Community Organization (WACO), which forced the city to help the residents it displaced. Rogers and others picketed and blocked bulldozers removing the housing stock in the Western Addition. Rogers went on to advise the Redevelopment Agency and serve as a San Francisco Housing Authority community-relations manager. According to her obituary, "Rogers fought until her last days for affordable housing and to restore the Fillmore's vibrancy." Above, she is standing after winning election as a WACO committee member. Redevelopment staff members are sitting at the table. At left, a Western Addition house is being moved at night. Rogers and others objected to such moves and to bulldozing homes. (Both, courtesy of the San Francisco Redevelopment Agency)

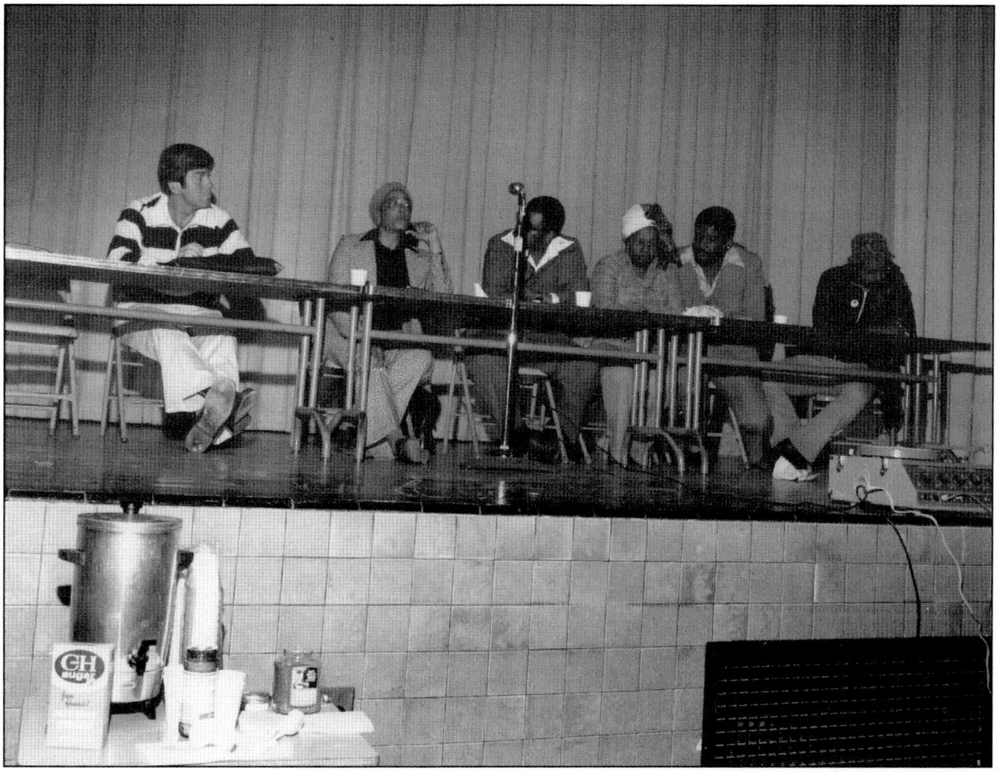

Members of the Western Addition Community Organization (WACO) meet around 1966–1970 to discuss the redevelopment plan for the area. Identified here are Essie Collins (second from left), Mary Rogers (fourth from left), and Arnold Townsend (fifth from left). (Courtesy of the San Francisco Redevelopment Agency.)

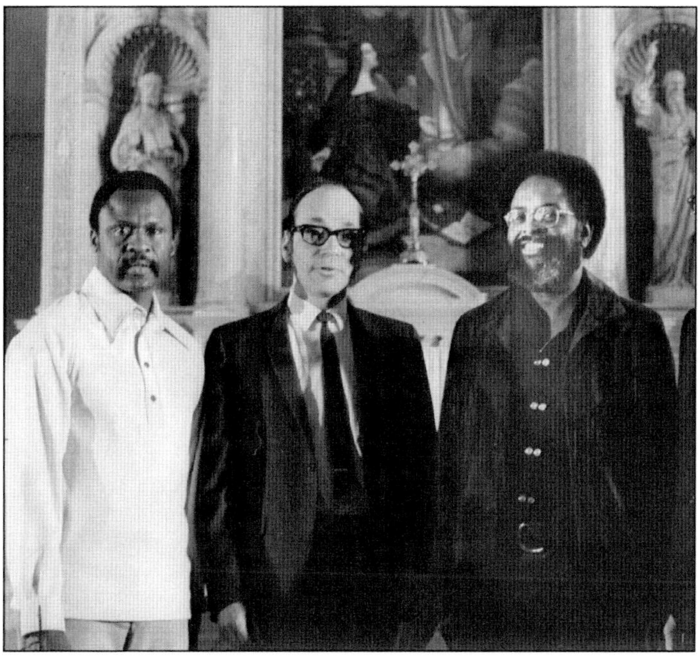

In this 1969 photograph are community activists Hannibal Williams (left), pastor Eugene Boyle (center), and Rev. Cecil Williams of Glide Memorial Church. (Courtesy of the Archives of the Archdiocese of San Francisco.)

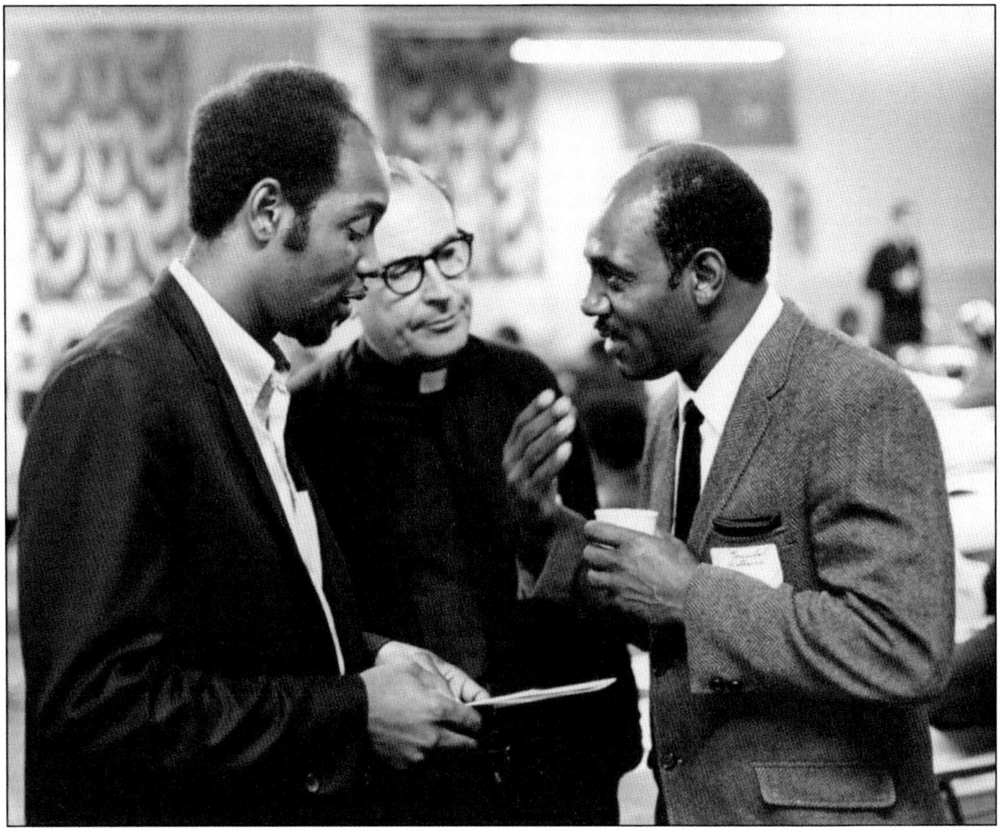

Pictured are Hannibal Williams (right), pastor Eugene Boyle (center), and an unidentified man at Sacred Heart Church in 1969. (Courtesy of the Archives of the Archdiocese of San Francisco.)

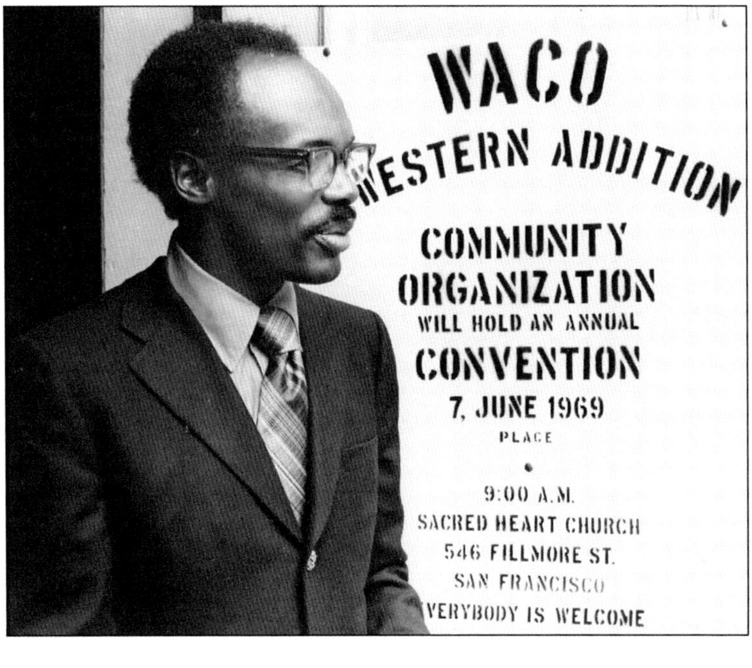

In 1969, Willie Brown attends the Western Addition Community Organization Convention held at Sacred Heart Church on Fillmore Street. (Courtesy of the Archives of the Archdiocese of San Francisco.)

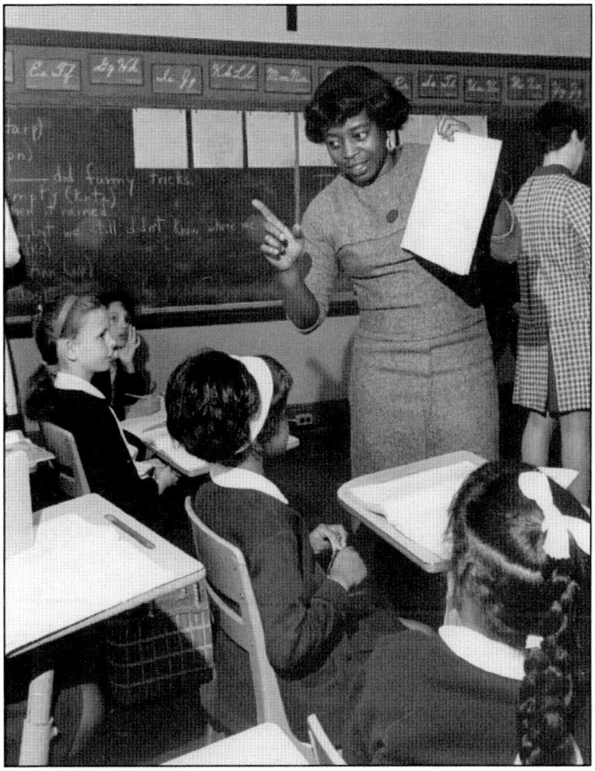

In the 1960s, Maxine Duncan, community member, serves as a volunteer teacher at Sacred Heart School on Fillmore Street in the Western Addition. (Courtesy of the Archives of the Archdiocese of San Francisco.)

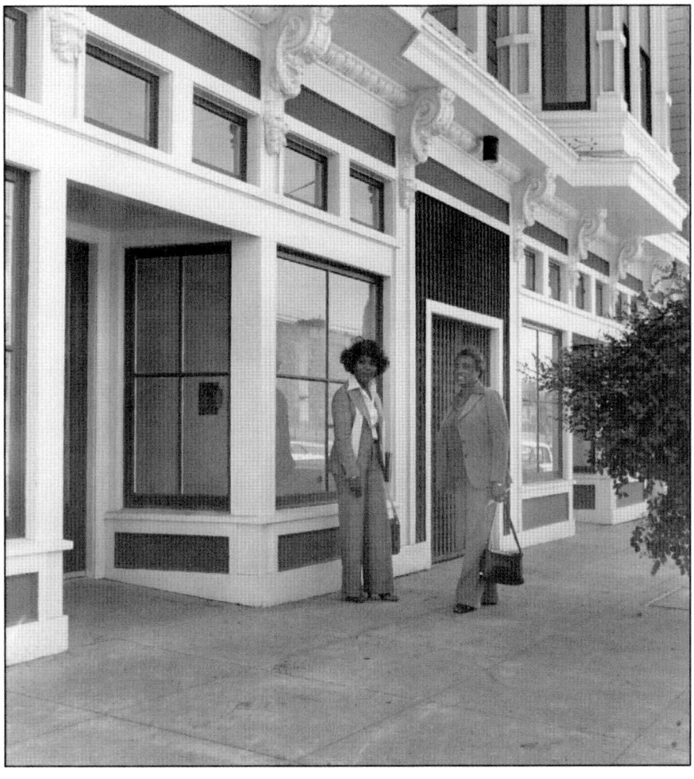

Essie Collins (right), a well-known businesswoman who served with Mary Rogers on WACO, stands with an unidentified woman in front of newly constructed offices in the Western Addition. Collins also served on the Western Addition Community Organization. (Courtesy of the San Francisco Redevelopment Agency.)

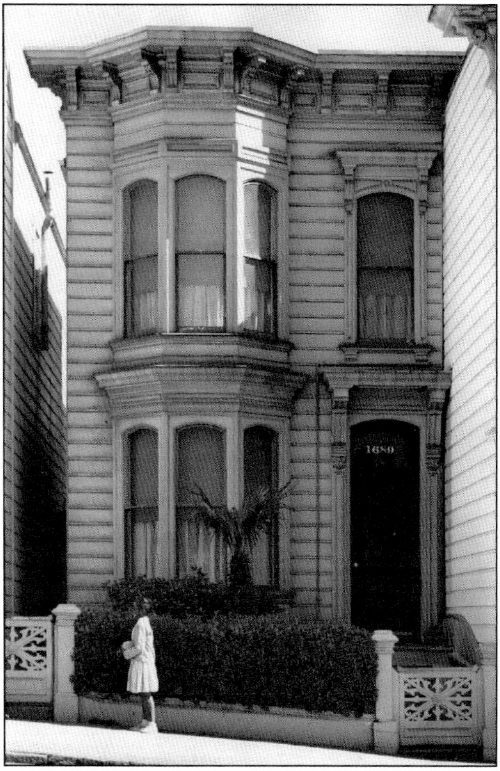

Gerri Sumner was a resident who lived on Geary Street as a young girl during the early stages of San Francisco's redevelopment program. She said in an interview, "Many children witnessed the removal of the housing stock in the neighborhood. Some of these children moved into newly built housing stock, while others moved to new neighborhoods in the city, as my family did." (Courtesy of the San Francisco Redevelopment Agency.)

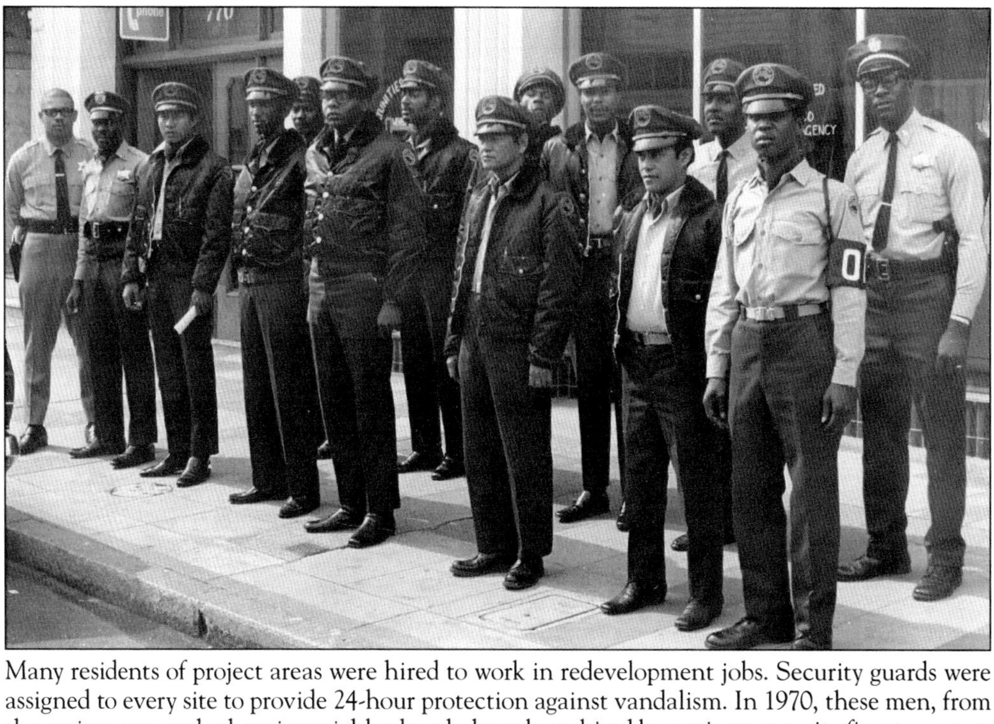

Many residents of project areas were hired to work in redevelopment jobs. Security guards were assigned to every site to provide 24-hour protection against vandalism. In 1970, these men, from the project area and other city neighborhoods, have been hired by a private security firm to protect redevelopment projects. (Courtesy of the San Francisco Redevelopment Agency.)

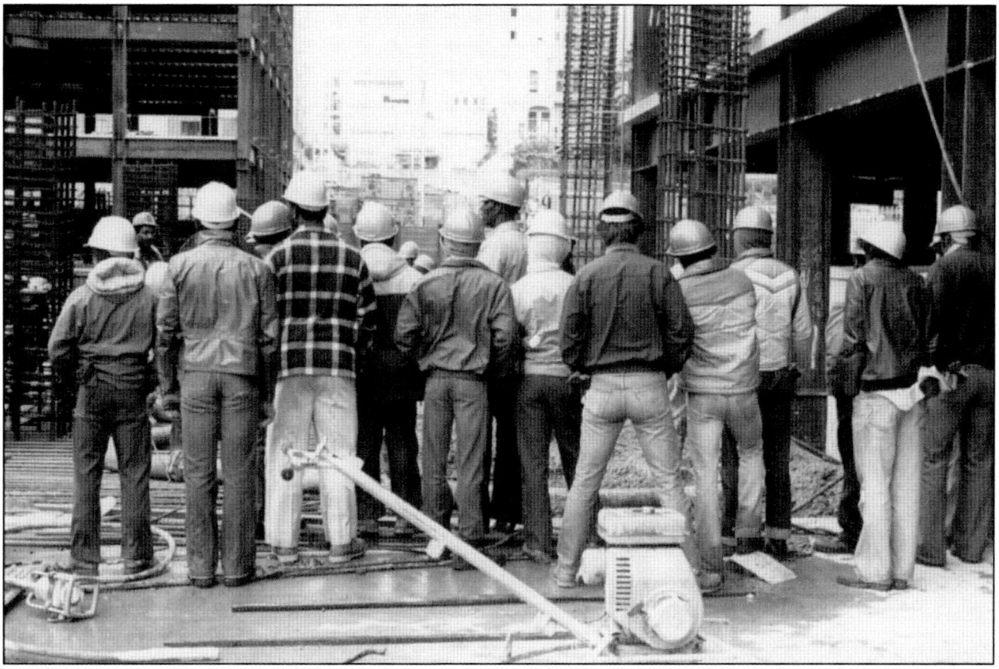

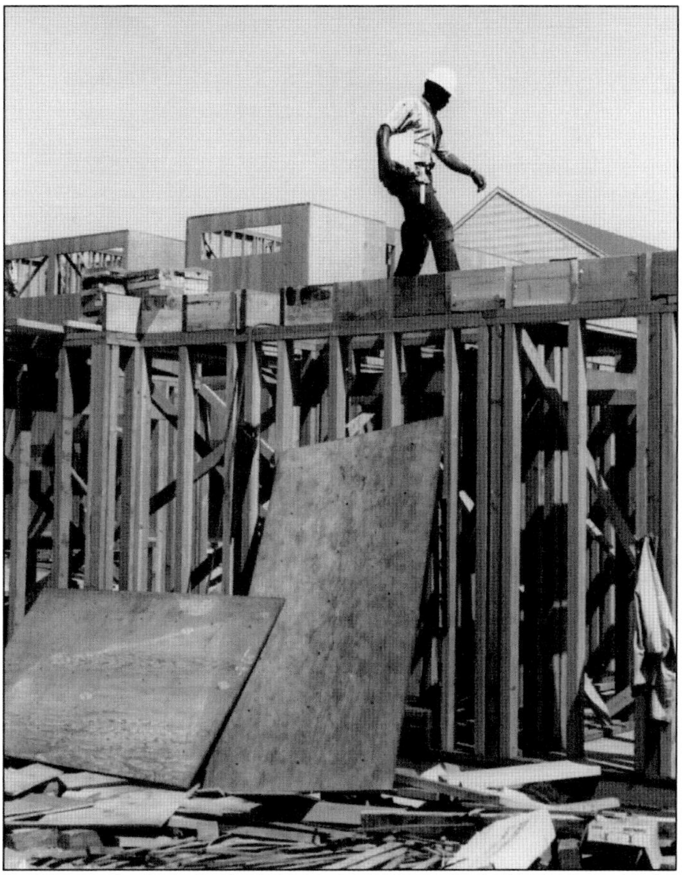

According to a resident of the Hunters Point project area, residents were able to benefit economically from the city's redevelopment projects. Many acquired new job skills that helped them into new careers. (Both, courtesy of the San Francisco Redevelopment Agency.)

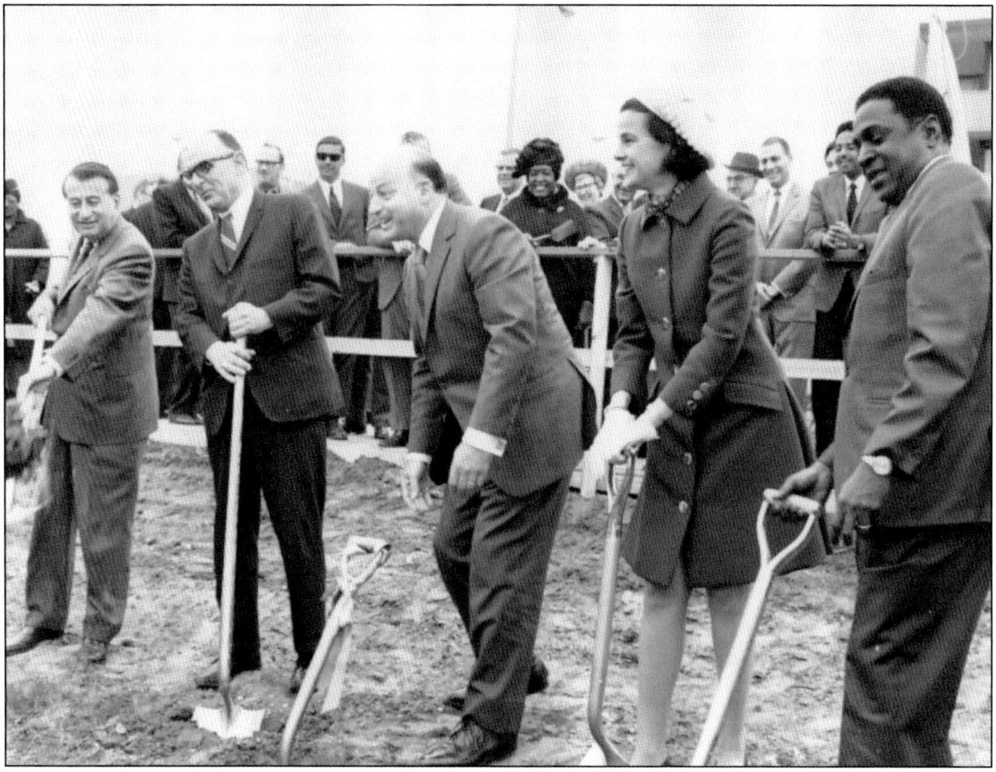

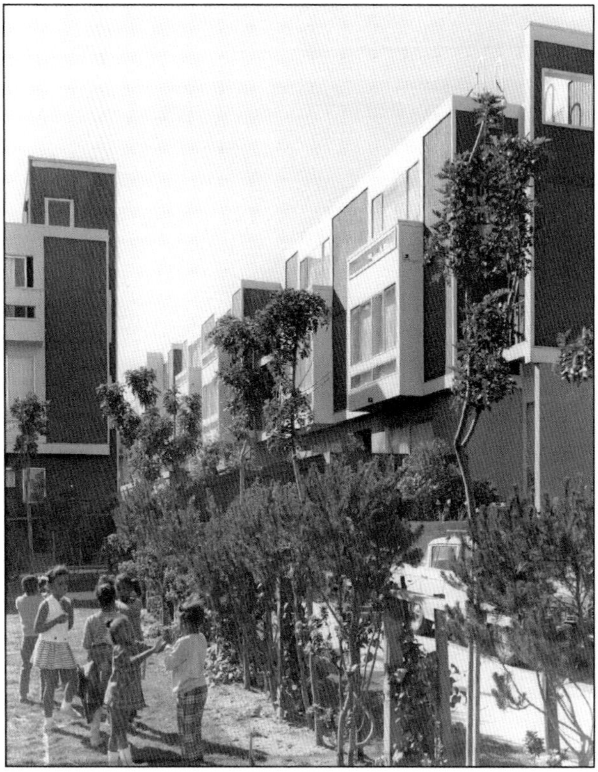

In 1970, from left to right, redevelopment director Justin Herman, Mayor Joseph Alioto, unidentified, and members of the board of supervisors Dianne Feinstein and Terry Francois hold a ground-breaking for a family housing development. In the photograph on the left, families dislocated by the redevelopment were able to move into newly constructed family housing. (Both, courtesy of the San Francisco Redevelopment Agency.)

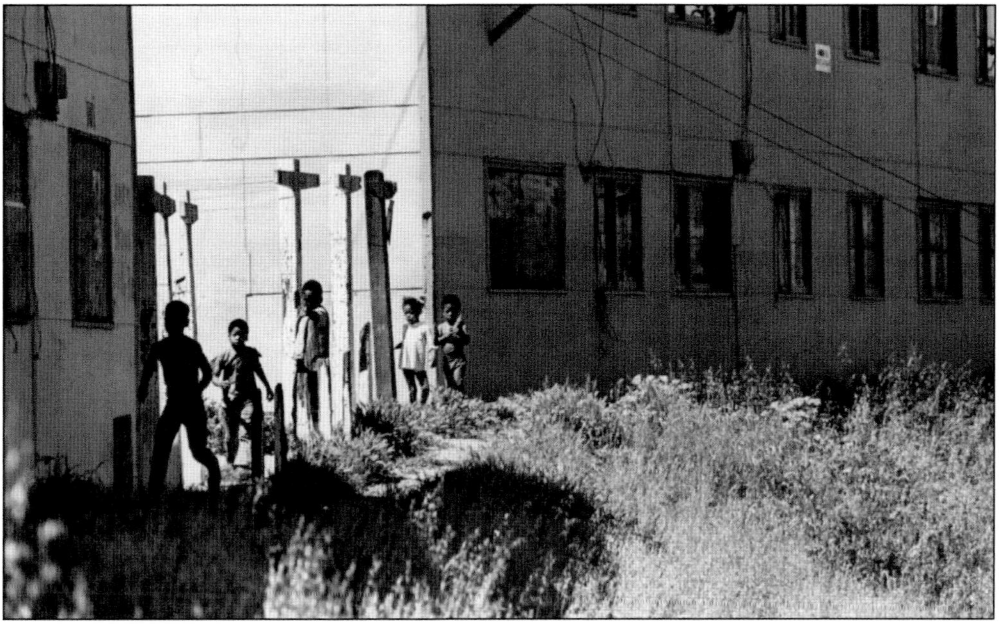

Based on resident interviews after the war, African American residents lost employment opportunities because of shipyard closures and relocation of other industries out of Hunters Point. The Pentagon offered Navy housing to the Housing Authority for public housing. Many of these complexes became low-income housing projects. Children played in unsafe areas, and overcrowding developed in the housing projects. In 1966, riots broke out in Hunters Point. (Above, courtesy of the Archives of the Archdiocese of San Francisco; below, courtesy of Oscar Davis.)

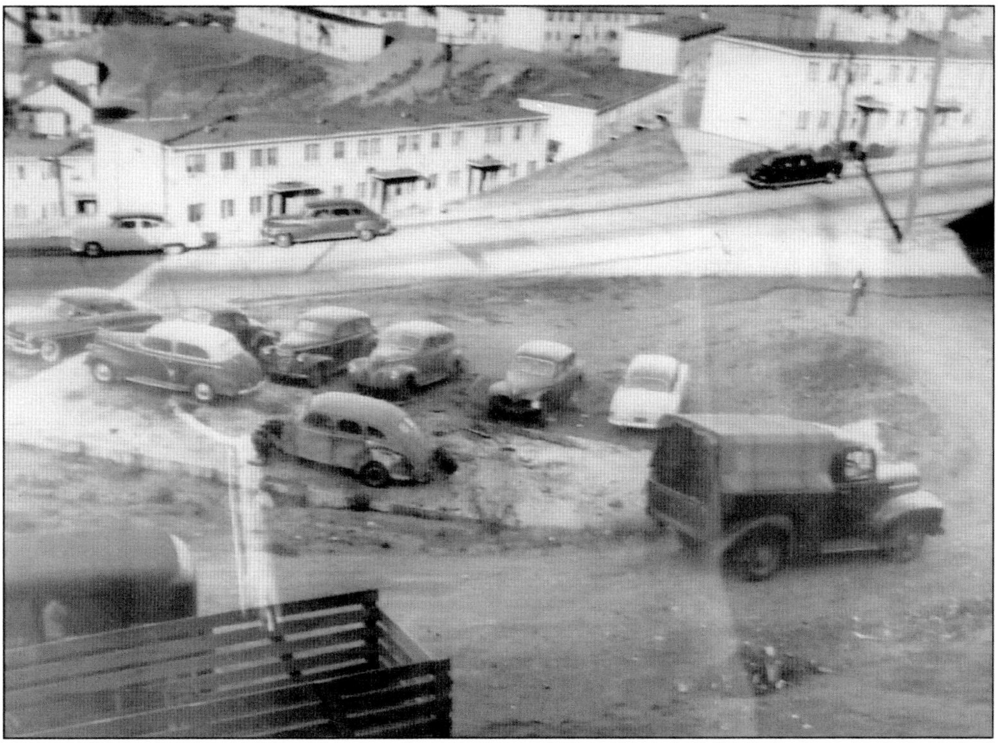

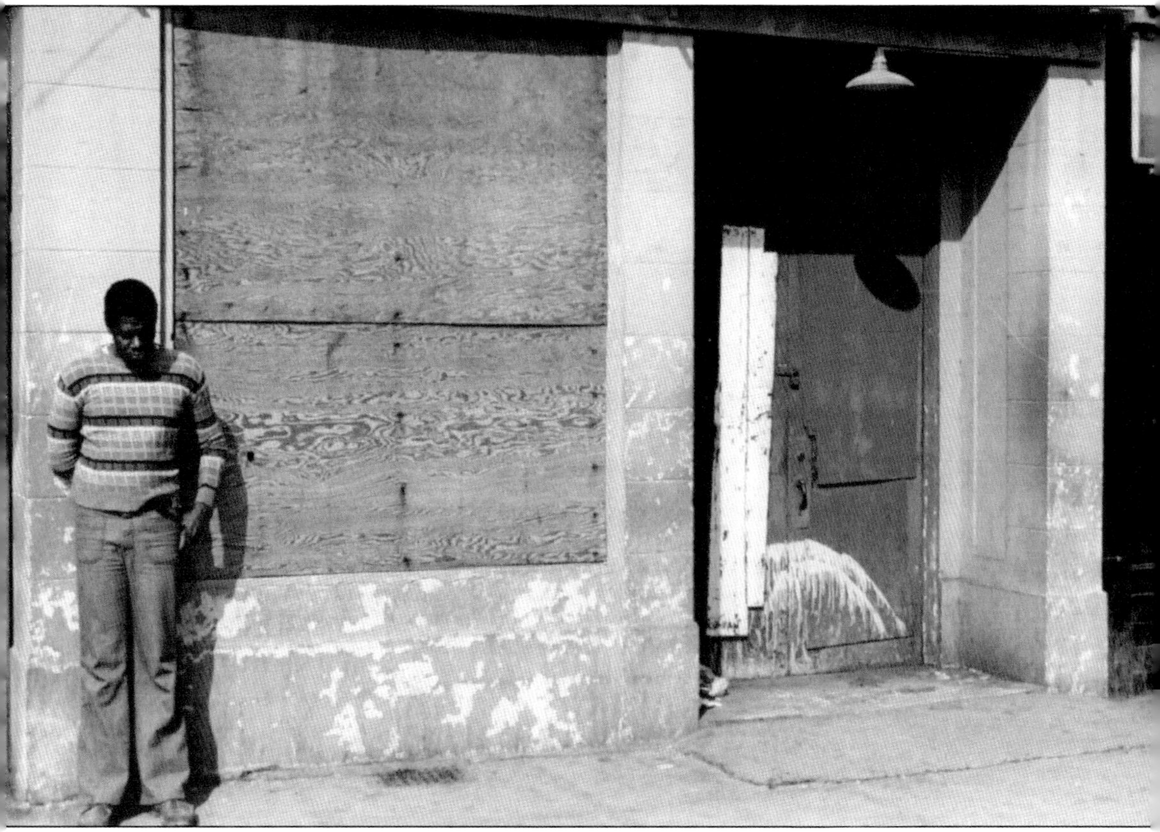

By 1966, many young men were disillusioned and could not find employment due to the deindustrialization of Bayview-Hunters Point. Many low-income families were displaced during urban renewal projects and had to relocate to communities in the East Bay or the South Bay. Those who could afford to moved to better neighborhoods outside of San Francisco, leaving behind neighborhoods with a high concentration of hopeless, low-income residents. With high unemployment and large numbers of welfare recipients, the neighborhood of Bayview-Hunters Point became a center for crime culminating in a riot in 1966. (Courtesy of the San Francisco Redevelopment Agency.)

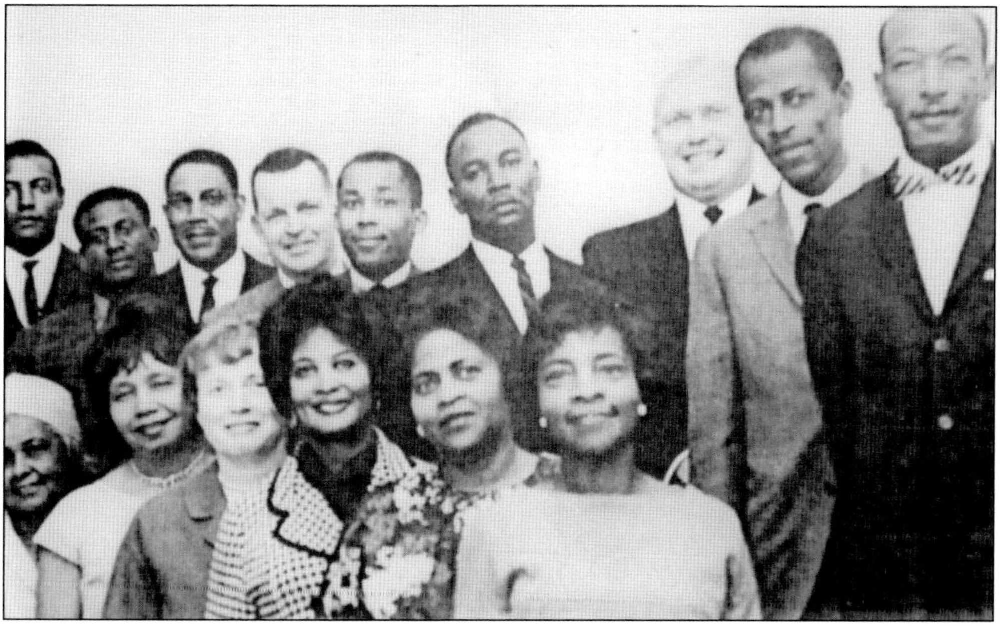

In 1964, the Bayview-Hunters Point Housing Committee was established. A few of its members are pictured in this photograph. Pictured, from left to right, are (first row) Makela Cashmere, Osceola Washington-Means, unidentified, Ruth Williams (wife of George Williams), and Essie Webb, and an unidentified niece of Nellie Dedman; (second row) John Dukes (left), the only man identified. This committee of community members accepted the responsibility to protect the rights of the citizens of Bayview-Hunters Point. According to Oscar James, an activist, they were highly respected by the residents of Bayview-Hunters Point. (Above, courtesy of Oscar Davis; below, courtesy of the Archives of the Archdiocese of San Francisco.)

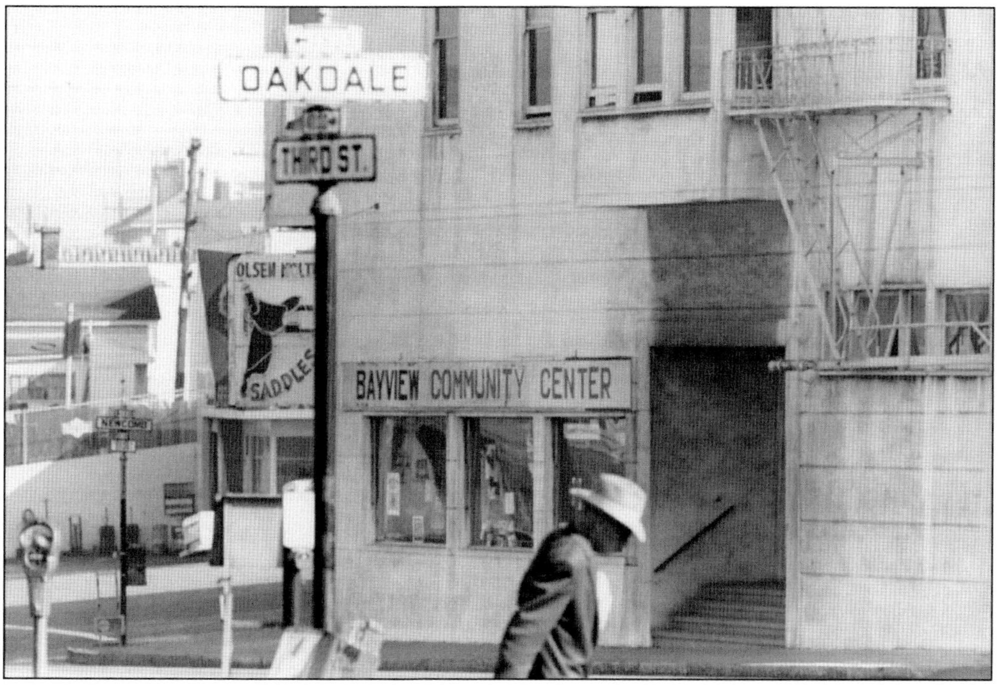

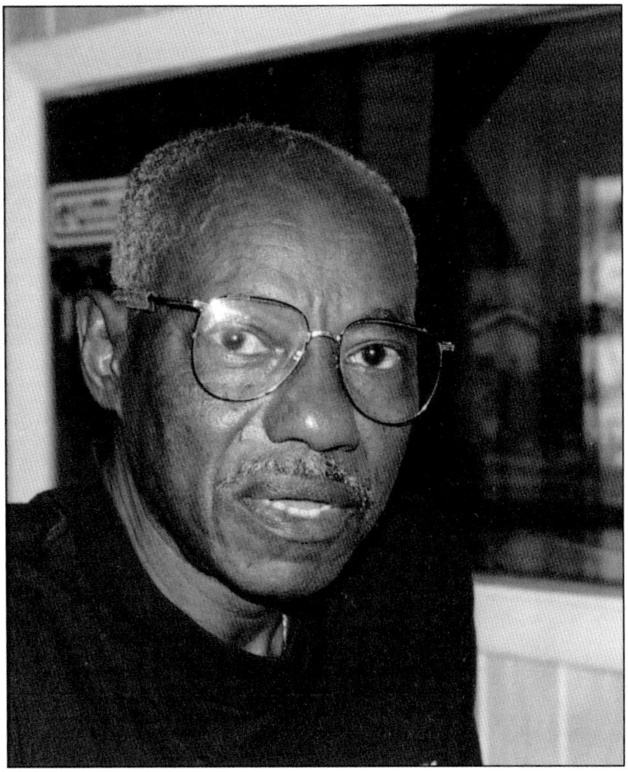

David Johnson began photographing his community in the 1940s. In 1945, Johnson was the first African American chosen by the renowned photographer Ansel Adams to enroll in his class at the California School of Fine Arts in San Francisco. Johnson photographed the lifestyle of the African American community, particularly the San Francisco Fillmore and Hunters Point neighborhoods from 1945 through the end of 1970s. His photographs recorded the history of the great jazz era of the Fillmore District during the 1940s and 1950s. Johnson and his son are shown below. (Both, courtesy of David Johnson.)

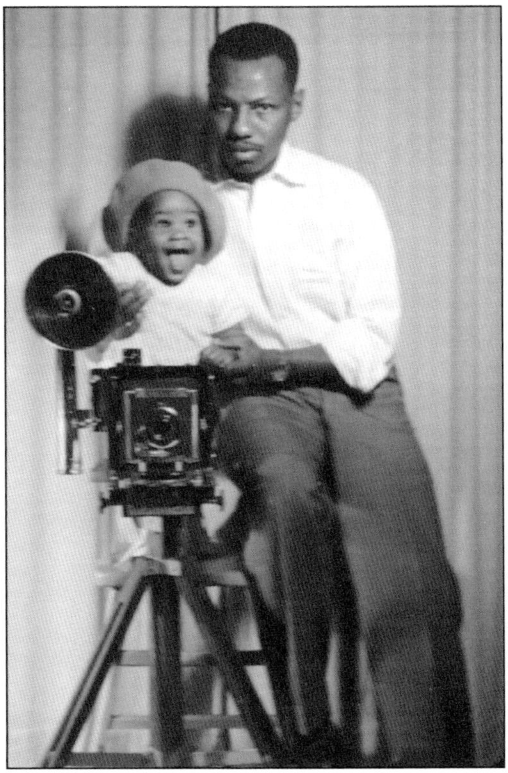

Four

1980–Present

After the Turmoil

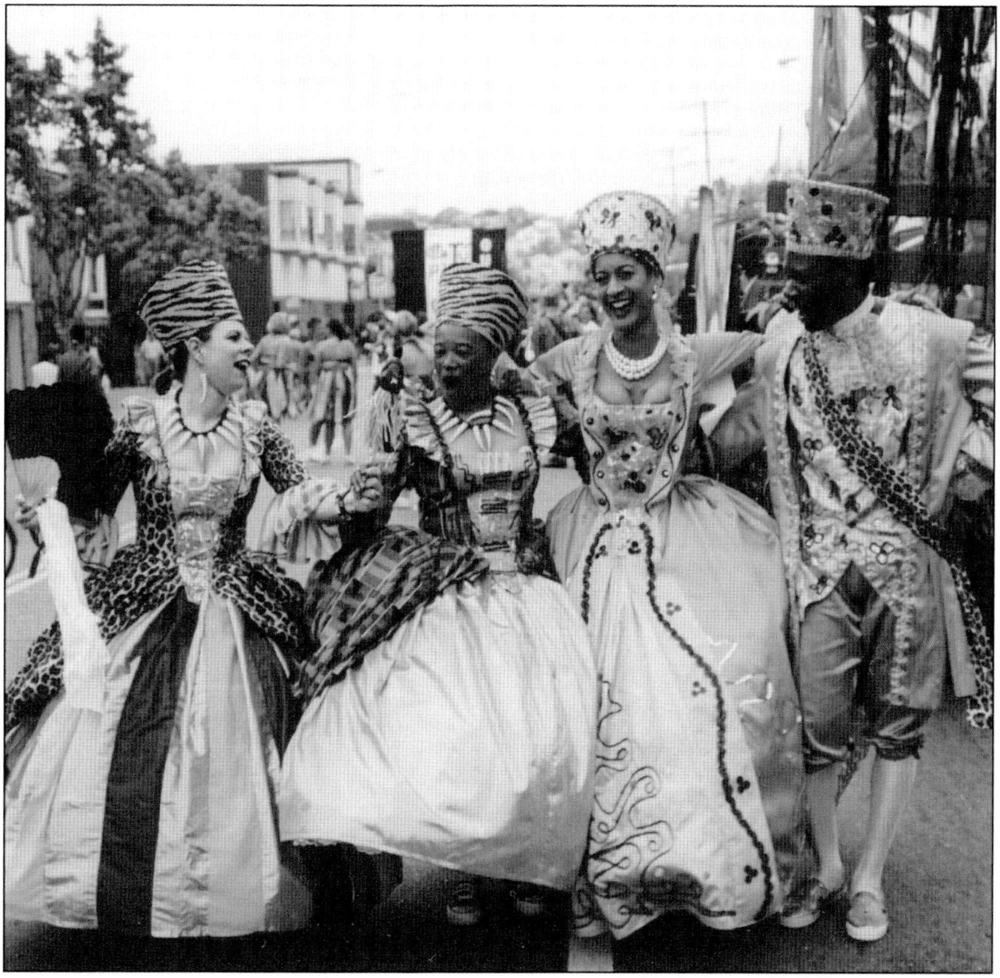

Since 1970, the city's African American population had been declining steadily. In 1980, there were 86,190 African Americans living in San Francisco. In 1990, the black population dropped to 79,039; by 2000, it fell to 58,791. Since 1980, African Americans have lived throughout San Francisco, instead of concentrating in one or two neighborhoods. Communities throughout the city celebrate a wide variety of heritage among their residents. Chinese New Year, Mardi Gras, Fillmore Jazz Festival, parades, and Gay Pride are just a few of the cultural events available to all residents and visitors. (Courtesy of Blanche Brown Collection.)

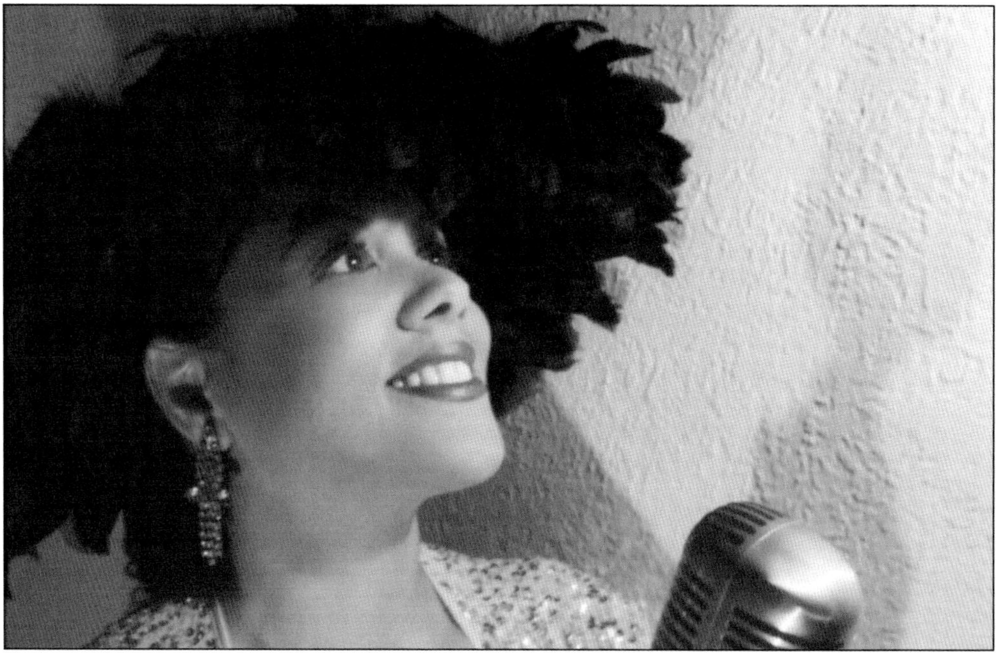

Kim Nalley, a favorite African American jazz artist, has performed globally, including at jazz festivals such as Monterey, Umbria Jazz, and Jazz at Lincoln Center. She traveled performing throughout Europe for several years before returning to San Francisco to reopen the club Jazz at Pearl's. During her time as owner and artistic director from 2003 to 2008, Nalley raised the club to international acclaim. She was taught piano by her great-grandmother and studied opera and theater in high school. Working her way through the University of California, Berkeley by singing in small dives and jam sessions, Nalley learned all of the intricacies of jazz the old-fashioned way. Music critic Phil Elwood and San Francisco Symphony director Michael Tilson Thomas discovered Nalley singing nightly to packed audiences at the Alta Plaza and quickly brought her to national attention. (Courtesy of Kim Nalley.)

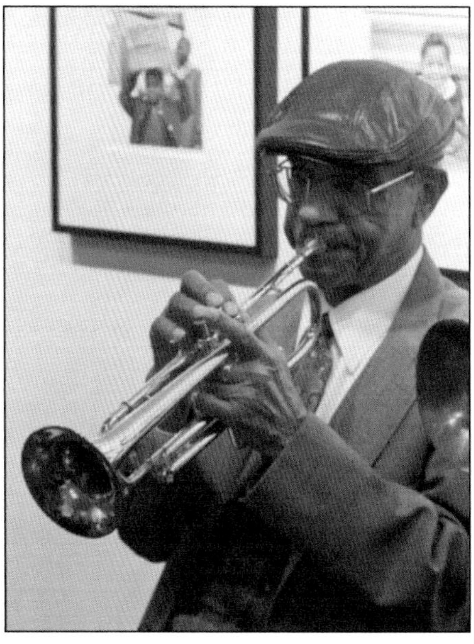

Allen Smith played in a band in the Fillmore District during the 1940s and 1950s. Today, he is still playing the horn. (Courtesy of the Jazz Heritage Center of San Francisco.)

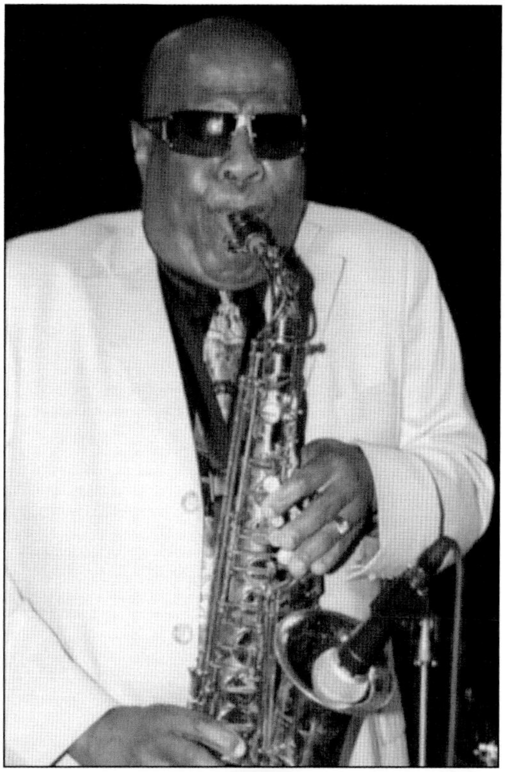

Jazz artists John Handy (right) and Frank Fisher (below) are musicians from the Fillmore jazz era. Today, they continue playing to audiences who love jazz. (Both, courtesy of the Jazz Heritage Center of San Francisco.)

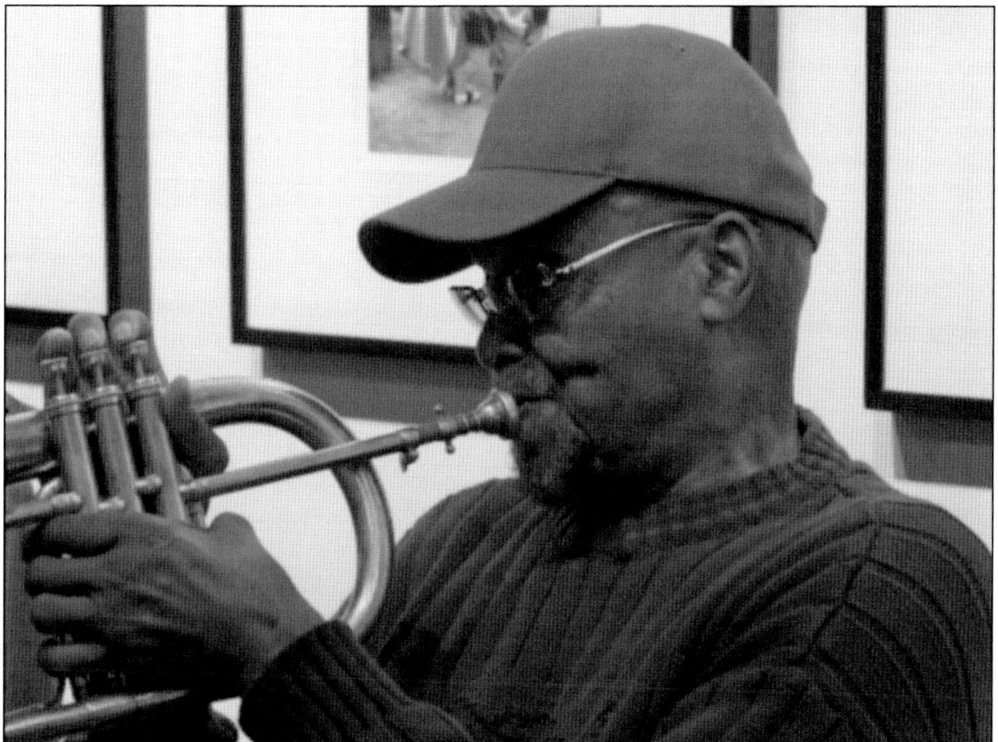

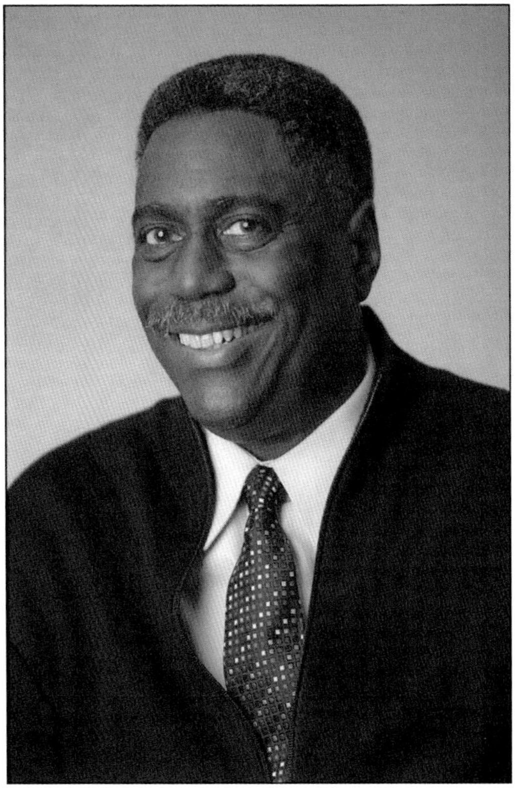

Stanley E. Williams (left) moved to San Francisco from Connecticut to pursue his vision for an African American arts institute. He and Quentin Easter (below), from Baltimore, Maryland, met in San Francisco. The two set out to establish the Lorraine Hansberry Theatre in 1981. The theater was named after Hansberry because she lived in San Francisco when her play *A Raisin in the Sun* opened on the Broadway stage in New York. Over the past 30 years, the Lorraine Hansberry Theatre has produced that play, the many plays by August Wilson, and others by a variety of playwrights. Yearly, the theater presents a holiday play, originally *Black Nativity* and more recently *Rejoice!*. Both Stanley and Quentin have received numerous awards and recognitions from San Francisco for their contributions to the city. After the passing of both men in 2010, the theater continues to thrive in the traditions established by its founders. (Left, courtesy of Bryan Davis Images. com; below, courtesy of Marc Paquette.)

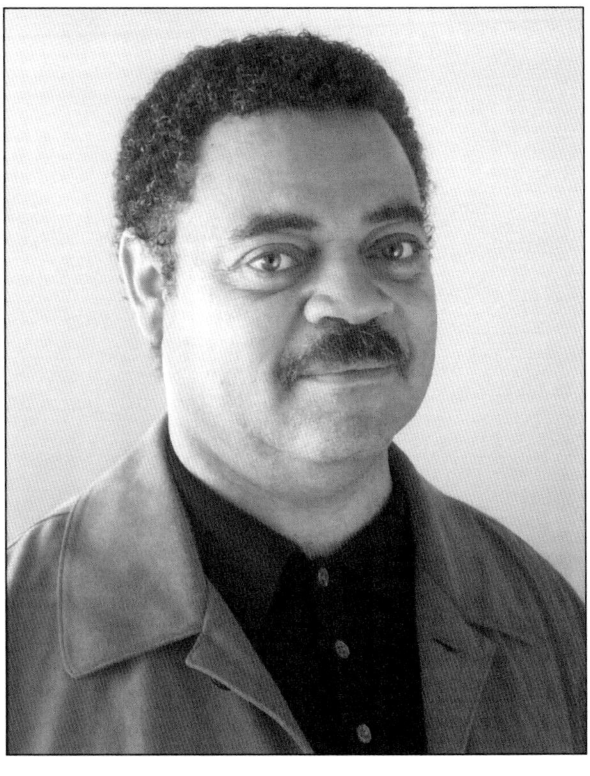

Peter Fitzsimmons, founding executive director of the Jazz Heritage Center (JHC) located on Fillmore Street in San Francisco, serves as the center's artistic director. Son of legendary jazz trumpeter F. Allen Smith, Fitzsimmons is dedicated to raising awareness about jazz and the influence of the Fillmore District and its effects on jazz and jazz musicians throughout the world. Critically acclaimed as an actor, director, and producer, Fitzsimmons brings a unique combination of business acumen and grassroots organizing to his role at the JHC. (Courtesy of the Jazz Heritage Center of San Francisco.)

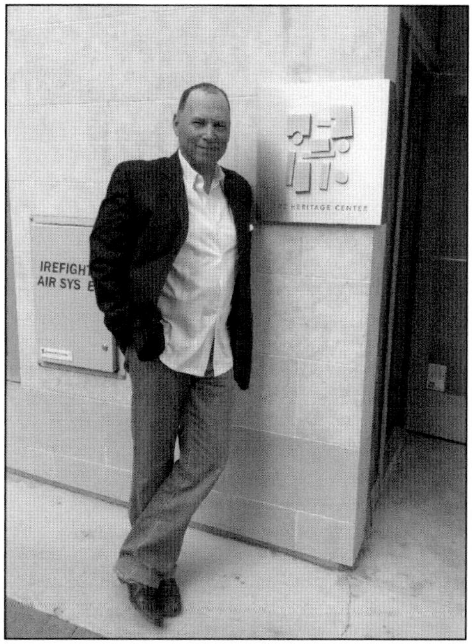

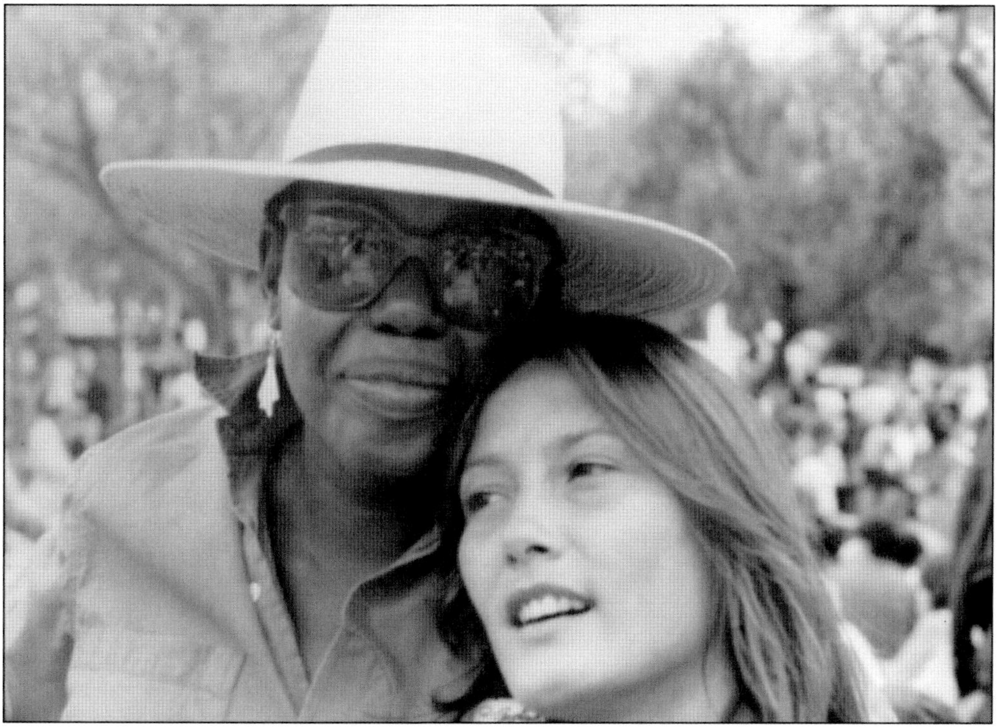

Adrienne Fuzee (left), a resident of San Francisco, was a curator for the San Francisco Arts Commission and was involved in different programs related to gays in the arts. Adrienne worked to bring awareness of gay and lesbians in the arts to San Francisco. She was a founding member of the city's Queer Cultural Center and was a member of Lesbians in the Visual Arts. Adrienne is seen in this photograph with her partner, Barbara Circa, at the 1986 Gay Day Parade. (Courtesy of Shades of San Francisco, San Francisco Public Library.)

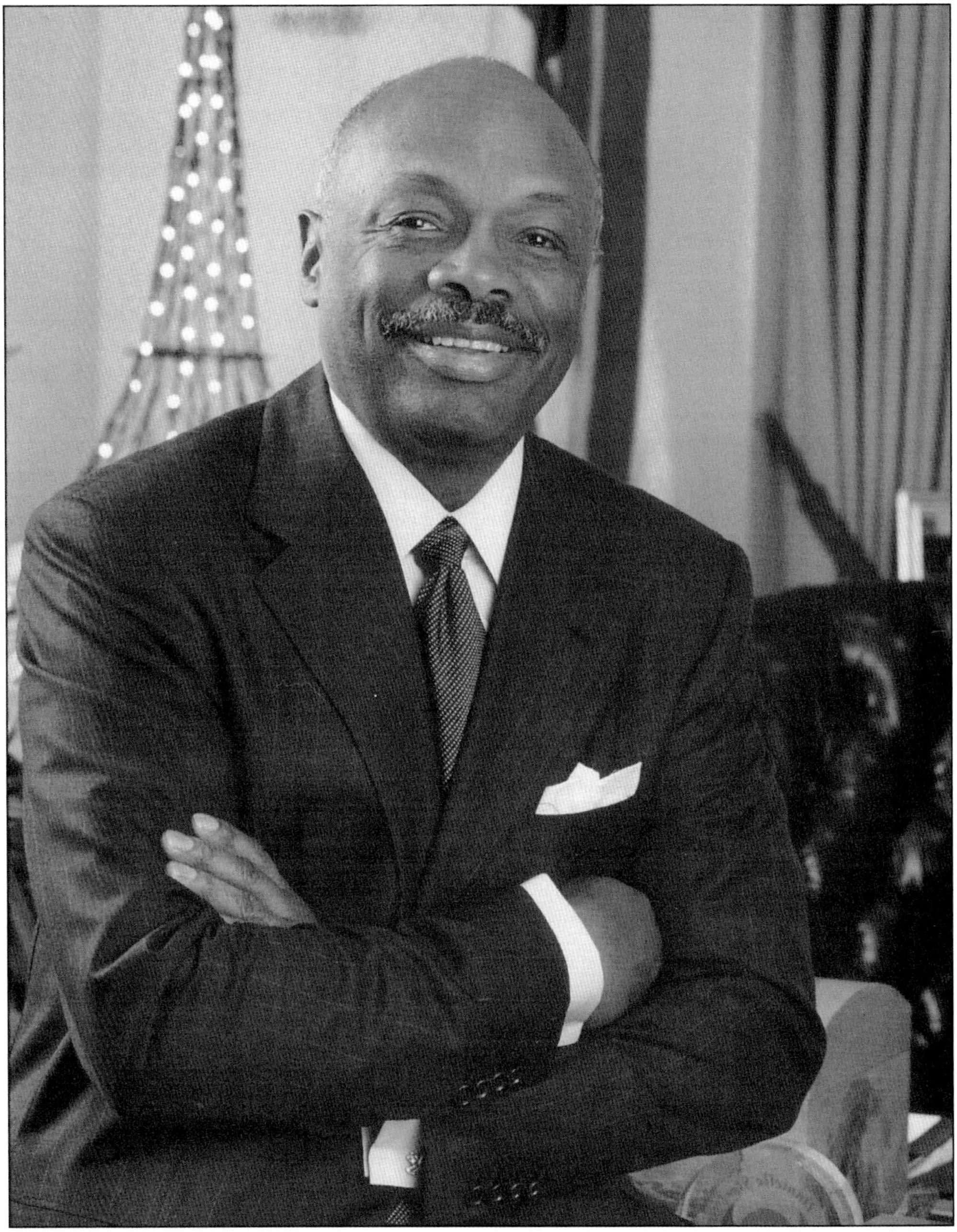

According to an article in the *Oakland Tribune* on Sunday, April 22, 1984, "Willie Brown is one of the most powerful black politicians in the nation." Willie Lewis Brown Jr. served over 30 years representing San Francisco in the California State Assembly. While in the assembly, Brown served 15 years as the speaker and then was San Francisco's 41st mayor from 1996 to 2004. Brown was born in Mineola, Texas, and moved to San Francisco in 1951. He graduated from San Francisco State College in 1955 and earned his Juris Doctor from the University of California Hastings College of Law in 1958. He practiced law until in 1964, when he was elected to the assembly. Brown has officially retired from politics and now advises other politicians. (Courtesy of Blanche Brown Collection.)

In 1957, Blanche and Willie Brown married. Willie was an attorney with the firm of Terry Francois. This photograph shows Willie and Blanch Brown (third and fourth from left) at their anniversary in the 1960s. The Browns resided in San Francisco for 40 years before relocating to Oakland. (Courtesy of Blanche Brown Collection.)

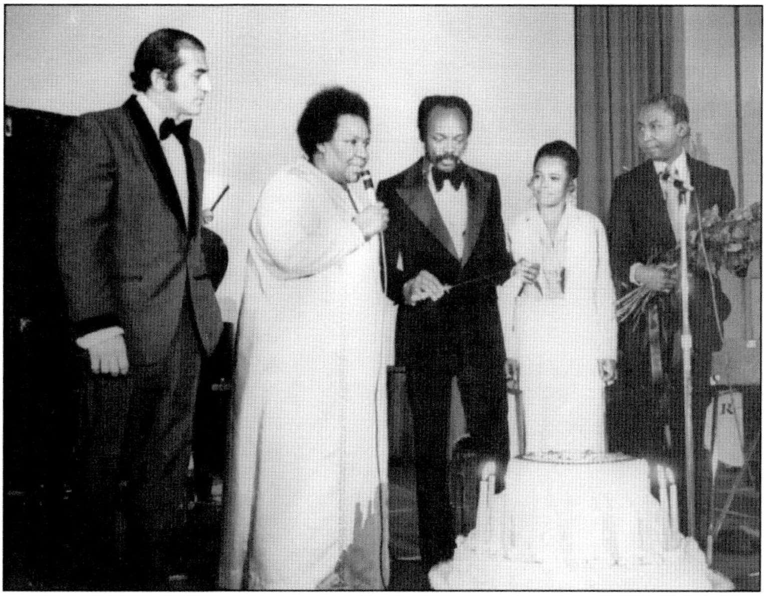

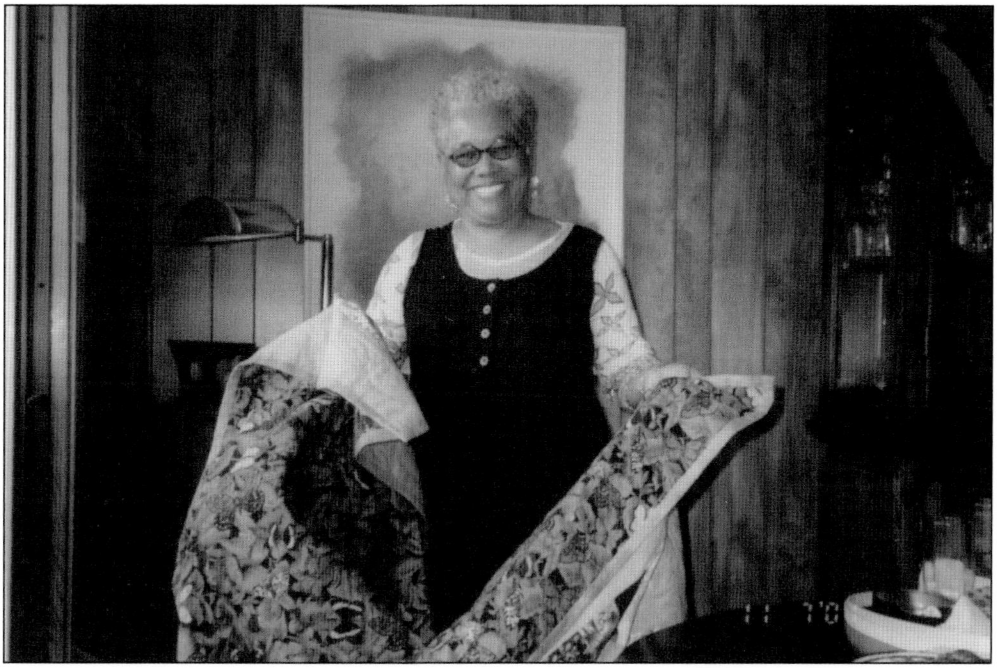

Blanche Brown became a dancer after completing a dance degree at San Francisco State University in 1975 at age 35. In 1980, she established Group Petit la Croix dance company in the Mission District, where she taught many San Francisco residents African and Haitian dances until the early 1990s. Brown saw her dance as a way to reach people. She taught dance at San Francisco State University for eleven years. Now, Brown has taken up the hobby of quilting in her spare time. (Courtesy of Blanche Brown Collection.)

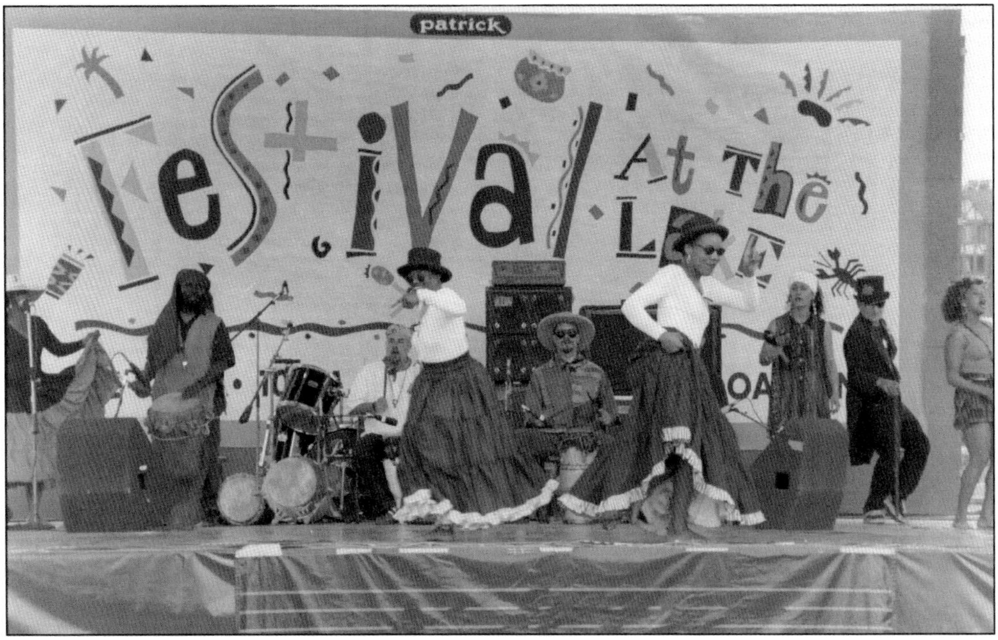

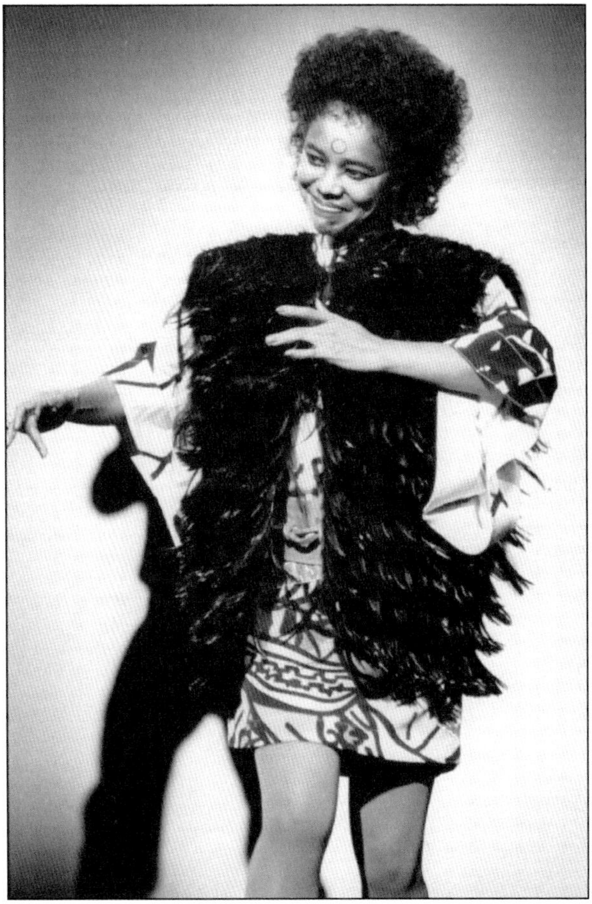

Blanche Brown (center, left) and dancers of Petit la Croix perform at the Festival at the Lake in 1994. They also danced at San Francisco's Carnival in 1990s. (Courtesy of Blanche Brown Collection.)

Seen here as a dance instructor in the 1980s, Brown was the first dance person to serve on the San Francisco Arts Commission. Appointed to the commission by Mayor George Moscone, she continued serving under Mayor Willie Brown. (Courtesy of Blanche Brown Collection.)

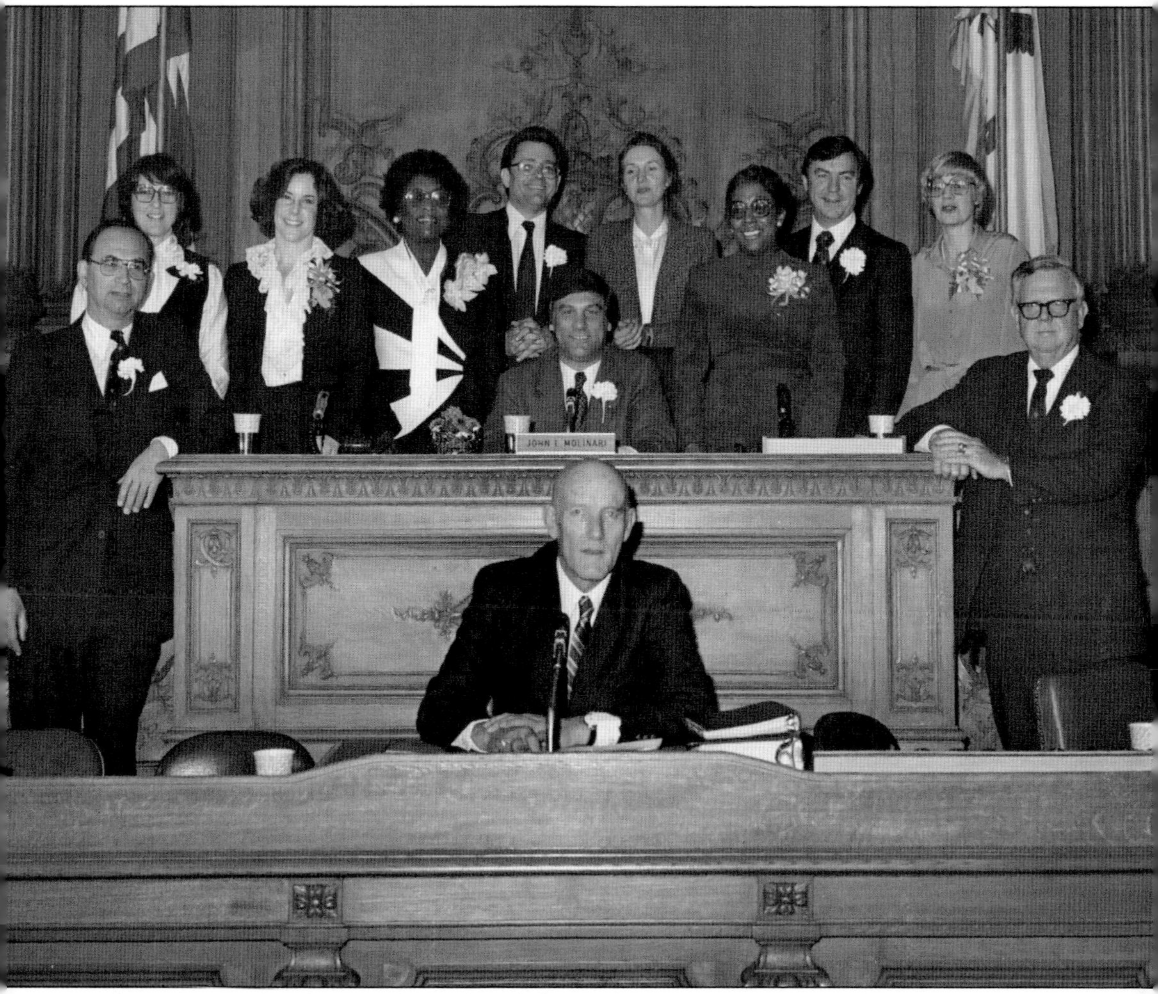

Board members in the photograph are, from left to right, Quenten Kapp, Carol R. Silver, Wendy Velder, Ella Hill Hutch, Harry Britt, Nancy Walker, Doris Ward, Richard Hongisto, Louise Renne, Lee Dobson, and John Malinario; the man in the foreground is identified as "the Clerk." In 1978, Ella Hill Hutch became the first African American elected to the San Francisco Board of Supervisors. She served until 1981. Hutch came to San Francisco shortly after World War II. She found a staff job with the International Longshore and Warehouse Union in the early 1950s. Hutch served as a member of the Fillmore Tenants Council. She organized a concert appearance by Paul Robeson and chaired the San Francisco chapter of the Labor Youth League. Hutch, along with 25 other African American women, joined the Democratic Women's Political Workshop in 1959, swept up by national civil rights activity and the excitement of John Kennedy's presidential campaign. From there, it was a short step to the Democratic County Central Committee in 1966, the Bay Area Rapid Transit (BART) board in 1974, and the board of supervisors in 1977, first from the Fillmore-centered District 4 and then citywide. Hutch based her campaign on government-financed, low-cost housing. Currently, a community center that provides youth recreational programs has been named after her. Doris Ward, who was later elected San Francisco assessor-recorder, served on the board of supervisors from 1980 to 1992. In 2000, Ward served as a California delegate to the Democratic National Convention. (Courtesy of San Francisco History Center, San Francisco Public Library.)

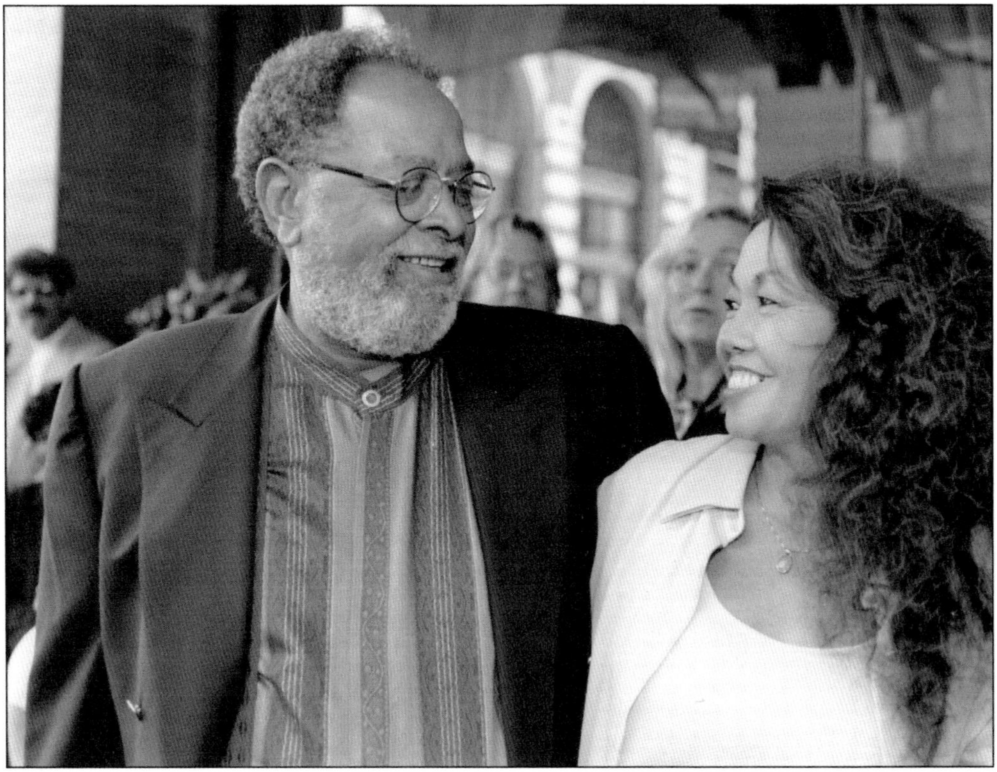

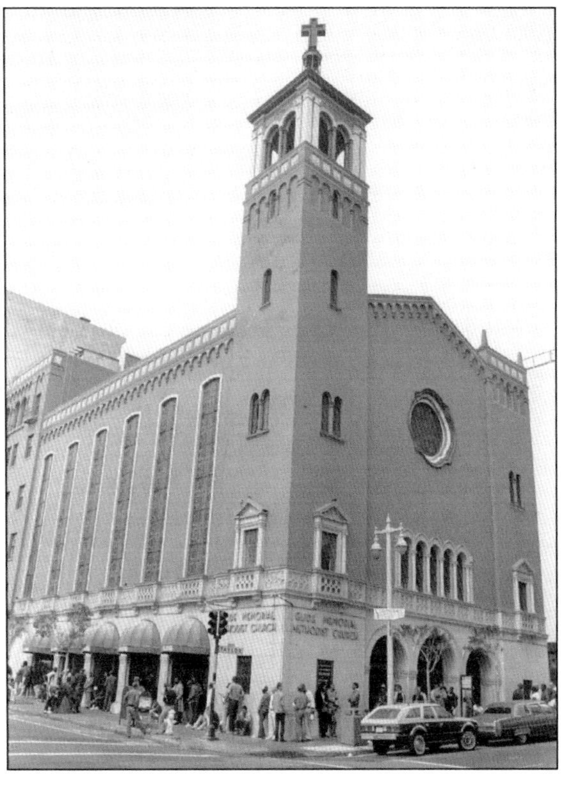

Rev. Cecil Williams, founder and minister of liberation of Glide Memorial United Methodist Church, was the first to expand the church beyond its traditional Methodist limits. For over 40 years, he developed a ministry of spirituality, compassion, and diversity. As minister, author, social activist, lecturer, community leader, and spokesperson for the poor and marginalized, Rev. Williams has been respected and recognized as a national leader on the forefront of change. Over the years, Williams and his wife, Janice Mirikitani (who is also cofounder of the ministry), have built over 87 comprehensive programs at Glide that provide education, recovery support, mental health care, job training, housing, and human services to those in need. (Both, courtesy of Glide.)

Rev. Cecil Williams emphasizes the celebration of life at Glide's Sunday-morning worship services. In a nontraditional and contemporary way, Glide focuses on reaching the souls of people by bringing them together in the spirit of the beloved community. Celebration means bringing hope even in the most despairing situations. Glide's celebrations are at the core of its program for people. (Both, courtesy of Glide.)

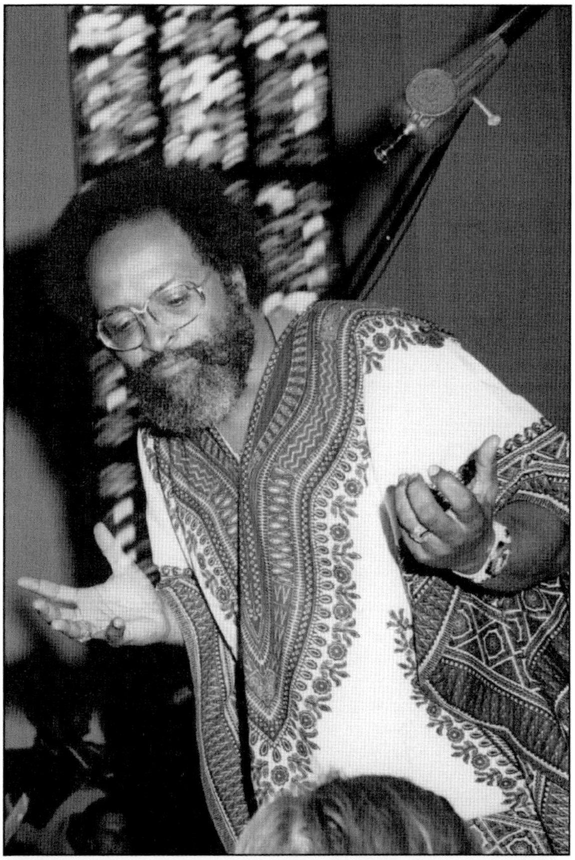

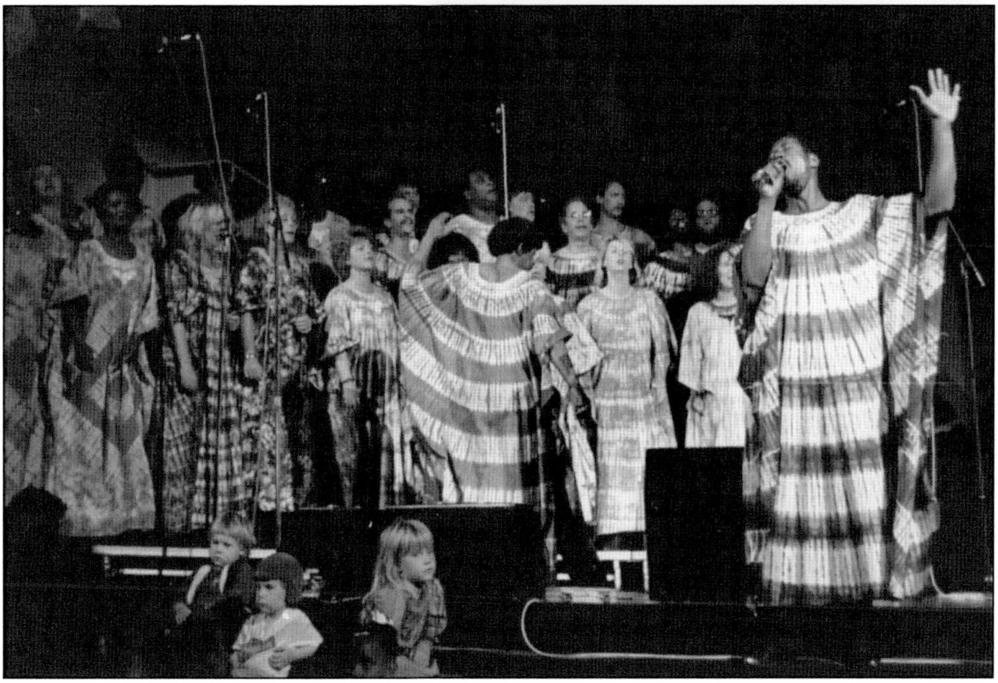

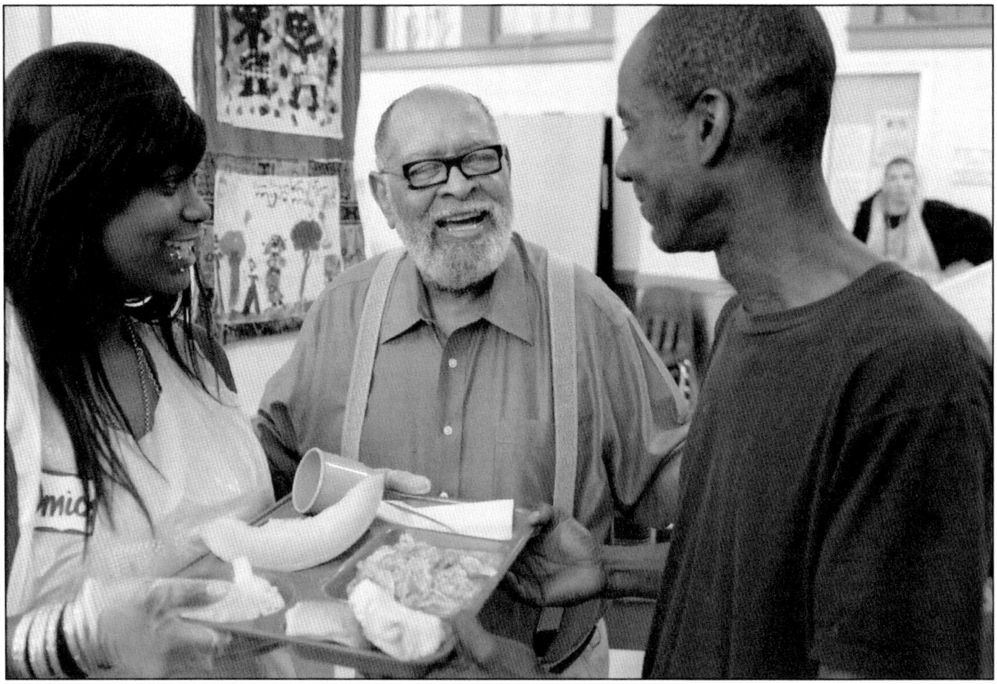

In 1969, Glide's social services were launched when a handful of volunteers began serving a Monday-night meal to poor and street people. Since then, Glide has become San Francisco's largest and most comprehensive provider of innovative services for hungry people throughout the city. The Glide free-meal program is the only program in San Francisco that serves three meals per day for 365 days annually, resulting in more than 750,000 meals served to the poor in one year. Glide believes its mission is where liberation and healing also occurs. Below, Rev. Williams and the men of the church take the cause for recovery to the streets of the Tenderloin District. (Both, courtesy of Glide.)

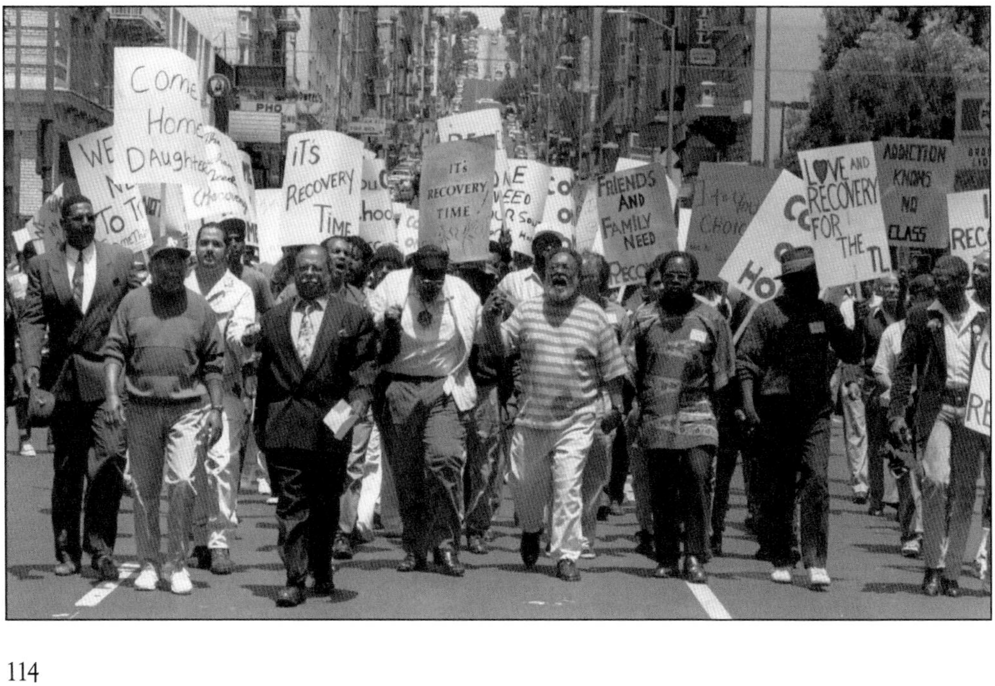

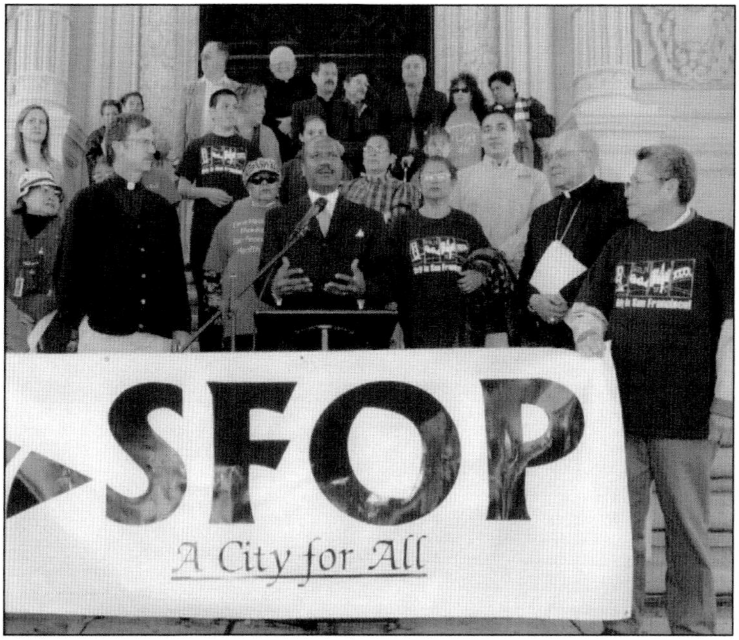

Rev. Boyd of Bethel AME Church (speaking) is an advocate for healthy meals for youth and sound housing for residents of San Francisco. (Courtesy of Bethel AME Church.)

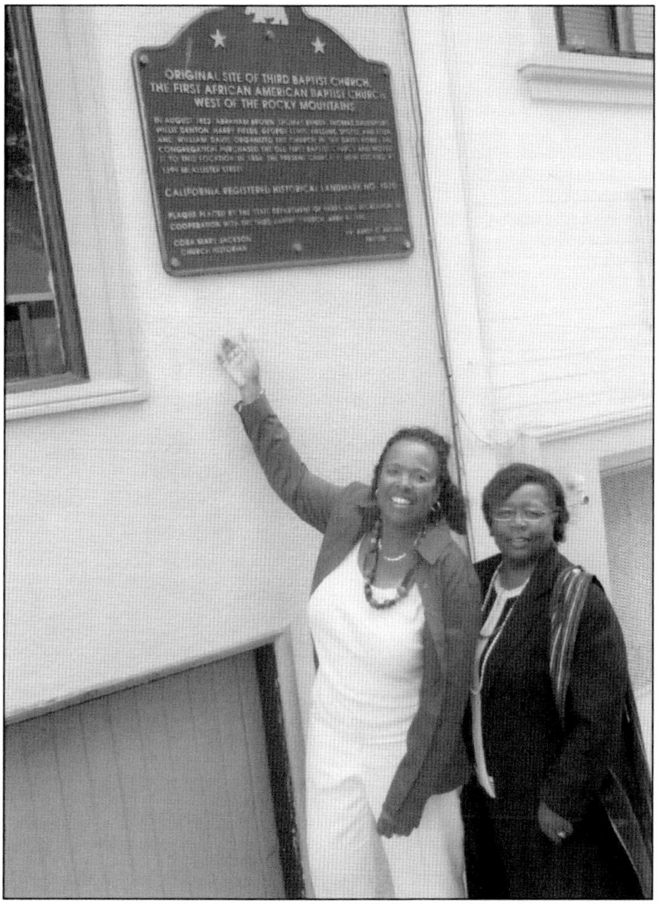

The historic landmark plaque is located on the side of a building on the southeast corner of Grant Avenue and Greenwich Street in North Beach. This was the site of the home of Eliza Davis and her husband, William, and was where the first meeting of pioneers in the 1850s was held that started the Third Baptist Church of San Francisco. Retired historian Ellen Carr of the Third Baptist Church stand to the far right of the plaque. (Courtesy of Ellen Carr.)

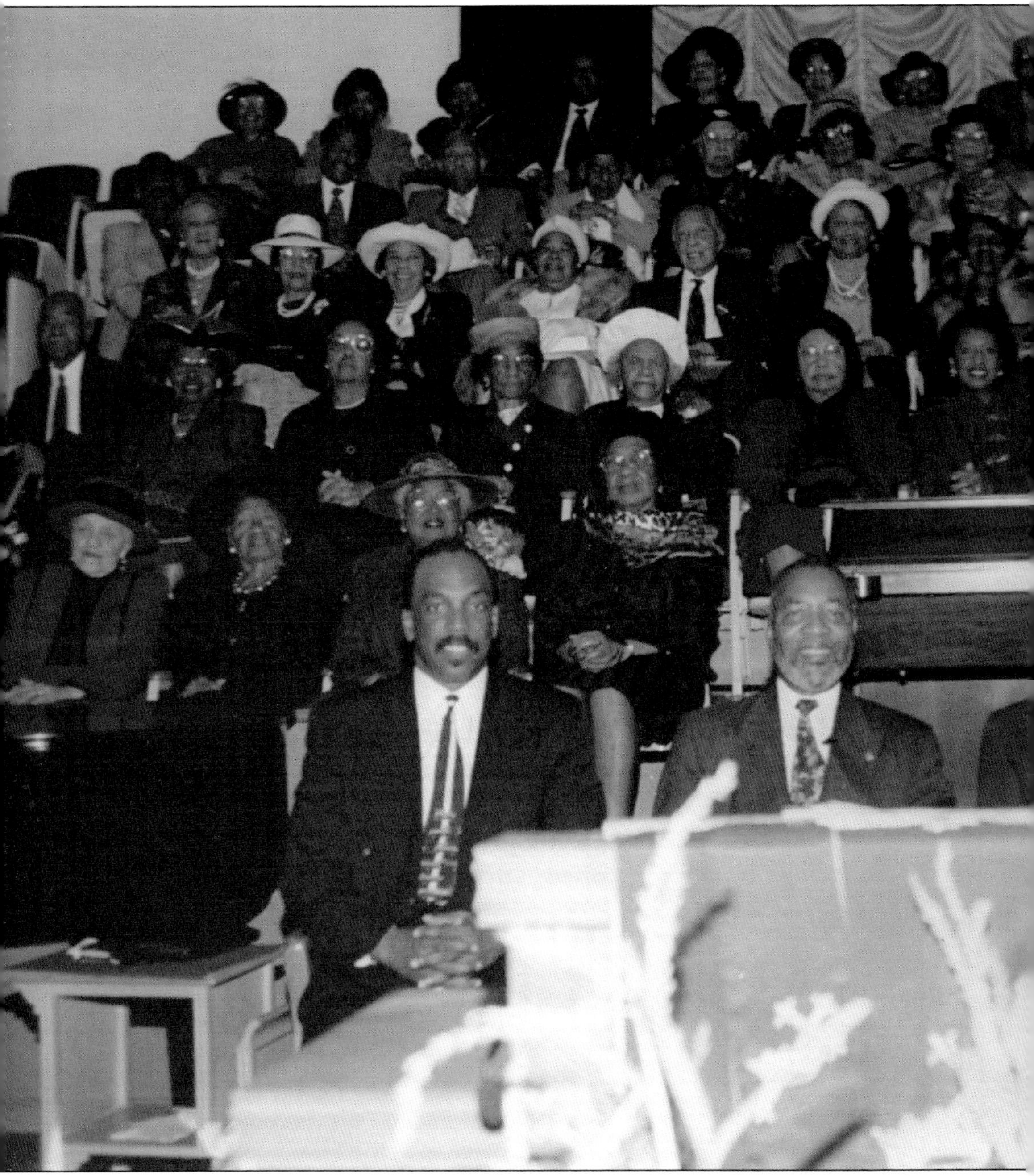

Annually, Dr. Amos Brown, pastor of Third Baptist Church, meets with the members who have served in the church for over 50 years. Here, he is seated to the right. Brown is a community leader and serves as president of the San Francisco branch of the NAACP. (Courtesy of Third Baptist historian Ellen Carr.)

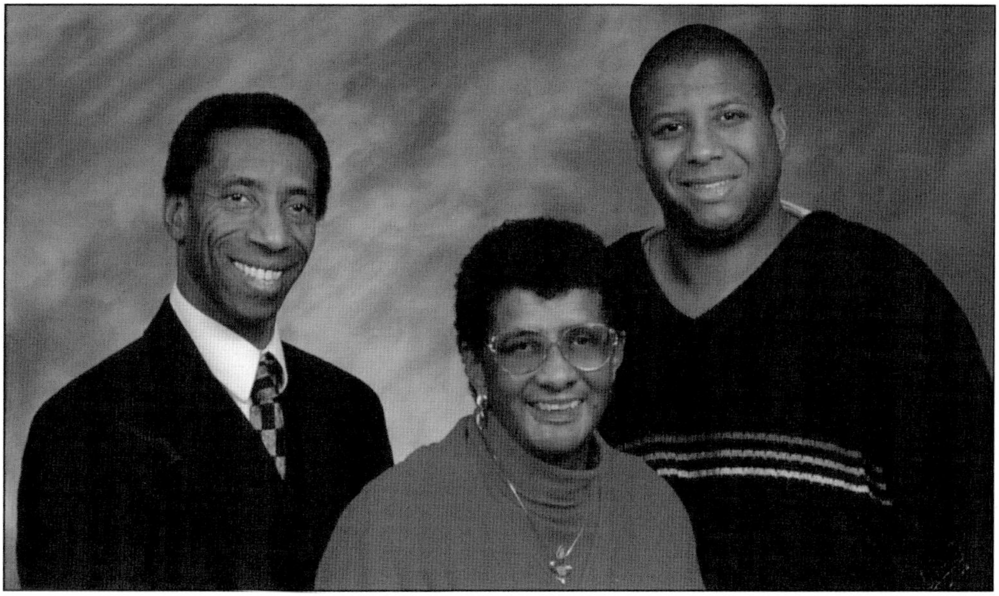

Phillip and Ethel Walker and son Travis are members of Third Baptist Church of San Francisco. Ethel is pictured below when receiving an appointment to the San Francisco Arts Commission. Then mayor Willie Brown is on the right; the other man is unidentified. With a doctorate in theater, she is a tenured professor (since 1989) at San Jose State University and has served as the dean of the theatre department. Phillip and Ethel founded the African American Drama Company in 1977. (Both, courtesy of the Walker family.)

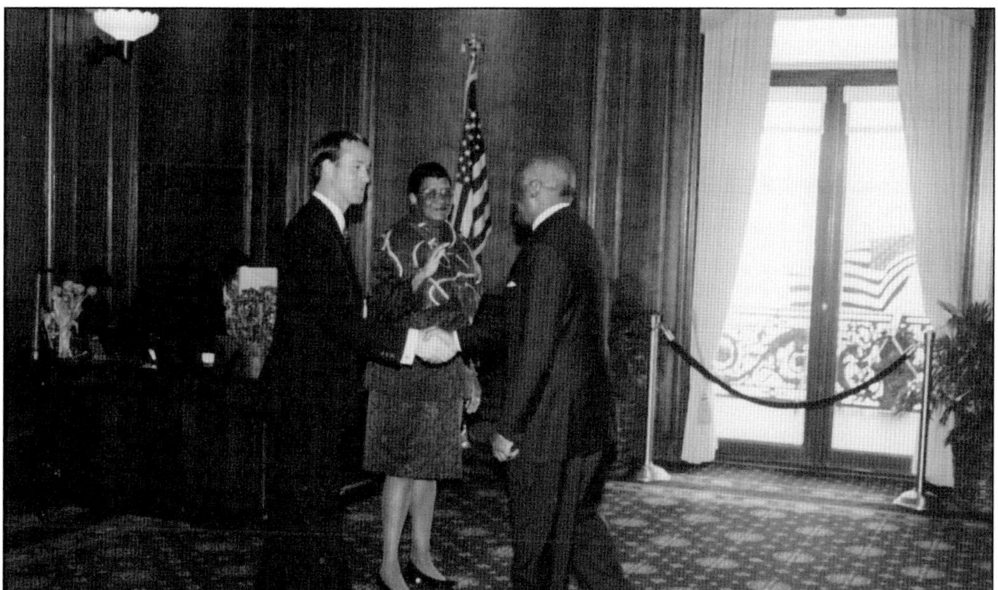

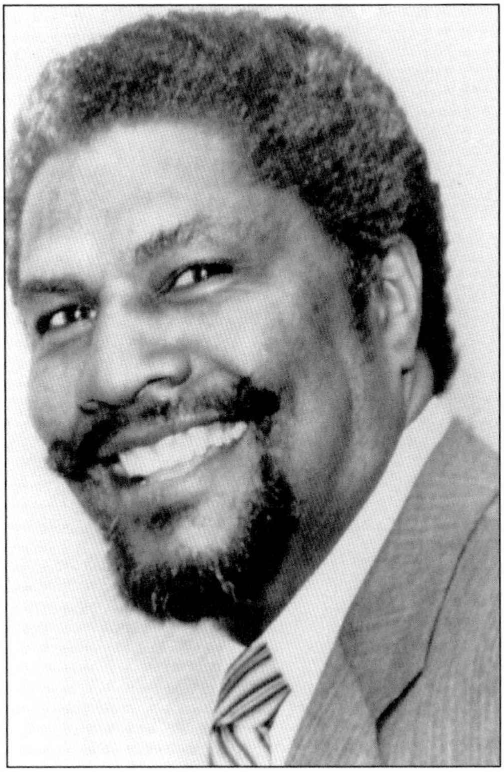

Nathan Hare taught sociology at Howard University from 1961 to 1968. He was recruited to head up the black studies department at San Francisco State College in 1968. Dismissed from San Francisco State College in 1969 as a result of the student strikes, Nathan began publication of *The Black Scholar: A Journal of Black Studies and Research*. Many have considered it the most important journal devoted to black issues. (Courtesy of Nathan and Julia Hare.)

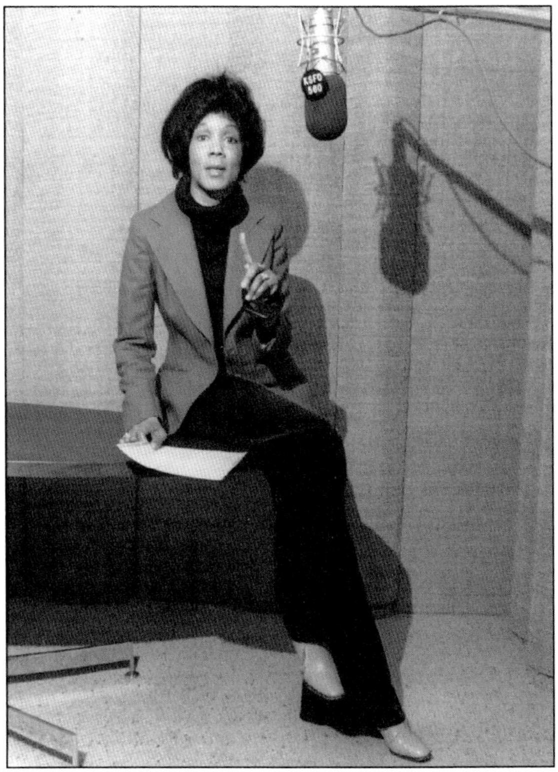

Dr. Julia Hare, a motivational speaker over the last 20 years, has addressed leading black leaders from around the country. Invited to give a motivational speech to the Congressional Black Caucus Institute on issues of education, health care, and economic opportunities for African Americans at the Democratic National Convention in 2004, Hare challenged national black leaders to tackle issues of black leadership at both local and national levels. (Courtesy of Nathan and Julia Hare.)

Originally from Oklahoma, Nathan and Julia Hare moved to San Francisco in 1969 from Washington, DC, when Nathan was hired to coordinate the black studies program at San Francisco State College. Julia, a concert pianist, is best known for her work in radio broadcasting as the first black director of community affairs at KSFO and her efforts in fighting housing discrimination in San Francisco during the 1970s and 1980s. Nathan, with doctorates in both sociology and psychology, is best known for his publication *The Black Scholar*, a magazine of the black movement. Julia applies her music intuition to her work today as a motivational speaker. She can read an individual, situation, or crowd quickly and goes from there. Over the years, Julia has performed recitals throughout San Francisco. Nathan and Julia are founders of the Black Think Tank. (Both, courtesy of Nathan and Julia Hare.)

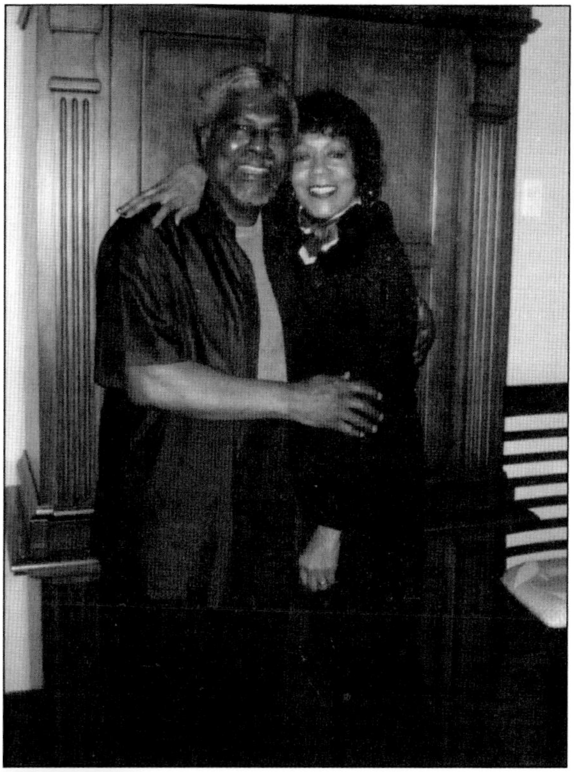

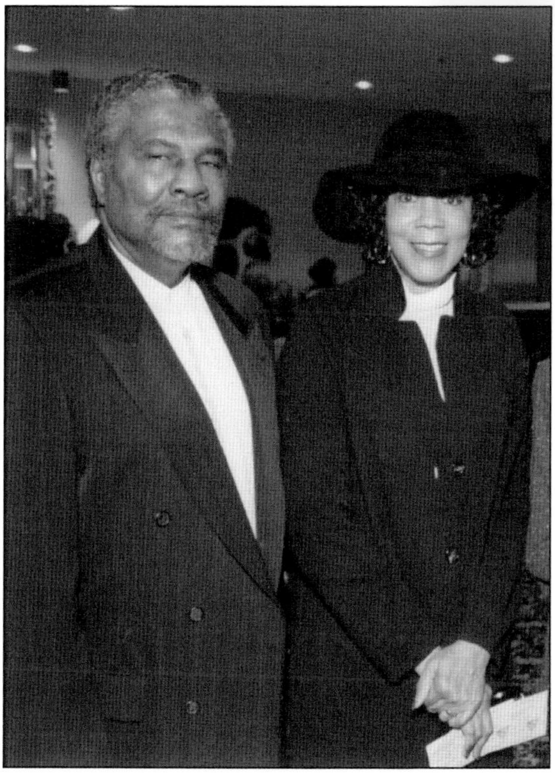

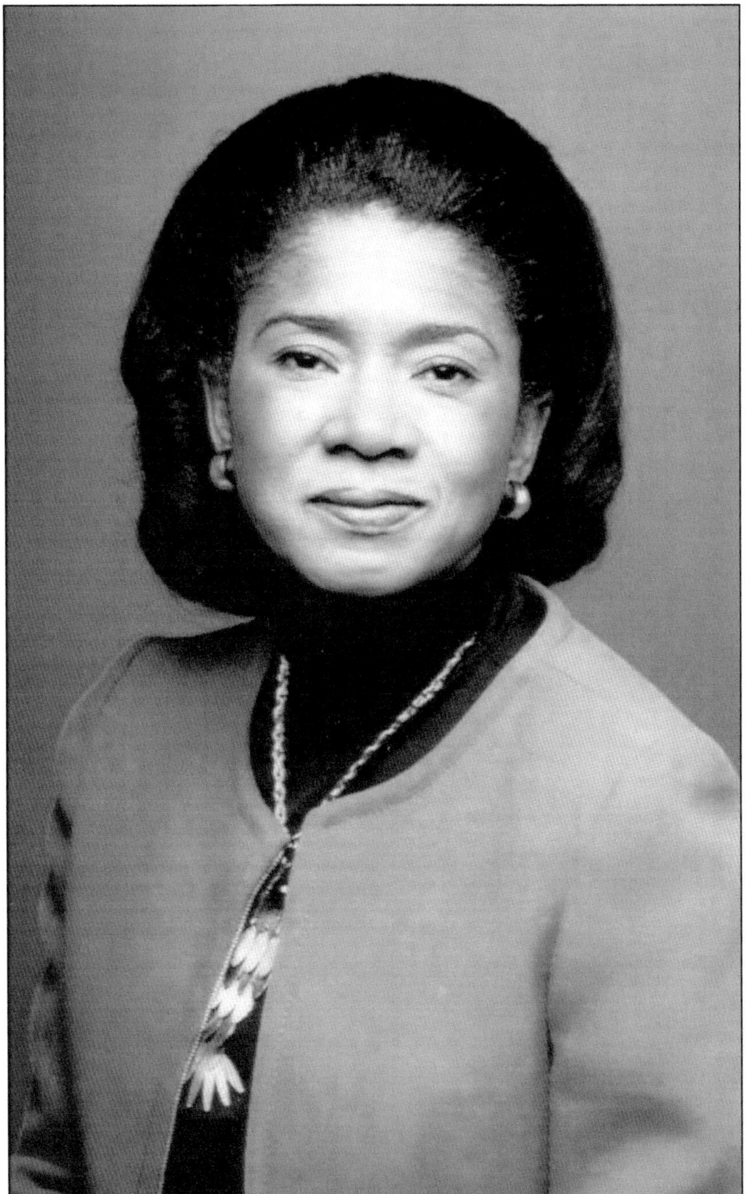

As the first black female television journalist in the West Coast, Belva Davis helped change the face and focus of television news. Davis was born to a 15-year-old Louisiana laundress during the Great Depression. In a career spanning half a century, Davis has reported many of the most explosive stories of the era, including the Berkeley student protests, the birth of the Black Panthers, the Peoples Temple cult that ended in the mass suicides at Jonestown, the assassinations of San Francisco's mayor George Moscone and supervisor Harvey Milk, and more. She has won eight local Emmys and a number of lifetime achievement awards. In 2010, Davis completed her autobiography, *Never in My Wildest Dreams: A Black Woman's Life in Journalism*. She is profiled in the Newseum, in Washington, DC, the world's first interactive museum of news. Davis continues to host a weekly news roundtable and special reports at KQED, one of the nation's leading PBS stations. (Courtesy of Belva Davis.)

As young teens, Raymond Westbrook (left) and Oscar Preston were best friends in San Francisco. Oscar was a well-known pianist in the 1960s. (Courtesy of Ross E. Westbrook and Dorothy Preston Word families.)

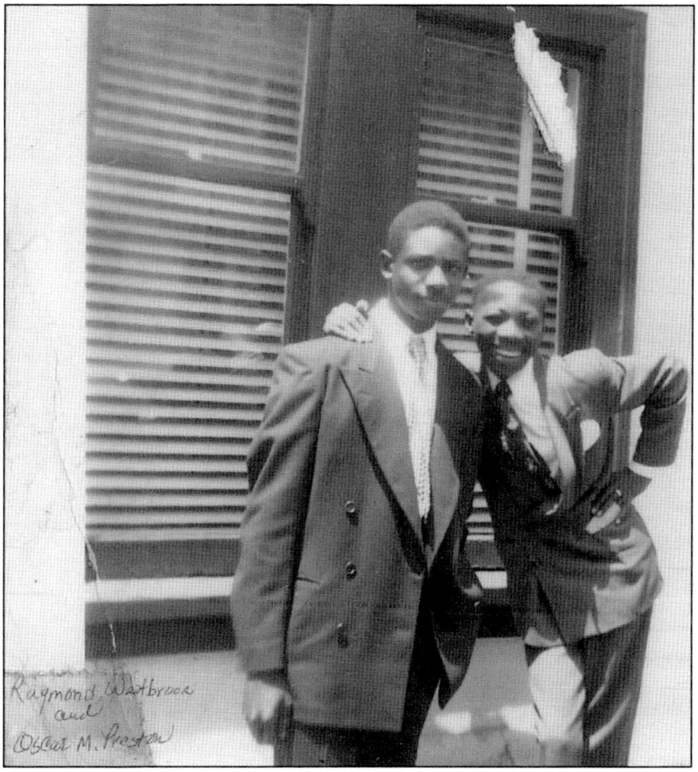

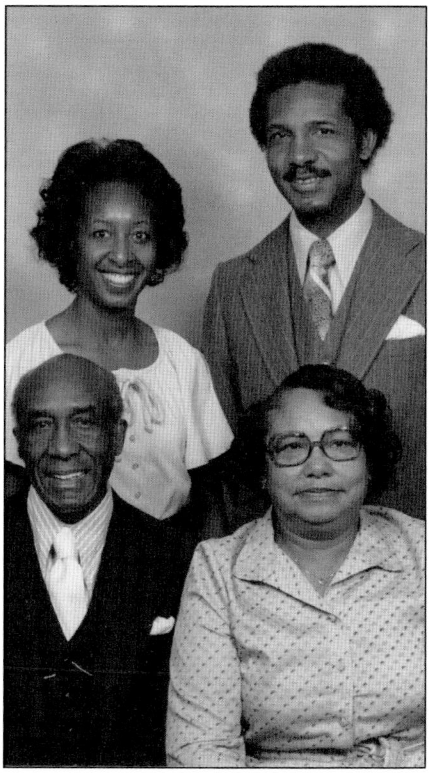

Ross E. Westbrook migrated to San Francisco from Austin, Texas, in 1942 in search of employment. As with so many African Americans, Westbrook found work in the shipyards and then sent for his wife, Mary, and their children, Raymond and LaZelle. Initially, the family lived in the Westside Housing project on Buchanan Street. By 1950, they purchased a two-story duplex on Scott Street. The Westbrooks joined Third Baptist Church. For 31 years, Mary worked at I. Magnin & Company in shipping and receiving. She retired in 1993. After shipyard work, Ross became a longshoreman and worked throughout the ports of San Francisco. Pictured are, from left to right, (first row) Ross and Mary; (second row) LaZelle and Raymond. Ross passed away in 1993, and Raymond is also deceased. (Courtesy of the Ross E. Westbrook family.)

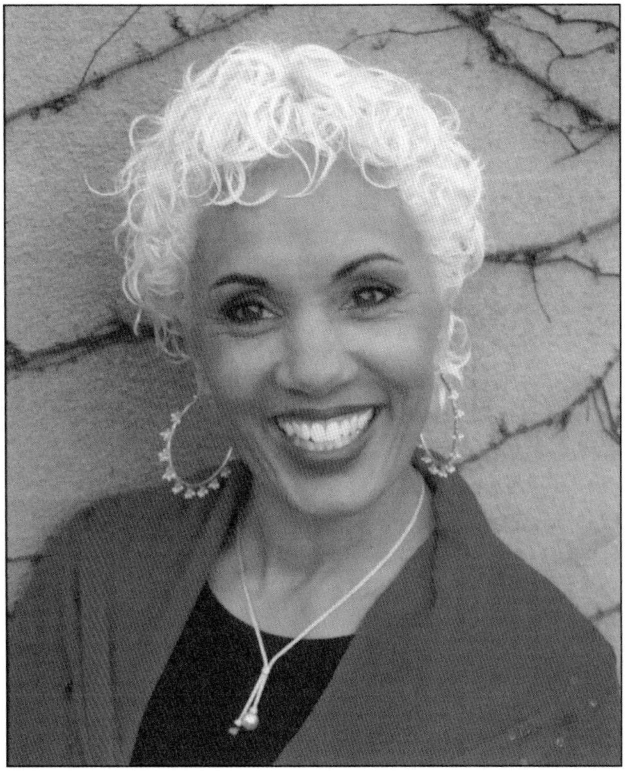

Deborah King Santana, daughter of musician Saunders King, is an author, philanthropist, and supporter of peace and social justice. Her memoir, *Space Between the Stars: My Journey to an Open Heart*, was published in March 2005. Santana is founder of Do A Little, a nonprofit whose mission is to support women in the areas of health, education, and happiness. (Courtesy of the King family.)

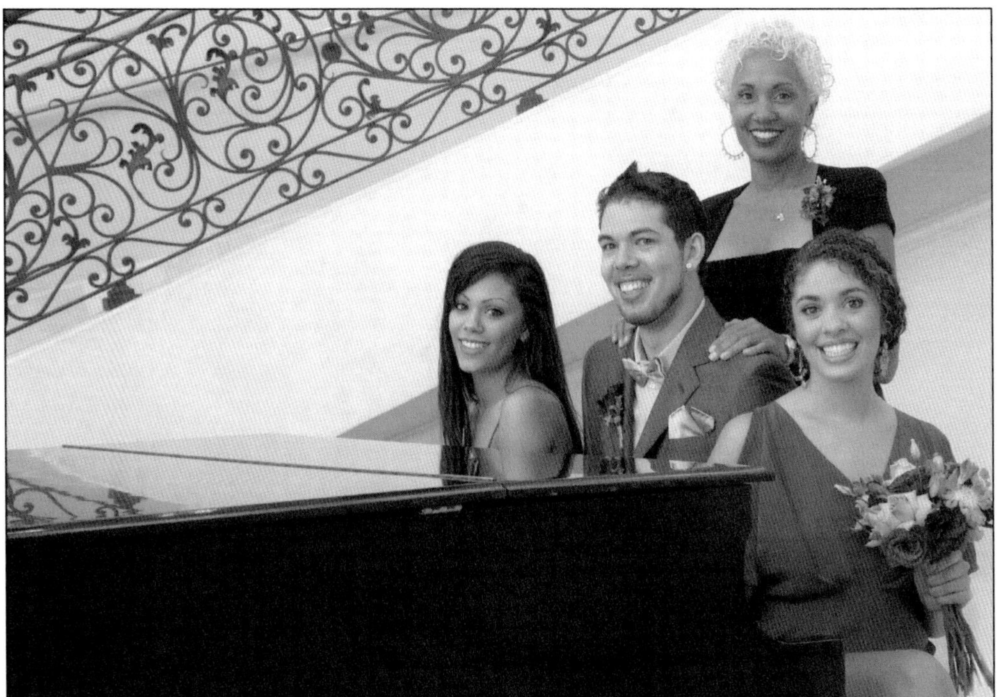

Deborah King Santana (standing) and her family—Angelica (left), Salvador, and Stella—are pictured here. (Courtesy of the King family.)

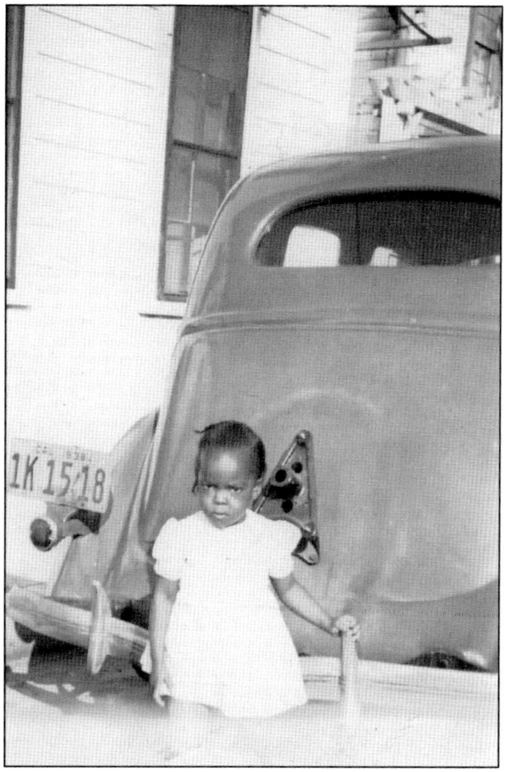

Gerry Sumner is standing in front of her father's car in 1939. Her dad, Jerrell Hudson, came to San Francisco after living and working in Santa Cruz as a cook at Beach Hill Inn. Eventually, Jerrell gained employment with the US Navy as a driver for its officers. Gerry, her parents, brothers, and sisters lived in the Fillmore District but moved to Ingleside during the early stages of the urban renewal project. Below, Gerry (left) is standing with her sister Maxine (right), brothers Jerry and Richard, and their grandmother. (Both, courtesy of the Gerry Sumner family.)

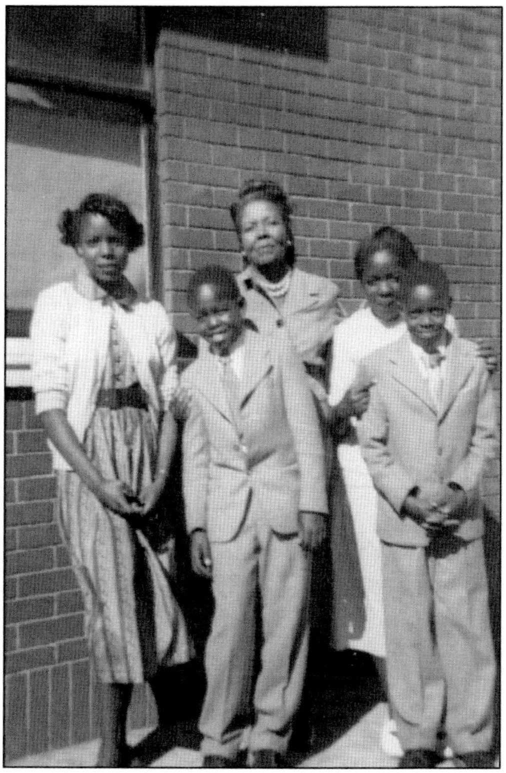

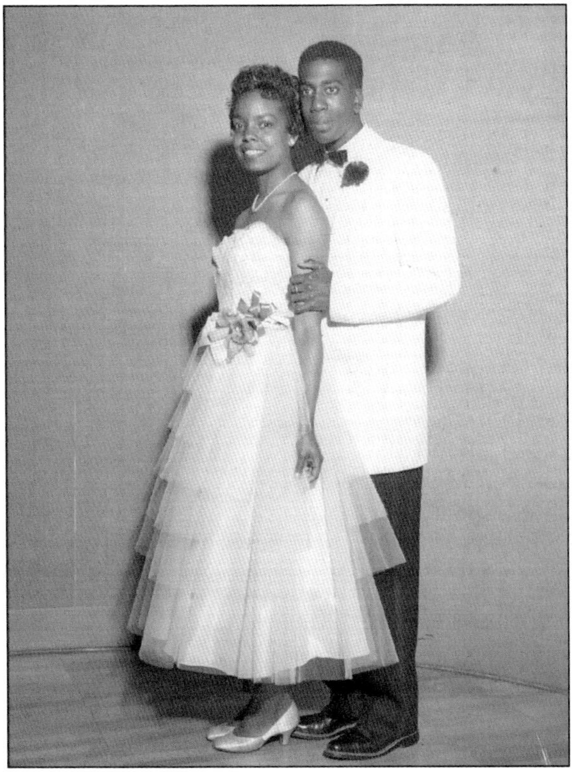

Gerry and Ron Sumner are pictured at the Galileo High School Prom in 1955. On June 14, 1957, high school sweethearts Gerry and Ron married. After the wedding, they moved to San Jose in search of a better environment for raising a family. For the past 30 years, Gerry has served her community by working as a teacher director. She has one son, Eric, and two granddaughters. In the below photograph, Gerry is with granddaughters Kaya (left) and Mia. (Both, courtesy of the Gerry Sumner family.)

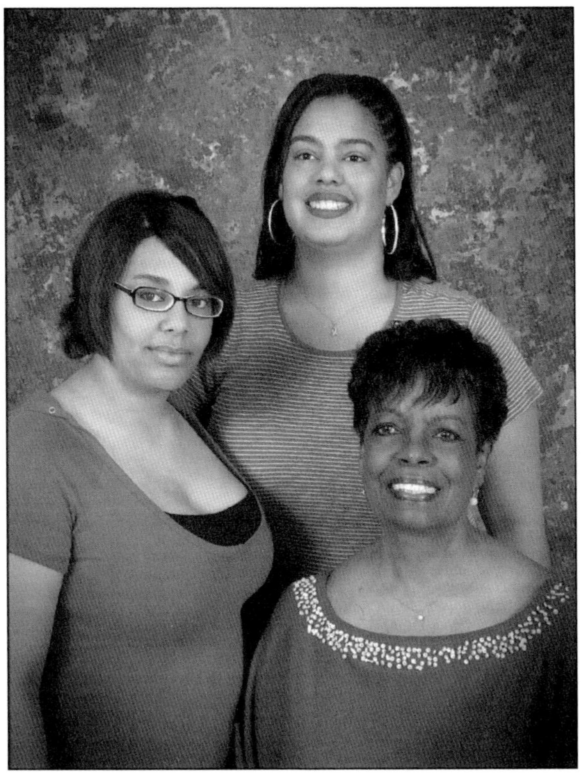

Oscar James, a community leader, was born in 1946 on Navy Road in the Bayview-Hunters Point community. With six brothers, Oscar had to go to work at age nine to help his parents provide for the family. In the 1970s, James became involved in community politics and joined the Joint Housing Committee, which was the watchdog of the Redevelopment Agency for the US Department of Housing and Urban Development (HUD). James was also elected to the Model Cities Commission during the 1970s. Many people in his community call him the historian of Bayview-Hunters Point. James has a passion for speaking up for the underdog to protect the rights of citizens. He retired from the San Francisco Redevelopment Agency. (Courtesy of Oscar James.)

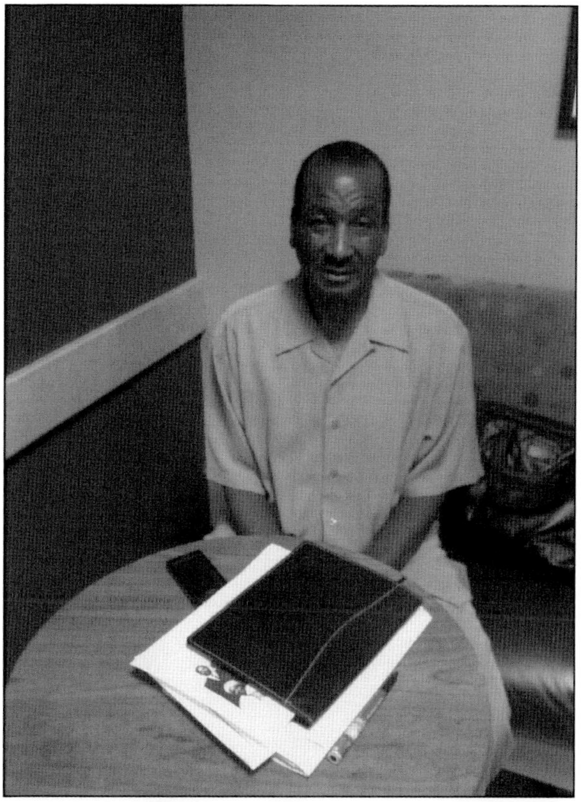

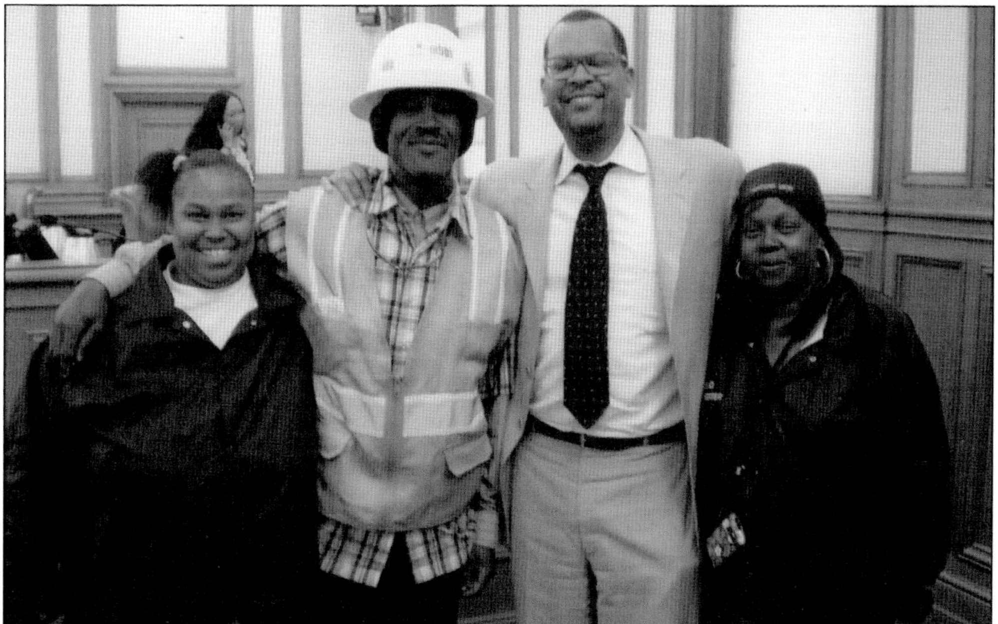

Residents of Bayview-Hunters Point and the redevelopment staff of San Francisco still work together to protect the rights of the residents throughout the redevelopment phase. (Courtesy of Oscar James.)

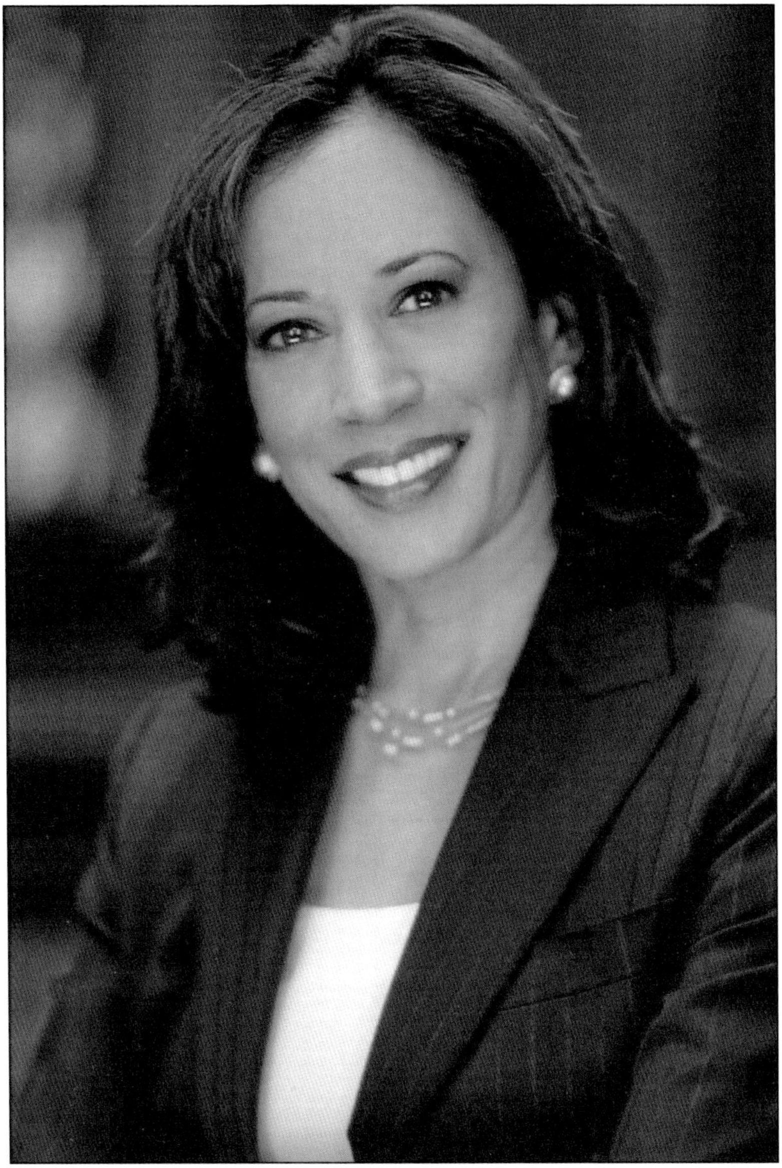

On January 3, 2011, Kamala D. Harris was sworn in as the 32nd attorney general of the state of California. She is the first woman, the first African American, and the first South Asian American to hold that office in California history. In 2003, Harris was elected as San Francisco's district attorney; she was overwhelmingly reelected to a second term in November 2007. As San Francisco's district attorney, Harris focused intensively on fighting violent crime. She expanded services to victims of crime and their families, combated gun violence in the city, and addressed issues of child assault, public integrity, and environmental crimes. Born and raised in the East Bay, Harris is the daughter of Dr. Shyamala Harris and attended public schools. She graduated from Howard University, regarded as among the most prestigious historically black universities, and then the University of California Hastings College of the Law in San Francisco. Attorney General Harris has spent her entire professional life in the trenches as a courtroom prosecutor. She is the author of the book *Smart on Crime: A Career Prosecutor's Plan to Make Us Safer.* (Courtesy of Kamala Harris.)

Bibliography

Adkins, Jan. *Literary Prose and Poetry in San Francisco's Black Newspapers, 1862–1885*. Ann Arbor, MI: ProQuest, 2010.

Beasley, Delilah. *The Negro Trail Blazers of California*. Fairfield, CA: James Stevenson, 2004.

Broussard, Albert S. *Black San Francisco: The Struggle for Racial Equality in the West, 1990–1954*. Lawrence, KS: University Press of Kansas, 1993.

Burke, Anne. "Remembering the Strike." *San Francisco State University Magazine*. Fall/Winter 2008. http://www.sfsu.edu/~sfsumag/archive/fall_08/strike.html.

Daniels, Douglas Henry. *Pioneer Urbanites: A Social and Cultural History of Black San Francisco*. Berkeley: University of California Press, 1991.

Davis, Belva. *Never in My Wildest Dreams: A Black Women's Life in Journalism*. Sausalito, CA: PoliPoint, 2010.

De Graaf, Lawrence, Kevin Mulroy, and Quintard Taylor, eds. *Seeking El Dorado: African Americans in California*. Seattle: University of Washington Press, 2001.

Freedman, Lew. *African American Pioneers of Baseball: A Biographical Encyclopedia*. Westport, CT: Greenwood, 2007.

Hill, Anthony Duane. "Anderon, Garland (1886–1939)." http://blackpast.org/?q=aah/anderson-garland-1886-1939.

Lapp, Rudolph. *Blacks in Gold Rush California*. New Haven, CT: Yale University Press, 1977.

Pepin, Elizabeth and Lewis Watts. *Harlem of the West: The San Francisco Fillmore Jazz Era*. San Francisco: Chronicle Books, 2008.

Santana, Deborah. *Space Between the Stars: My Journey to an Open Heart*. New York: Random House, 2005.

Thurman, Sue Bailey. *Pioneers of Negro Origin in California*. Henderson, NV: Acme, 1952.

Tompkins, E. Berkeley. *Black Ahab: William T. Shorey, Whaling Master*. San Francisco, California Historical Society, 1972.

Wilkerson, Isabel. *The Warmth of Other Suns: The Epic Story of America's Great Migration*. New York: Random House, 2010.

Withers, Ernest C. *Negro League Baseball*. New York: Harry N. Abrams, 2004.

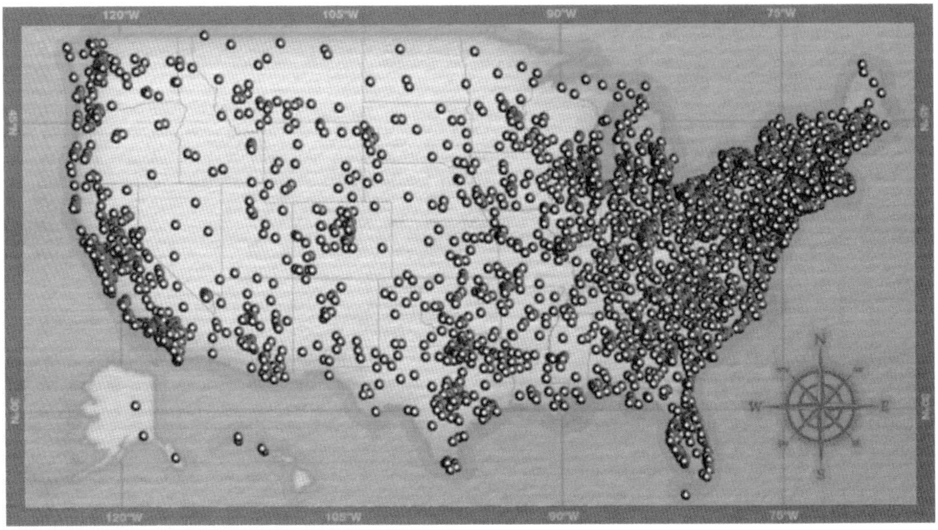